# THE TONY AWARDS®

THE AMERICAN THEATRE WING PRESENTS

# THE
# TONY
## AWARDS®

A CELEBRATION OF EXCELLENCE IN THEATRE

*by* EILA MELL *foreword by* AUDRA McDONALD

BLACK DOG
& LEVENTHAL
PUBLISHERS
NEW YORK

# CONTENTS

Audra McDonald in 2016, after winning her sixth Tony and becoming the most decorated performer in Tony history

# FOREWORD

As a little girl I had always dreamed of being on Broadway. But my dream wasn't as big as it should have been.

Let me explain. Growing up in Fresno, California, meant that it was too expensive to just fly off to New York to see Broadway shows whenever I wanted. Most touring shows didn't come through to Fresno, so if we wanted to see one, we had to drive three hours south to L.A. or three and a half hours north to San Francisco.

So how did I fuel my love of musical theatre? My parents would buy me cast albums of Broadway shows, like *The Wiz, Dreamgirls, Evita, A Chorus Line, Ain't Misbehavin'*, and *Funny Girl*. I would listen to them over and over and wear the records out on my little Mickey Mouse record player. I memorized every word of "I'm the Greatest Star"; I would stand on my bed singing "Don't Cry for Me Argentina" to my stuffed animals; I'd make up my own dance moves to "God I Hope I Get It"; I'd grab a hairbrush and sing "Dreamgirls." And every June one of the most powerful ways of fueling my dreams was to watch the Tony Awards. It was a chance for me to really see what those shows looked like. Suddenly, those disembodied voices from the records came to life, fully realized. I could see Patti LuPone's fire and power as she sang "A New Argentina," Jennifer Holliday bringing down the house with "And I Am Telling You I'm Not Going," and Lena Horne singing to my little soul "If You Believe."

That was in the days pre–cell phones, DVRs, and bootleg recordings. Watching the Tonys every year was the way I could journey closest to the real thing, get the closest look at what my dream could be. It was always such a visceral experience. Not only was I excited by the performances I was seeing but I could also fully imagine myself performing them. There was something in my body, like the "quickening" Martha Graham advised Agnes de Mille about. I still feel that when I sit in a theater and watch other people perform, where my body almost feels like it's doing what they're doing up onstage. So I'd watch and dream and worry. Yes, worry, because as a little Black girl, I knew there weren't that many shows featuring Black performers. My worry was always would there be enough, or *any*, shows for people who looked like me by the time I got there? But still I dreamed...

---

Nicholas Hytner cast me as Carrie Pipperidge in the 1994 production of *Carousel* at Lincoln Center Theater. People certainly took notice of the color-blind casting of me and Shirley Verrett, who played Nettie Fowler. That season, some of the only Black representation happening on Broadway was in *Carousel*. That show was a turning point in my life.

I was privileged to win my first Tony because of that show, and then my career changed so quickly. A few months later I had my first meeting with Terrence McNally, who asked me to be in his new play, *Master Class*. I went right into that show after *Carousel*. That recognition from the Tonys allowed me the privilege of not being pigeonholed as an actor, and it allowed me the opportunity to be considered for any type of role. With *Carousel*, I was given the opportunity be a part of the breaking down of barriers for people of color in theatre. Often I think today about all the other young, undiscovered actors of color who could

and should have had careers in theatre if only there had been more opportunity. I'm heartened to see that in the years since, things have begun to change. There is more work to be done, but I do see the change. Today we don't just have color-blind casting. Now we have color-full casting. The stories and storytellers are beginning to be more diversified, and inclusive in every sense. This only adds to the power the theatre has to heal, illuminate, educate, and ultimately to transform.

---

The night I won the Tony for playing Billie Holiday in *Lady Day at Emerson's Bar & Grill* was an out-of-body experience in the same way that all of those nights happened for me: I sort of float out of my body and time stands still. It was so overwhelming when they called my name that I didn't comprehend it at all. It felt like it was happening to someone else. That win put me in the company of Angela Lansbury and Julie Harris, as the performers with the most Tonys. To be in that esteemed company is an incredible honor and, in some ways, still very hard for me to grasp. But I also look at it as a way of inspiring younger generations of theatre makers. Especially young theatre makers of color. Me—music theatre–obsessed little Audra from Fresno, California—being in that esteemed company shows them that they can do it too. Not only can they do it, but they can excel, be celebrated, and exceed their wildest dreams. Someday, some of them will win many more Tonys than I have, and I will be the first to cheer them on.

It is such a special honor to win a Tony Award. But I know that there is no daylight between me and all the theatre makers who have not been recognized with a Tony Award (yet!). Anytime you stand in front of an audience, whether it's an audience of three or three thousand, you are making art. You don't have to be on Broadway to create that magic and to be a brilliant artist. Theatre happens anywhere and everywhere.

So dare to dream. Dream as big as you can and then after all of that...dream even bigger.

---

**AUDRA McDONALD**

# INTRODUCTION

The theatre brings communities together. It is one of the few communal experiences we still have. It brings us together and allows us to have insight in a way that streaming something at home does not. The troubles we face as a world are not going to be made better by going away from each other. The theatre is a way that we can come together. We've been evolving as a society and certainly as a theatre industry.

The American Theatre Wing is about American theatre across the country, but I think the most important thing we do is that we create a pipeline into the industry that is diverse. Secondarily to that, we elevate the artist who is often hidden. We make it possible for people to spend a lifetime in the theatre, from the Title 1 schools that we support where we introduce the theatre, to training opportunities, all the way up to providing essential acknowledgment of an artist's work that allows the artist to get more work. We are there for a life cycle. We are also dedicated to making sure the playing field is as equitable as possible. You have to see it to believe it. When James Earl Jones and Chita Rivera won Lifetime Achievement Awards, you cannot underestimate the power of that. To quote Kenny Leon, "Lifetime Achievement tells kids of color everywhere that they can not only be in the theatre; they can have a lifetime in the theatre." We're working on all angles through the life cycle because we want these stories to be told; we need these stories to be told. Our society depends on it. When you have representation, you're saying to everyone that your voice matters.

Awards are not perfect, but we believe they matter. They can help to create opportunities for artists that they wouldn't otherwise get. You see it when people get it young, but then Cicely Tyson was in her nineties when she got her Tony, and it seemed to matter a lot to her. More importantly, it mattered to the history of the Tonys. It is about excellence.

Anniversaries are an important moment to reflect. We're looking back at seventy-five years to where we came from so we can charter the future. We're not perfect, but we're making strides. This book is a visual representation of what can happen when a community comes together, and will provide a road map for the next seventy-five years.

**HEATHER HITCHENS, PRESIDENT & CEO**
**EMILIO SOSA, CHAIR**
**AMERICAN THEATRE WING**

Heather Hitchens

Emilio Sosa

# A NOTE TO THE READER

This book is a commemoration
of over seventy-five years of the
American Theatre Wing and the actors,
playwrights, composers, lyricists,
directors, designers, choreographers,
and other working professionals
who give us all so much to celebrate.

These pages are filled with interviews,
stories, and memories from the people
who were there and who are now
a part of Tony history.

the **1940s**

The inscription on the back of a Tony award from 1947

# WINNERS ○ 1947

**AUTHOR (PLAY):** Arthur Miller, *All My Sons*

**ORIGINAL SCORE (MUSIC AND/OR LYRICS)**
**WRITTEN FOR THE THEATRE:** Kurt Weill, *Street Scene*

**ACTOR IN A LEADING ROLE IN A PLAY:**
José Ferrer, *Cyrano de Bergerac*; Fredric March, *Years Ago*

**ACTRESS IN A LEADING ROLE IN A PLAY:**
Ingrid Bergman, *Joan of Lorraine*; Helen Hayes, *Happy Birthday*

**ACTRESS IN A FEATURED ROLE IN A MUSICAL:**
Patricia Neal, *Another Part of the Forest*

**ACTOR IN A FEATURED ROLE IN A MUSICAL:** David Wayne, *Finian's Rainbow*

**SCENIC DESIGN:** David Folks, *Henry VIII*

**COSTUME DESIGN:** Lucinda Ballard, *Happy Birthday*, *Another Part of the Forest*,
*Street Scene*, *John Loves Mary*, *The Chocolate Soldier*

**DIRECTION (PLAY OR MUSICAL):** Elia Kazan, *All My Sons*

**CHOREOGRAPHY:** Agnes de Mille, *Brigadoon*; Michael Kidd, *Finian's Rainbow*

**SPECIAL TONY AWARD:** Dora Chamberlain; Mr. and Mrs. Ira Katzenberg;
Jules Leventhal; Burns Mantle; P.A. MacDonald; Vincent Sardi

**KATHLEEN MARSHALL:** Agnes de Mille was a pioneer. She was a woman choreographing on Broadway at a time when there weren't many women on creative teams. She moved plots forward through dance and created characters for her dancers. They were not anonymous identical members of the chorus; they were unique individuals and real people. I try to emulate that in my work.

**RUBEN SANTIAGO-HUDSON:** As an artist José Ferrer was the epitome of excellence in every way. An actor and director who destroyed every barrier and stereotype imposed upon him. A proud Puerto Rican from Santurce, Princeton graduate, Oscar winner, multiple Tony Award winner, Golden Globe winner, National Medal of Arts Honor recipient, and recipient of a host of other recognitions and achievements. José Ferrer is the benchmark of what all artists should look to as an example of grace, style, perseverance, and infinite brilliance. José Ferrer was a beacon of light in an often too dark business, and specifically for me as a Puerto Rican he is my shining star.

A ticket from the inaugural Tony Awards

The program from the very first Tony Awards

José Ferrer as Cyrano de Bergerac

# WINNERS ○ 1948

**PLAY:** *Mister Roberts*, Thomas Heggen and Joshua Logan

**AUTHOR (PLAY):** Thomas Heggen and Joshua Logan, *Mister Roberts*

**PRODUCER (PLAY):** Leland Hayward, *Mister Roberts*

**ACTOR IN A LEADING ROLE IN A PLAY:**
Henry Fonda, *Mister Roberts*; Paul Kelly, *Command Decision*;
Basil Rathbone, *The Heiress*

**ACTRESS IN A LEADING ROLE IN A PLAY:** Judith Anderson, *Medea*;
Katharine Cornell, *Antony and Cleopatra*; Jessica Tandy, *A Streetcar Named Desire*

**ACTOR IN A LEADING ROLE IN A MUSICAL:**
Paul Hartman, *Angel in the Wings*

**ACTRESS IN A LEADING ROLE IN A MUSICAL:**
Grace Hartman, *Angel in the Wings*

**SCENIC DESIGN:** Horace Armistead, *The Medium*

**COSTUME DESIGN:** Mary Percy Schenck, *The Heiress*

**DIRECTION:** Joshua Logan, *Mister Roberts*

**CHOREOGRAPHY:** Jerome Robbins, *High Button Shoes*

**CONDUCTOR AND MUSICAL DIRECTOR:** Max Meth, *Finian's Rainbow*

**OUTSTANDING PERFORMANCE BY NEWCOMERS:** June Lockhart,
*For Love or Money*; James Whitmore, *Command Decision*

**REGIONAL THEATRE TONY AWARD:**
Robert Porterfield; Virginia Barter Theatre

**SPECIAL TONY AWARD:** Rosalind Gilder; Vera Allen;
Experimental Theatre, Inc.; the cast of *The Importance of Being
Earnest*; Robert W. Dowling; George Pierce; Mary Martin; Joe E. Brown

**STAGE TECHNICIAN:** George Gebhardt

Antoinette Perry, co-founder of the American Theatre Wing
and namesake of the Tony Award

FOR LOVE OR MONEY

THE PLAYBILL

REGISTERED IN U.S. PATENT OFFICE

FOR HENRY MILLER'S THEATRE

**JUNE LOCKHART** The Tony for my performance in F. Hugh Herbert's *For Love or Money* was the first time a Tony was awarded for Outstanding Newcomer. Of course, I was thrilled to win! Appearing in the show was a joy, and it meant so much to me to be part of and acknowledged by the community of theatre professionals.

In those days, the award was a medallion, with my initials on one side. I wore it on my charm bracelet for many years. I donated that original gold medallion; it is on display at the Smithsonian.

(Top to bottom) John Loder, Vicki Cummings, and June Lockhart on the cover of the *Playbill* for *For Love or Money*

# WINNERS ○ 1949

**PLAY:** *Death of a Salesman*, Arthur Miller
Produced by Kermit Bloomgarden, Walter Fried

**MUSICAL:** *Kiss Me, Kate*
Produced by Saint-Subber, Lemuel Ayers

**BOOK OF A MUSICAL:** Bella and Sam Spewack, *Kiss Me, Kate*

**ORIGINAL SCORE (MUSIC AND/OR LYRICS) WRITTEN FOR THE THEATRE:**
Cole Porter, *Kiss Me, Kate*

**ACTOR IN A LEADING ROLE IN A PLAY:** Rex Harrison, *Anne of the Thousand Days*

**ACTRESS IN A LEADING ROLE IN A PLAY:** Martita Hunt, *The Madwoman of Chaillot*

**ACTOR IN A LEADING ROLE IN A MUSICAL:** Ray Bolger, *Where's Charley?*

**ACTRESS IN A LEADING ROLE IN A MUSICAL:** Nanette Fabray, *Love Life*

**ACTOR IN A FEATURED ROLE IN A PLAY:** Arthur Kennedy, *Death of a Salesman*

**ACTRESS IN A FEATURED ROLE IN A PLAY:** Shirley Booth, *Goodbye, My Fancy*

**SCENIC DESIGN:** Jo Mielziner, *Sleepy Hollow, Summer and Smoke,*
*Anne of the Thousand Days, Death of a Salesman, South Pacific*

**COSTUME DESIGN:** Lemuel Ayers, *Kiss Me Kate*

**DIRECTION:** Elia Kazan, *Death of a Salesman*

**CHOREOGRAPHY:**
Gower Champion, *Lend an Ear*

**CONDUCTOR AND MUSICAL DIRECTOR:**
Max Meth, *As the Girls Go*

Nanette Fabray, Ray Bolger, and Shirley Booth with
their Tony medallions

**JULES FISHER:** Jo Mielziner is one of the few scenic designers who did his own lighting for every show in his long career. He was brilliant at understanding how the play should be told. A lot of the staging in *Death of a Salesman* was affected by Jo. The ability to get the brother from the upstairs bedroom downstairs in the blink of an eye was Jo's idea. He was a big influence for me.

Mildred Dunnock, Lee J. Cobb, Arthur Kennedy, and Cameron Mitchell on Jo Mielziner's set for *Death of a Salesman*

# the 1950s

Helen Hayes with 1950 Tony winners Sidney Blackmer and Shirley Booth

# WINNERS ◎ 1950

**PLAY:** *The Cocktail Party*, T.S. Eliot
Produced by Gilbert Miller

**MUSICAL:** *South Pacific*
Produced by Leland Hayward, Oscar Hammerstein II,
Joshua Logan, Richard Rodgers

**BOOK OF A MUSICAL:** Oscar Hammerstein II and
Joshua Logan, *South Pacific*

**ORIGINAL SCORE (MUSIC AND/OR LYRICS) WRITTEN FOR THE THEATRE:**
Richard Rodgers, *South Pacific*

**ACTOR IN A LEADING ROLE IN A PLAY:** Sidney Blackmer, *Come Back, Little Sheba*

**ACTRESS IN A LEADING ROLE IN A PLAY:** Shirley Booth, *Come Back, Little Sheba*

**ACTOR IN A LEADING ROLE IN A MUSICAL:** Ezio Pinza, *South Pacific*

**ACTRESS IN A LEADING ROLE IN A MUSICAL:** Mary Martin, *South Pacific*

**ACTOR IN A FEATURED ROLE IN A MUSICAL:** Myron McCormick, *South Pacific*

**ACTRESS IN A FEATURED ROLE IN A MUSICAL:** Juanita Hall, *South Pacific*

**SCENIC DESIGN:** Jo Mielziner, *The Innocents*

**COSTUME DESIGN:** Aline Bernstein, *Regina*

**DIRECTION:** Joshua Logan, *South Pacific*

**CHOREOGRAPHY:** Helen Tamiris, *Touch and Go*

**CONDUCTOR AND MUSICAL DIRECTOR:** Maurice Abravanel, *Regina*

**SPECIAL TONY AWARD:** Maurice Evans; Philip Faversham; Brock Pemberton

**STAGE TECHNICIAN:** Joe Lynn, *Miss Liberty*

**ANDRÉ BISHOP:** Rodgers and Hammerstein are timeless when they're in the hands of a good director and a good production. The social import of their shows has suddenly come to the forefront again. Directors like Bartlett Sher emphasize that. The racial aspects of *South Pacific*, the political aspects of *The King and I*, the dynamic between men and women in *Carousel* were all emphasized in our productions at Lincoln Center Theater.

**BARTLETT SHER:** What people forget about Rodgers and Hammerstein is they were so daring in the way they were pushing the whole form forward. When we watch it now, it feels very traditional, but they did things nobody had done up to then. They took on subjects no one would dare take on when it came to musicals. They were highly experimental. Hammerstein loved pushing it forward. They had the first death in a musical. Nobody had ever imagined doing anything like *South Pacific*. The idea that you would do *King and I* set somewhere in Thailand was new. *Oklahoma!* was the first musical that used the songs to move the story forward and had a giant ballet sequence in it which Agnes de Mille choreographed. It's insane when you think of how they moved musicals forward and how they were unafraid to take real risks. They had incredible success doing it. Lin-Manuel Miranda has said that the opening of *Oklahoma!* was as radical in 1943 as *Hamilton*. Nobody had ever seen anything like it; it was that edgy and complex. In 2019 Daniel Fish did this miraculous experimental version, which was based on the original experimental musical. Rodgers and Hammerstein knew there were controversial issues in the show. They put it more into the subtext than Daniel's production, but they were aware of the themes they were trying to take on. They were really trying to push the envelope to see what the musical could reach to in terms of statements about America and who we are, and to capture a sound of who we were at the time. They knew all of that, and they were fully immersed in that ability.

Helen Hayes, center, with, from left, Leland Hayward, Oscar Hammerstein II, Joshua Logan, Myron McCormick, Richard Rodgers, and Juanita Hall, all from *South Pacific*

(From left) Isabel Bigley, Tennessee Williams, and Uta Hagen

# WINNERS ◎ 1951

**PLAY:** *The Rose Tattoo*, Tennessee Williams
Produced by Cheryl Crawford

**MUSICAL:** *Guys and Dolls*
Produced by Cy Feuer, Ernest H. Martin

**ORIGINAL SCORE (MUSIC AND/OR LYRICS) WRITTEN FOR THE THEATRE:**
Irving Berlin, *Call Me Madam*

**ACTOR IN A LEADING ROLE IN A PLAY:** Claude Rains, *Darkness at Noon*

**ACTRESS IN A LEADING ROLE IN A PLAY:** Uta Hagen, *The Country Girl*

**ACTOR IN A LEADING ROLE IN A MUSICAL:** Robert Alda, *Guys and Dolls*

**ACTRESS IN A LEADING ROLE IN A MUSICAL:** Ethel Merman, *Call Me Madam*

**ACTOR IN A FEATURED ROLE IN A PLAY:** Eli Wallach, *The Rose Tattoo*

**ACTRESS IN A FEATURED ROLE IN A PLAY:** Maureen Stapleton, *The Rose Tattoo*

**ACTOR IN A FEATURED ROLE IN A MUSICAL:** Russell Nype, *Call Me Madam*

**ACTRESS IN A FEATURED ROLE IN A MUSICAL:** Isabel Bigley, *Guys and Dolls*

**SCENIC DESIGN:** Boris Aronson, *The Rose Tattoo*, *The Country Girl*, *Season in the Sun*

**COSTUME DESIGN:** Miles White, *Bless You All*

**DIRECTION (PLAY OR MUSICAL):**
George S. Kaufman, *Guys and Dolls*

**CHOREOGRAPHY:** Michael Kidd, *Guys and Dolls*

**CONDUCTOR AND MUSICAL DIRECTOR:**
Lehman Engel, *The Consul*

**SPECIAL TONY AWARD:** Ruth Green

**STAGE TECHNICIAN:** Richard Raven,
*The Autumn Garden*

Boris Aronson's sketch of the set for *The Rose Tattoo*

# WINNERS ◎ 1952

PLAY: *The Fourposter*, Jan de Hartog

MUSICAL: *The King and I*

ACTOR IN A LEADING ROLE IN A PLAY: José Ferrer, *The Shrike*

ACTRESS IN A LEADING ROLE IN A PLAY: Julie Harris, *I Am a Camera*

ACTOR IN A LEADING ROLE IN A MUSICAL: Phil Silvers, *Top Banana*

ACTRESS IN A LEADING ROLE IN A MUSICAL: Gertrude Lawrence, *The King and I*

ACTOR IN A FEATURED ROLE IN A PLAY: John Cromwell, *Point of No Return*

ACTRESS IN A FEATURED ROLE IN A PLAY: Marian Winters, *I Am a Camera*

ACTOR IN A FEATURED ROLE IN A MUSICAL: Yul Brynner, *The King and I*

ACTRESS IN A FEATURED ROLE IN A MUSICAL: Helen Gallagher, *Pal Joey*

SCENIC DESIGN: Jo Mielziner, *The King and I*

COSTUME DESIGN: Irene Sharaff, *The King and I*

DIRECTION (PLAY OR MUSICAL): José Ferrer, *The Shrike*, *The Fourposter*, *Stalag 17*

CHOREOGRAPHY: Robert Alton, *Pal Joey*

CONDUCTOR AND MUSICAL DIRECTOR: Max Meth, *Pal Joey*

SPECIAL TONY AWARD: Judy Garland, Edward Kook, Charles Boyer

STAGE TECHNICIAN: Peter Feller, *Call Me Madam*

Yul Brynner and Gertrude Lawrence in *The King and I*, wearing costumes designed by Irene Sharaff

Oscar Hammerstein II, Gertrude Lawrence, Richard Rodgers, Helen Hayes, Phil Silvers, Judy Garland, and Yul Brynner

# WINNERS ◯ 1953

**PLAY:** *The Crucible*, Arthur Miller
Produced by Kermit Bloomgarden

**MUSICAL:** *Wonderful Town*
Produced by Robert Fryer

**ACTOR IN A LEADING ROLE IN A PLAY:** Tom Ewell, *The Seven Year Itch*

**ACTRESS IN A LEADING ROLE IN A PLAY:** Shirley Booth, *Time of the Cuckoo*

**ACTOR IN A LEADING ROLE IN A MUSICAL:** Thomas Mitchell, *Hazel Flagg*

**ACTRESS IN A LEADING ROLE IN A MUSICAL:** Rosalind Russell, *Wonderful Town*

**ACTOR IN A FEATURED ROLE IN A PLAY:** John Williams, *Dial M for Murder*

**ACTRESS IN A FEATURED ROLE IN A PLAY:** Beatrice Straight, *The Crucible*

**ACTOR IN A FEATURED ROLE IN A MUSICAL:** Hiram Sherman, *Two's Company*

**ACTRESS IN A FEATURED ROLE IN A MUSICAL:** Sheila Bond, *Wish You Were Here*

**SCENIC DESIGN:** Raoul Pène Du Bois, *Wonderful Town*

**COSTUME DESIGN:** Miles White, *Hazel Flagg*

**DIRECTION (PLAY OR MUSICAL):** Joshua Logan, *Picnic*

**CHOREOGRAPHY:** Donald Saddler, *Wonderful Town*

**CONDUCTOR AND MUSICAL DIRECTOR:** Lehman Engel, *Wonderful Town* and Gilbert and Sullivan Season

**SPECIAL TONY AWARD:** Beatrice Lillie; Danny Kaye; Equity Community Theatre

**STAGE TECHNICIAN:** Abe Kurnit, *Wish You Were Here*

Beatrice Lillie and Thomas Mitchell

# WINNERS ◎ 1954

Audrey Hepburn, Dolores Gray, and Jo Van Fleet

PLAY: *The Teahouse of the August Moon*, John Patrick
Produced by Maurice Evans, George Schaefer

MUSICAL: *Kismet*
Produced by Charles Lederer

ACTOR IN A LEADING ROLE IN A PLAY:
David Wayne, *The Teahouse of the August Moon*

ACTRESS IN A LEADING ROLE IN A PLAY: Audrey Hepburn, *Ondine*

ACTOR IN A LEADING ROLE IN A MUSICAL: Alfred Drake, *Kismet*

ACTRESS IN A LEADING ROLE IN A MUSICAL: Dolores Gray, *Carnival in Flanders*

ACTOR IN A FEATURED ROLE IN A PLAY: John Kerr, *Tea and Sympathy*

ACTRESS IN A FEATURED ROLE IN A PLAY: Jo Van Fleet, *The Trip to Bountiful*

ACTOR IN A FEATURED ROLE IN A MUSICAL: Harry Belafonte,
*John Murray Anderson's Almanac*

ACTRESS IN A FEATURED ROLE IN A MUSICAL: Gwen Verdon, *Can-Can*

SCENIC DESIGN: Peter Larkin, *Ondine*, *The Teahouse of the August Moon*

COSTUME DESIGN: Richard Whorf, *Ondine*

DIRECTION (PLAY OR MUSICAL):
Alfred Lunt, *Ondine*

CHOREOGRAPHY:
Michael Kidd, *Can-Can*

CONDUCTOR AND MUSICAL DIRECTOR:
Louis Adrian, *Kismet*

STAGE TECHNICIAN:
John Davis, *Picnic*

David Wayne, Audrey Hepburn, and Faye Emerson

# WINNERS ◎ 1955

**PLAY:** *The Desperate Hours*, Joseph Hayes
Produced by Howard Erskine, Joseph Hayes

**MUSICAL:** *The Pajama Game*
Produced by Frederick Brisson, Robert Griffith, Harold Prince

**ACTOR IN A LEADING ROLE IN A PLAY:** Alfred Lunt, *Quadrille*

**ACTRESS IN A LEADING ROLE IN A PLAY:** Nancy Kelly, *The Bad Seed*

**ACTOR IN A LEADING ROLE IN A MUSICAL:** Walter Slezak, *Fanny*

**ACTRESS IN A LEADING ROLE IN A MUSICAL:** Mary Martin, *Peter Pan*

**ACTOR IN A FEATURED ROLE IN A PLAY:** Francis L. Sullivan,
*Witness for the Prosecution*

**ACTRESS IN A FEATURED ROLE IN A PLAY:** Patricia Jessel, *Witness for the Prosecution*

**ACTOR IN A FEATURED ROLE IN A MUSICAL:** Cyril Ritchard, *Peter Pan*

**ACTRESS IN A FEATURED ROLE IN A MUSICAL:** Carol Haney, *The Pajama Game*

**SCENIC DESIGN:** Oliver Messell, *House of Flowers*

**COSTUME DESIGN:** Cecil Beaton, *Quadrille*

**DIRECTION (PLAY OR MUSICAL):**
Robert Montgomery, *The Desperate Hours*

**CHOREOGRAPHY:** Bob Fosse, *The Pajama Game*

**CONDUCTOR AND MUSICAL DIRECTOR:** Thomas Schippers,
*The Saint of Bleecker Street*

**SPECIAL TONY AWARD:** Proscenium Productions

**STAGE TECHNICIAN:** Richard Rodda, *Peter Pan*

Rosalind Russell, Sybil Trubin, Carol Haney, Helen Hayes, Nancy Kelly, and Elizabeth Montgomery, who was there accepting on behalf of her father, Robert Montgomery

# WINNERS ◎ 1956

**PLAY:** *The Diary of Anne Frank*, Frances Goodrich and Albert Hackett
Produced by Kermit Bloomgarden

**MUSICAL:** *Damn Yankees*, George Abbott and Douglass Wallop
Produced by Frederick Brisson, Robert Griffith, Harold Prince in association with Albert B. Taylor

**ACTOR IN A LEADING ROLE IN A PLAY:** Paul Muni, *Inherit the Wind*

**ACTRESS IN A LEADING ROLE IN A PLAY:** Julie Harris, *The Lark*

**ACTOR IN A LEADING ROLE IN A MUSICAL:** Ray Walston, *Damn Yankees*

**ACTRESS IN A LEADING ROLE IN A MUSICAL:** Gwen Verdon, *Damn Yankees*

**ACTOR IN A FEATURED ROLE IN A PLAY:** Ed Begley, *Inherit the Wind*

**ACTRESS IN A FEATURED ROLE IN A PLAY:** Una Merkel, *The Ponder Heart*

**ACTOR IN A FEATURED ROLE IN A MUSICAL:** Russ Brown, *Damn Yankees*

**ACTRESS IN A FEATURED ROLE IN A MUSICAL:** Lotte Lenya, *The Threepenny Opera*

**SCENIC DESIGN:** Peter Larkin, *Inherit the Wind*, *No Time for Sergeants*

**COSTUME DESIGN:** Alvin Colt, *Pipe Dream*

**DIRECTION (PLAY OR MUSICAL):** Tyrone Guthrie, *The Matchmaker*

**CHOREOGRAPHY:** Bob Fosse, *Damn Yankees*

**CONDUCTOR AND MUSICAL DIRECTOR:** Hal Hastings, *Damn Yankees*

**SPECIAL TONY AWARD:**
City Center; Fourth Street Chekhov Theatre;
The Shakespearewrights; *The Threepenny
Opera*; The Theatre Collection of the
N.Y. Public Library

**STAGE TECHNICIAN:** Harry Green, *Middle
of the Night*, *Damn Yankees*

Ed Begley, Gwen Verdon,
Una Merkel, and Ray Walston

Julie Harris, Paul Muni, and Helen Hayes

**JUDY PRINCE:** Hal was thrilled to be a Tony winner. I'm looking at twenty-one of them now. In the early days the show was produced by Alex Cohen. We would all gather in our seats, and he would go up and down in the aisles to the nominees. He'd say, "Hi, Hal, how was your summer?" It felt like a school picnic. It was just a lot of people who were in the theatre and had a real feel of family. The Tonys always gave Hal a feeling of continuity; it reminded him how long he'd been in the theatre. That meant a lot to him. He loved being a part of the theatre community. His motto was always the day after the Tony Awards or the day after a show opened, he would be working on his next show.

**CHITA RIVERA:** Hal Prince was full of ideas and allowed his actors to have the freedom pick and choose the right solutions for them. I didn't know where to go when I played the Spider Woman. He allowed me to take the time to find her.

**JOHN KANDER:** Hal Prince was a marvelous, volatile, super talented producer of theatre. *Cabaret* was a wonderful, exciting experience. *Zorba* was Hal's idea, and that was a rich, exciting time. My experiences with Hal were very fulfilling.

**ANDREW LLOYD WEBBER:** I always wanted to work with Hal Prince. I wish I'd known he wanted to direct *Jesus Christ Superstar*. I never got the telegram that he sent. *Evita* was our first collaboration, and I knew he was exactly the right person to direct *The Phantom of the*

*Opera*. He really understood how important it was that a show look visually right. He said, "You can't listen to a musical if you can't look at it." That's a very important mantra. The look of a show can make or break it, especially a musical.

Hal Prince in 1995, holding his Tony Award for Best Director of a Musical for *Show Boat*.

# WINNERS ◔ 1957

**PLAY:** *Long Day's Journey into Night*, Eugene O'Neill
Produced by Leigh Connell, Theodore Mann, José Quintero

**MUSICAL:** *My Fair Lady*
Produced by Herman Levin

**ACTOR IN A LEADING ROLE IN A PLAY:**
Frederic March, *Long Day's Journey into Night*

**ACTRESS IN A LEADING ROLE IN A PLAY:** Margaret Leighton, *Separate Tables*

**ACTOR IN A LEADING ROLE IN A MUSICAL:** Rex Harrison, *My Fair Lady*

**ACTRESS IN A LEADING ROLE IN A MUSICAL:** Judy Holliday, *Bells Are Ringing*

**ACTOR IN A FEATURED ROLE IN A PLAY:** Frank Conroy, *The Potting Shed*

**ACTRESS IN A FEATURED ROLE IN A PLAY:** Peggy Cass, *Auntie Mame*

**ACTOR IN A FEATURED ROLE IN A MUSICAL:** Sydney Chaplin, *Bells Are Ringing*

**ACTRESS IN A FEATURED ROLE IN A MUSICAL:** Edith Adams, *Li'l Abner*

**SCENIC DESIGN:** Oliver Smith, *My Fair Lady*

**COSTUME DESIGN:** Cecil Beaton, *My Fair Lady*

**DIRECTION (PLAY OR MUSICAL):** Moss Hart, *My Fair Lady*

**CHOREOGRAPHY:** Michael Kidd, *Li'l Abner*

**CONDUCTOR AND MUSICAL DIRECTOR:**
Franz Allers, *My Fair Lady*

**SPECIAL TONY AWARD:** American Shakespeare Festival;
Jean-Louis Barrault; Robert Russell Bennett; William
Hammerstein; Paul Shyre

**STAGE TECHNICIAN:** Howard McDonald, *Major Barbara*

Sydney Chaplin and
Edith Adams

(Seated, from left) Sydney Chaplin, Peggy Cass, and Moss Hart (Standing, from left)
Judy Holliday, Rex Harrison, Margaret Leighton, Fredric March, and Edith Adams

# WINNERS ◎ 1958

PLAY: *Sunrise at Campobello*, Dore Schary
Produced by Lawrence Langner, Theresa Helburn, Armina Marshall, Dore Schary

MUSICAL: *The Music Man*
Produced by Kermit Bloomgarden, Herbert Greene in association with Frank Productions

ACTOR IN A LEADING ROLE IN A PLAY: Ralph Bellamy, *Sunrise at Campobello*

ACTRESS IN A LEADING ROLE IN A PLAY: Helen Hayes, *Time Remembered*

ACTOR IN A LEADING ROLE IN A MUSICAL: Robert Preston, *The Music Man*

ACTRESS IN A LEADING ROLE IN A MUSICAL: Thelma Ritter,
*New Girl in Town*; Gwen Verdon, *New Girl in Town*

ACTOR IN A FEATURED ROLE IN A PLAY: Henry Jones, *Sunrise at Campobello*

ACTRESS IN A FEATURED ROLE IN A PLAY: Anne Bancroft, *Two for the Seesaw*

ACTOR IN A FEATURED ROLE IN A MUSICAL: David Burns, *The Music Man*

ACTRESS IN A FEATURED ROLE IN A MUSICAL: Barbara Cook, *The Music Man*

SCENIC DESIGN: Oliver Smith, *West Side Story*

COSTUME DESIGN: Motley, *The First Gentleman*

DIRECTION (PLAY OR MUSICAL): Vincent J. Donehue, *Sunrise at Campobello*

CHOREOGRAPHY: Jerome Robbins, *West Side Story*

CONDUCTOR AND MUSICAL DIRECTOR:
Herbert Greene, *The Music Man*

SPECIAL TONY AWARD: New York Shakespeare
Festival; Mrs. Martin Beck; Circle in the Square;
Phoenix Theatre; Esther Hawley

STAGE TECHNICIAN: Harry Romar,
*Time Remembered*

Robert Preston, Thelma Ritter, Helen Hayes, and Ralph Bellamy

Chita Rivera (left) and the cast of *West Side Story* performing Jerome
Robbins's choreography; set design by Oliver Smith

**CHITA RIVERA:** I called Jerome Robbins Big Daddy. If he had told me to leap off a seven-story building and land on my left foot and take two steps forward, I would have done it, because I really believed in him. He taught me that you never get anything worthwhile unless you really work hard for it. I learned so much from him, and I was better off from working with him. He cast me in my very first show, *Call Me Madam*. I was one of four principal characters in the show. I had no idea how valuable that was at the time.

**JASON ALEXANDER:** Jerry Robbins did meticulous research when he began a project. He was a very exacting person, but he was very exacting with himself too. He was not a casual creator. He was a dedicated and serious creator. As a result, no one would ever mark something for Jerry Robbins. No one gave him 90 percent at a rehearsal. The reason his dancers were more extraordinary than other dancers is because he didn't teach them moves; he taught them their characters…how they were telling the story with their bodies. He imbued dancers with character and intention.

Jerry came up through a school of thinking that you break an artist, and then you train them. That's how Jerry was treated, and I think he felt that was the way others needed to be treated as well. It could make him cruel at times. On occasions he would take talented people and shut them down or remove them from a role or make them feel unworthy. It was heartbreaking to see. I knew his heart; I saw his heart. He did not want to be cruel. On our opening night of *Jerome Robbins' Broadway* he was in my dressing room weeping. I said, "You can't possibly be nervous. It's glorious. It's everything you could ever want it to be." He said, "I know. I just don't want it to end." He loved all of it and everyone. Even the ones he tortured; he loved them. But it was such a complicated, complex relationship. I feel very blessed to have gotten to know him a little bit and see into his heart in those moments. And he could be so kind and so generous, too. If a little kid came into the rehearsal space, he was Santa Claus. He was magical with children. But I do believe he had a demon he could not exorcise.

**BERNADETTE PETERS** I was a kid and Robert Preston was an established actor when I worked with him. The day after we had done a show he said, "That scene went a different way last night…That's good." What he was saying was we didn't have to get stuck and do the show by rote. We were in the moment, and that's all we need to do. That was so freeing when he told me that. That's the best advice I ever got working with someone, and I never forgot it.

# WINNERS ◎ 1959

PLAY: *J.B.*, Archibald MacLeish
Produced by Alfred de Liagre Jr.

MUSICAL: *Redhead*, Herbert and Dorothy Fields, Sidney Sheldon, and David Shaw
Produced by Robert Fryer, Lawrence Carr

ACTOR IN A LEADING ROLE IN A PLAY: Jason Robards Jr., *The Disenchanted*

ACTRESS IN A LEADING ROLE IN A PLAY: Gertrude Berg, *A Majority of One*

ACTOR IN A LEADING ROLE IN A MUSICAL: Richard Kiley, *Redhead*

ACTRESS IN A LEADING ROLE IN A MUSICAL: Gwen Verdon, *Redhead*

ACTOR IN A FEATURED ROLE IN A PLAY: Charlie Ruggles,
*The Pleasure of His Company*

ACTRESS IN A FEATURED ROLE IN A PLAY: Julie Newmar, *The Marriage-Go-Round*

ACTOR IN A FEATURED ROLE IN A MUSICAL: Russell Nype, *Goldilocks*;
Leonard Stone, *Redhead*

ACTRESS IN A FEATURED ROLE IN A MUSICAL: Pat Stanley, *Goldilocks*

SCENIC DESIGN: Donald Oenslager, *A Majority of One*

COSTUME DESIGN: Rouben Ter-Arutunian, *Redhead*

DIRECTION (PLAY OR MUSICAL): Elia Kazan, *J.B.*

CHOREOGRAPHY: Bob Fosse, *Redhead*

CONDUCTOR AND MUSICAL DIRECTOR: Salvatore Dell'Isola, *Flower Drum Song*

SPECIAL TONY AWARD: John Gielgud; Howard Lindsay and Russell Crouse;
Cast of *La Plume de Ma Tante* (Pamela Austin, Colette Brosset, Roger Caccia,
Yvonne Constant, Genevieve Coulombel, Robert Dhery, Michael Kent,
Jean Lefevre, Jacques Legras, Michael Modo, Pierre Olaf, Nicole Parent,
Ross Parker, and Henri Pennec)

STAGE TECHNICIAN: Sam Knapp, *The Music Man*

Tony winners Jason Robards Jr., Gwen Verdon, and Richard Kiley with Claudette Colbert and Bud Collyer

**ACTRESS–MUSICAL STAR**                                                      WRITE-INS

Miyoshi Umeki                 ||

Gwen Verdon                   ||||| ||||| ||||| ||||| |||| ||||    28 ✓

**ACTOR–DRAMATIC FEATURED or SUPPORTING**

Marc Connelly                 //||

George Grizzard               ||||| |

Walter Matthau                ||||| |

Robert Morse                  / ||                                  13 ✓

Charlie Ruggles               ||||| ||||| |||

George Scott

**ACTRESS–DRAMATIC FEATURED or SUPPORTING**

Maureen Delany                |||||

Dolores Hart                  ||||| |||                            8 ✓

Julie Newmar                  ||||| |||

Nan Martin                    ||||| ||

Bertice Reading               / |||

**ACTOR–MUSICAL FEATURED or SUPPORTING**

Russell Nype        7         || |||||      Joyce the Grosi 1

Leonard Stone       7         | |||||       Pierre My 1 5
    Ed. Kennedy                |

**ACTRESS–MUSICAL FEATURED or SUPPORTING**

Julienne Marie                / ||          Estelle Grosst 1

Pat Stanley                   ||||| ||||| ⑪    Pamela Austin 1
    Sissenden                  ||
        OR
Supporting Cast of La Plume de Ma Tante  ||||| ||||| |      (11 + 2)  13

**SCENIC DESIGNER**

Boris Aronson  ||||| |       Donald Oenslager  ||||| ||||| |||    13 ✓

Ballou         |             Teo Otto           |||

Ben Edwards    |||           Oliver Smith       1

Oliver Messel  |||||

---

**COSTUME DESIGNER**

Castillo                      |||||

Dorothy Jeakins               |||

Oliver Messel                 ||||| ||

Irene Sharaff                 ||||| ||

Rouben-Ter-Aruntunian         ||||| |||                           8 ✓

**DIRECTOR**

Peter Brook                   ||||| |

Robert Dhery                  |

William Gaskill               ||

Peter Glenville               //                                  11 ✓

Elia Kazan                    ||||| ||||| |

Cyril Ritchard                ||||| |

Dore Schary                   |||

**CHOREOGRAPHER**

Agnes De Mille                ||||| ||||

Bob Fosse                     ||||| ||||| ||                       12 ✓

Carol Haney                   |||||

Onna White                    |||

**MUSICAL DIRECTOR**

Jay Blackton                  ||||| ||

Salvatore Dell'Isola          ||||| ||||                          9 ✓

Lehman Engel                  ||||| |

Gershon Kingsley              ||

**TECHNICIAN**

Edward Fitzgerald     4

Thomas Flynn          3

Sam Knapp             || + ||                                     17 ✓

Comden Green 1        Lindsay & Crows
                      Gielgud

Handwritten voting tallies from the 12th Annual Tony Awards in 1959

Gwen Verdon, 1959 Tony winner, with Ingrid Bergman, 1947 Tony winner

**JULIE NEWMAR:** My mother was in the Ziegfeld Follies, and when I was growing up, she always told me, "If you make it on Broadway, you've made it." I started as a dancer, and *The Marriage-Go-Round* was my very first acting job. I was in stellar company with Charles Boyer and Claudette Colbert. I learned so much just by being in their presence. The way they worked, their manners, their rapport with the audience. The show ran for a year and a month to standing room only. The only reason that it had to close was because Charles Boyer had a movie commitment in the south of France.

When you're up there accepting, you're not aware of what's happening or what you're saying or what's going on. You're just in the thrill state. It's important to thank your producer. You're there to sell tickets. An artist can't be appreciated unless that artist can fill seats.

People go to the theatre to be moved, elevated, to have the light turned on their souls. We, the artists, are the safe distraction from the ordinary grind of life. Occasionally, some show or performance hits the theatrical jackpot and will be remembered fifty years later. Theatre is the real deal—you had to be there. It is a head-on collision of spontaneity as well as transformation. Theatre has always been my first love.

The Tony is beautiful. The design of it is exquisite. I love how it spins around. I have it on a shelf in my den. After I won the Tony for that first performance, I thought it wise to enroll in acting school. I wanted to live up to the award. Winning means you will be grateful to many people.

Julie Newmar, center, with Charles Boyer and Claudette Colbert in *The Marriage-Go-Round*

# ACCEPTANCE SPEECHES THROUGH THE YEARS

Very wise choice. **BRIAN BEDFORD (1971)**

**TOMMY TUNE (2015):** Right now I'm thinking about Texas in the fifties. You see, my father's great dream for me was the same as every Texas father's dream for their firstborn son. They wanted us all to leave Texas, go to New York, and dance in the chorus of a Broadway show. And I did and I loved every single time step, especially tonight. This is a great honor....I want to thank each and every one of you who...through the years, have either attended or contributed to my Broadway offerings. They would not have worked without you. We know that Broadway has a universal mystique, and I am proud and humbled to be a part of our Broadway universe. It's vast and inclusive, and I believe that all of it—all of it—is simply an expression of love. What I did for love. What we do for love. My cup runneth over. On with the show!

Anthony Crivello and Tommy Tune

**MARSHALL W. MASON (2016):** On this night forty years ago, after I lost the first of my five nominations to the ever excellent Ellis Rabb I went to the party at the Waldorf Astoria, where [a] theatre critic taunted me: "Too bad you didn't win." I told him I thought the true honor lay in being nominated. He scoffed, "Nobody remembers the nominees, only who won." I'm very happy that you proved him wrong by remembering me. So for all you nominees this year, let me just say congratulations. Nobody at the Tony Awards is a loser. Everybody's a winner....To my artistic soulmate, the great Lanford Wilson, who celebrated the spirit of America more eloquently than anyone of his generation. Lance, this is for us.

I tell my kids every day that bad behavior and hysteria and tantrums and tears will get them nowhere. I don't quite know how to explain this.

**MARCIA GAY HARDEN (2009)**

**DAVEED DIGGS (2016):** When I was in preschool we were supposed to do a performance for the parents, and I didn't want to do it. My mom talked to the teacher, she came back she said you don't have to do it but you have to do something. And I said I want to do a gymnastics routine with my dad. And a couple of days later my dad showed up with me in matching rainbow tights and we did this gymnastics routine in front of the parents at the preschool. And the important thing about that story to me is that (1) my mom gave me permission to do something that everybody else wasn't doing and (2) my dad supported me and made it possible. I think a lot of us are here because people in our lives did that.

**DAVID HYDE PIERCE (2007):** I made my Broadway debut twenty-five years ago as the waiter in Chris Durang's *Beyond Therapy*, and the first words I ever spoke on a Broadway stage were "I'm sorry, we're going to have to ask you to leave." And I'm sitting here tonight, and I'm reminded of Raul's amazing performance and my dear friend Michael Cerveris, and Gavin, who tap dances on the ceiling, and Jonathan, who has so much talent at a young age that I have to go take a nap and I think, *Oh yeah, they're going to call my name. They're going to say, "David Hyde Pierce, I'm sorry, we're going to have to ask you to leave."*

David Hyde Pierce, Elizabeth Franz, and Christine Baranski

**CHRISTINE EBERSOLE (2007):** I left Hollywood when they told me I was over the hill, and now I'm standing here with this most distinguished award for what I consider to be the role of a lifetime. I'm over the hill in the role of a lifetime. This is so encouraging….This is for the Edies. May they live in our hearts forever, because those who take the journey when they come and see *Grey Gardens*, they help us get in touch with our humanity and our innate goodness.

**JEANINE TESORI (2015):** I didn't realize that a career in music was available to women until 1981. I saw the magnificent Linda Twine conduct [*Lena Horne: The Lady and Her Music*]. And that was my "Ring of Keys" moment, which, by the way, is not a song of love. It's a song of identification, because for girls you have to see it to be it. And I'm so proud to be standing here with Lisa Kron. We stand here on the shoulders of other women who've come before us: Mary Rodgers, Tania León, Linda Twine.

I already get to do *Something Rotten* eight times a week, so this feels like an embarrassment of riches. **CHRISTIAN BORLE (2015)**

**BRIAN YORKEY (2009):** For all those of you in this room and out there in America who are crazy enough to attempt something like an original musical, we salute you, and for what it's worth, two things we've learned: First, if you're working on something you believe in, keep going no matter how long it takes.
**TOM KITT (2009):** And second, find people who believe in it as much as you do and stand by you.

**GREGORY CLARKE (2009):** This is enormously generous, although it does of course give me an enormous problem because I now have to tell my parents that I don't actually work in a bank.

**REED BIRNEY (2016):** I've been an actor for almost forty-two years...but thirty-five of them were pretty bad. I just couldn't get anything going. So the last eight have been great. But the thing that was always great wherever I was, whatever level I was on, were the amazing people I got to work with.

# the 1960s

# WINNERS ◎ 1960

PLAY: *The Miracle Worker*, William Gibson
Produced by Fred Coe

MUSICAL: *The Sound of Music*, Howard Lindsay and Russel Crouse; *Fiorello!*,
Jerome Weidman and George Abbott
Produced by Leland Hayward, Richard Halliday, Rodgers and Hammerstein,
*The Sound of Music*; Robert E. Griffith and Harold S. Prince, *Fiorello!*

ACTOR IN A LEADING ROLE IN A PLAY: Melvyn Douglas, *The Best Man*

ACTRESS IN A LEADING ROLE IN A PLAY: Anne Bancroft, *The Miracle Worker*

ACTOR IN A LEADING ROLE IN A MUSICAL: Jackie Gleason, *Take Me Along*

ACTRESS IN A LEADING ROLE IN A MUSICAL: Mary Martin, *The Sound of Music*

ACTOR IN A FEATURED ROLE IN A PLAY: Roddy McDowall, *The Fighting Cock*

ACTRESS IN A FEATURED ROLE IN A PLAY: Anne Revere, *Toys in the Attic*

ACTOR IN A FEATURED ROLE IN A MUSICAL: Tom Bosley, *Fiorello!*

ACTRESS IN A FEATURED ROLE IN A MUSICAL: Patricia Neway, *The Sound of Music*

SCENIC DESIGN OF A PLAY: Howard Bay, *Toys in the Attic*

SCENIC DESIGN OF A MUSICAL: Oliver Smith, *The Sound of Music*

COSTUME DESIGN: Cecil Beaton, *Saratoga*

DIRECTION OF A PLAY: Arthur Penn, *The Miracle Worker*

DIRECTION OF A MUSICAL: George Abbott, *Fiorello!*

CHOREOGRAPHY: Michael Kidd, *Destry Rides Again*

CONDUCTOR AND MUSICAL DIRECTOR:
Frederick Dvonch, *The Sound of Music*

SPECIAL TONY AWARD: John D. Rockefeller III;
James Thurber and Burgess Meredith

STAGE TECHNICIAN: John Walters, *The Miracle Worker*

Winners in the lead acting categories (L to R): Mary Martin, Jackie Gleason, Anne Bancroft, and Melvyn Douglas

Oliver Smith's set design for *The Sound of Music*

Elizabeth Seal, winner of Actress in a Leading Role in a Musical, accepting her award from Cyril Ritchard and Mary Martin, 1955 co-stars and winners for *Peter Pan*

# WINNERS ◎ 1961

**PLAY:** *Becket*, Jean Anouilh, translated by Lucienne Hill
Produced by David Merrick

**MUSICAL:** *Bye Bye Birdie*
Produced by Edward Padula in association with L. Slade Brown

**ACTOR IN A LEADING ROLE IN A PLAY:** Zero Mostel, *Rhinoceros*

**ACTRESS IN A LEADING ROLE IN A PLAY:** Joan Plowright, *A Taste of Honey*

**ACTOR IN A LEADING ROLE IN A MUSICAL:** Richard Burton, *Camelot*

**ACTRESS IN A LEADING ROLE IN A MUSICAL:** Elizabeth Seal, *Irma La Douce*

**ACTOR IN A FEATURED ROLE IN A PLAY:** Martin Gable, *Big Fish, Little Fish*

**ACTRESS IN A FEATURED ROLE IN A PLAY:** Colleen Dewhurst, *All the Way Home*

**ACTOR IN A FEATURED ROLE IN A MUSICAL:** Dick Van Dyke, *Bye Bye Birdie*

**ACTRESS IN A FEATURED ROLE IN A MUSICAL:** Tammy Grimes, *The Unsinkable Molly Brown*

**SCENIC DESIGN OF A PLAY:** Oliver Smith, *Becket*

**SCENIC DESIGN OF A MUSICAL:** Oliver Smith, *Camelot*

**COSTUME DESIGN OF A PLAY:** Motley, *Becket*

**COSTUME DESIGN OF A MUSICAL:** Adrian and Tony Duquette, *Camelot*

**DIRECTION OF A PLAY:** Sir John Gielgud, *Big Fish, Little Fish*

**DIRECTION OF A MUSICAL:** Gower Champion, *Bye Bye Birdie*

**CHOREOGRAPHY:** Gower Champion, *Bye Bye Birdie*

**CONDUCTOR AND MUSICAL DIRECTOR:** Franz Allers, *Camelot*

**SPECIAL TONY AWARD:** David Merrick; The Theatre Guild

**STAGE TECHNICIAN:** Teddy Van Bemmel, *Becket*

Shirley Booth, Richard Burton, Elizabeth Seal, and Zero Mostel

Richard Burton, Julie Andrews, and the cast of *Camelot*; set design by Oliver Smith and costume design by Adrian

Chita Rivera and Dick Van Dyke in *Bye Bye Birdie*

Diahann Carroll, Robert Morse, Margaret Leighton, and Paul Scofield

# WINNERS ◎ 1962

**PLAY:** *A Man for All Season*, Robert Bolt
Produced by Robert Whitehead, Roger L. Stevens

**MUSICAL:** *How to Succeed in Business without Really Trying*
Produced by Cy Feuer, Ernest Martin

**BOOK OF A MUSICAL:** Abe Burrows, Jack Weinstock, and Willie Gilbert, *How to Succeed in Business without Really Trying*

**ORIGINAL SCORE (MUSIC AND/OR LYRICS) WRITTEN FOR THE THEATRE:** Richard Rodgers, *No Strings*

**ACTOR IN A LEADING ROLE IN A PLAY:** Paul Scofield, *A Man for All Seasons*

**ACTRESS IN A LEADING ROLE IN A PLAY:** Margaret Leighton, *The Night of the Iguana*

**ACTOR IN A LEADING ROLE IN A MUSICAL:** Robert Morse, *How to Succeed in Business without Really Trying*

**ACTRESS IN A LEADING ROLE IN A MUSICAL:** Anna Maria Alberghetti, *Carnival*; Diahann Carroll, *No Strings*

**ACTOR IN A FEATURED ROLE IN A PLAY:** Walter Matthau, *A Shot in the Dark*

**ACTRESS IN A FEATURED ROLE IN A PLAY:** Elizabeth Ashley, *Take Her, She's Mine*

**ACTOR IN A FEATURED ROLE IN A MUSICAL:** Charles Nelson Reilly, *How to Succeed in Business without Really Trying*

**ACTRESS IN A FEATURED ROLE IN A MUSICAL:** Phyllis Newman, *Subways Are for Sleeping*

**SCENIC DESIGN:** Will Steven Armstrong, *Carnival*

**COSTUME DESIGN:** Lucinda Ballard, *The Gay Life*

**DIRECTION OF A PLAY:** Noel Willman, *A Man for All Seasons*

**DIRECTION OF A MUSICAL:** Abe Burrows, *How to Succeed in Business without Really Trying*

**CHOREOGRAPHY:** Joe Layton, *No Strings*; Agnes de Mille, *Kwamina*

**CONDUCTOR AND MUSICAL DIRECTOR:** Elliot Lawrence, *How to Succeed in Business without Really Trying*

**SPECIAL TONY AWARD:** Brooks Atkinson; Franco Zeffirelli; Richard Rodgers

Phyllis Thaxter, Art Carney, and Elizabeth Ashley in *Take Her, She's Mine*

**ELIZABETH ASHLEY:** Even after all these years, I'm grateful to have gotten a Tony. It gives you a leg up in terms of getting work. Even decades later, producers know they can always put it behind your name in the advertising. I got my Tony before the ceremony was televised. Back in those days, the ceremony was a very grand dinner in the ballroom of the Waldorf Astoria. At that time, the only people who were involved or invited to attend the Tonys were theatre people. There were no movie stars. It was truly about nothing but the theatre. It's hard to believe, but in those days, one could be a star in the theatre without appearing in a sitcom or in the movies—like my idols Kim Stanley, Geraldine Page, and Julie Harris.

I think I won for two reasons: Art Carney and George Abbott. George Abbott had for decades been the most legendary and respected director in the Broadway theatre. Art Carney was really the "above the title" star of *Take Her, She's Mine* because it was the first time he'd been onstage since retiring from the iconic television show *The Honeymooners*. When you have George Abbott directing and Art Carney starring, what could go wrong? I was a real newcomer and a very young girl who had gotten a comedy role. In those days, there was no such thing as a female comedic ingenue. There had been tremendous publicity about who was going to get this role. I know they auditioned every "it girl" like Carol Lynley and Jane Fonda for that part. George Abbott kept saying no. He finally said to his daughter Judy Abbott, who was head of casting at George Abbott's office, and Hal Prince, who was an assistant in his office, that he wanted the most peculiar girl in New York. As a last-ditch attempt, I was called in for a cold reading, and I got the part.

To this day there are things that I learned working with George Abbott that I still rely on and preach incessantly to many of the young actors and directors that I work with. He was a strict disciplinarian. He instilled a strict work ethic in all his cast and crew, and they were the better for it. The most important thing I learned from George Abbott was to always play the truth, and never play for a laugh. He was a monument who stood against cheapness of any kind.

Winning was thrilling. I had great training from Sanford Meisner at the Neighborhood Playhouse, Lee Strasberg and the Actors Studio, and Philip Burton, who taught Shakespeare, which all prepared me, but winning was a definite surprise!

# WINNERS ◎ 1963

**PLAY:** *Who's Afraid of Virginia Woolf?*, Edward Albee
Produced by Theatre 1963, Richard Barr, Clinton Wilder

**MUSICAL:** *A Funny Thing Happened on the Way to the Forum*
Produced by Harold Prince

**BOOK OF A MUSICAL:** Burt Shevelove and Larry Gelbart,
*A Funny Thing Happened on the Way to the Forum*

**ORIGINAL SCORE (MUSIC AND/OR LYRICS) WRITTEN FOR THE THEATRE:**
Lionel Bart, *Oliver!*

**ACTOR IN A LEADING ROLE IN A PLAY:** Arthur Hill, *Who's Afraid of Virginia Woolf?*

**ACTRESS IN A LEADING ROLE IN A PLAY:** Uta Hagen, *Who's Afraid of Virginia Woolf?*

**ACTOR IN A LEADING ROLE IN A MUSICAL:** Zero Mostel, *A Funny Thing Happened on the Way to the Forum*

**ACTRESS IN A LEADING ROLE IN A MUSICAL:** Vivien Leigh, *Tovarich*

**ACTOR IN A FEATURED ROLE IN A PLAY:** Alan Arkin, *Enter Laughing*

**ACTRESS IN A FEATURED ROLE IN A PLAY:** Sandy Dennis, *A Thousand Clowns*

**ACTOR IN A FEATURED ROLE IN A MUSICAL:**
David Burns, *A Funny Thing Happened on the Way to the Forum*

**ACTRESS IN A FEATURED ROLE IN A MUSICAL:**
Anna Quayle, *Stop the World—I Want to Get Off*

**SCENIC DESIGN:** Sean Kenny, *Oliver!*

**COSTUME DESIGN:**
Anthony Powell, *The School for Scandal*

Sean Kenny's set design for *Oliver!*

DIRECTION OF A PLAY: Alan Schneider, *Who's Afraid of Virginia Woolf?*

DIRECTION OF A MUSICAL: George Abbott, *A Funny Thing Happened on the Way to the Forum*

CHOREOGRAPHY: Bob Fosse, *Little Me*

CONDUCTOR AND MUSICAL DIRECTOR: Donald Pippin, *Oliver!*

SPECIAL TONY AWARD: W. McNeil Lowry; Irving Berlin; Alan Bennett, Peter Cook, Jonathan Miller, and Dudley Moore

STAGE TECHNICIAN: Solly Pernick, *Mr. President*

ALAN ARKIN: When I won, I got up onstage and said, "I knew I was going to walk home with one of these, because my uncle Ken manufactures and designs them. He said if I didn't win, he was going to give me one anyway." That was the extent of my speech!

*Enter Laughing* turned my life upside down and inside out. We opened during a newspaper strike, so everybody was concerned there wouldn't be any reviews. But the television reviews were just sensational.

I thought I was going to get fired. The rumor was that Carl Reiner wanted to fire me because I took the show so seriously—I mean, it was Broadway!—that I wasn't funny for a long time. Then out of town I said, "Ah, screw it. I'm just going to have a good time." Then everything clicked into place.

*Enter Laughing* was interesting, to say the least. I was working with a lot of maniacs. Alan Mowbray was constantly drunk—so drunk that I had to say his lines as if I didn't hear them and repeat them every night. Sylvia Sidney played my mother in the show. I was getting so many laughs that she got furious. Her name was above the title, and at that point, my name had not been. One night I heard her screaming from her dressing room, "Ten years from now he will be nothing and I will still be Sylvia Sidney!" Ten years later I badly wanted to find her address and knock on her door and say, "Ten years ago you said in ten years I will be nothing and you will still be Sylvia Sidney. It's ten years, and you are nothing and I am Sylvia Sidney!" I never actually did it!

Irving Jacobson and Alan Arkin in *Enter Laughing*

# WINNERS ◎ 1964

**PLAY:** *Luther*, John Osborne Produced by David Merrick

**MUSICAL:** *Hello, Dolly!* Produced by David Merrick

**PRODUCER (PLAY):** Herman Shumlin, *The Deputy*

**BOOK OF A MUSICAL:** Michael Stewart, *Hello, Dolly!*

**ORIGINAL SCORE (MUSIC AND/OR LYRICS) WRITTEN FOR THE THEATRE:**
Jerry Herman, *Hello, Dolly!*

**ACTOR IN A LEADING ROLE IN A PLAY:** Alec Guinness, *Dylan*

**ACTRESS IN A LEADING ROLE IN A PLAY:** Sandy Dennis, *Any Wednesday*

**ACTOR IN A LEADING ROLE IN A MUSICAL:** Bert Lahr, *Foxy*

**ACTRESS IN A LEADING ROLE IN A MUSICAL:** Carol Channing, *Hello, Dolly!*

**ACTOR IN A FEATURED ROLE IN A PLAY:** Hume Cronyn, *Hamlet*

**ACTRESS IN A FEATURED ROLE IN A PLAY:** Barbara Loden, *After the Fall*

**ACTOR IN A FEATURED ROLE IN A MUSICAL:** Jack Cassidy, *She Loves Me*

**ACTRESS IN A FEATURED ROLE IN A MUSICAL:**
Tessie O'Shea, *The Girl Who Came to Supper*

**SCENIC DESIGN:** Oliver Smith, *Hello, Dolly!*

**COSTUME DESIGN:** Freddy Wittop, *Hello, Dolly!*

**DIRECTION OF A PLAY:** Mike Nichols, *Barefoot in the Park*

**DIRECTION OF A MUSICAL:** Gower Champion, *Hello, Dolly!*

**CHOREOGRAPHY:** Gower Champion, *Hello, Dolly!*

**CONDUCTOR AND MUSICAL DIRECTOR:**
Shepard Coleman, *Hello, Dolly!*

**SPECIAL TONY AWARD:** Eva Le Gallienne

Tessie O'Shea and Jack Cassidy

ROBIN WAGNER: I was Oliver Smith's assistant when we did *Hello, Dolly!* He used to draw on three-by-five cards. Sometimes he even painted them. His sketches were gorgeous. His paint elevations were beautiful. They were like real paintings.

During previews Oliver went to Peru and had no desire to come back, so I stood in for him. Gower Champion was directing and made a lot of changes. He wanted a new set for "Before the Parade Passes By." I called Oliver at the Monasterio Hotel in Cusco. Oliver had a fabulous library at his house in Brooklyn Heights. He told me the names of the books he wanted me to get, and what design elements to look for in each of them. The shop was able to build it exactly the way Oliver described it to me over the phone. He was able to design by telephone!

*Hello Dolly!* winners (L to R): Gower Champion, Jerry Herman, Carol Channing, David Merrick, and Freddy Wittop

# WINNERS ◎ 1965

---

PLAY: *The Subject Was Roses*, Frank Gilroy
Produced by Edgar Lansbury

MUSICAL: *Fiddler on the Roof* Produced by Harold Prince

AUTHOR (PLAY): Neil Simon, *The Odd Couple*

PRODUCER (PLAY): Claire Nichtern, *Luv*

BOOK OF A MUSICAL: Joseph Stein, *Fiddler on the Roof*

ORIGINAL SCORE (MUSIC AND/OR LYRICS) WRITTEN FOR THE THEATRE:
Jerry Bock and Sheldon Harnick, *Fiddler on the Roof*

ACTOR IN A LEADING ROLE IN A PLAY: Walter Matthau, *The Odd Couple*

ACTRESS IN A LEADING ROLE IN A PLAY: Irene Worth, *Tiny Alice*

ACTOR IN A LEADING ROLE IN A MUSICAL: Zero Mostel, *Fiddler on the Roof*

ACTRESS IN A LEADING ROLE IN A MUSICAL: Liza Minnelli, *Flora, the Red Menace*

ACTOR IN A FEATURED ROLE IN A PLAY: Jack Albertson, *The Subject Was Roses*

ACTRESS IN A FEATURED ROLE IN A PLAY: Alice Ghostley,
*The Sign in Sidney Brustein's Window*

ACTOR IN A FEATURED ROLE IN A MUSICAL: Victor Spinetti, *Oh, What a Lovely War*

ACTRESS IN A FEATURED ROLE IN A MUSICAL: Maria Karnilova, *Fiddler on the Roof*

SCENIC DESIGN: Oliver Smith, *Baker Street*, *Luv*, *The Odd Couple*

COSTUME DESIGN: Patricia Zipprodt, *Fiddler on the Roof*

DIRECTION OF A PLAY: Mike Nichols, *Luv*, *The Odd Couple*

DIRECTION OF A MUSICAL: Jerome Robbins, *Fiddler on the Roof*

CHOREOGRAPHY: Jerome Robbins, *Fiddler on the Roof*

SPECIAL TONY AWARD: Gilbert Miller, Oliver Smith

---

Lead acting winners (L to R): Walter Matthau, Irene Worth, Liza Minnelli, and Zero Mostel

**SHELDON HARNICK:** Being a Tony winner means that I'm recognized and as a very capable theatre lyricist, and that I'll continue to work. Winning a Tony made me more valuable as a lyricist, and I think I got hired more often because of it.

**DAVID ROCKWELL:** Boris Aronson provided me with my earliest inspiration, starting with his work on *Fiddler on the Roof*—my very first Broadway show. I do believe, sitting there, watching *Fiddler on the Roof* at the age of twelve, that the entire course of my professional life was charted in that afternoon.

# WINNERS ○ 1966

PLAY: *Marat/Sade*, Peter Weiss, English version by Geoffrey Skelton
Produced by David Merrick Arts Foundation

MUSICAL: *Man of La Mancha*
Produced by Albert W. Seldon, Hal James

ORIGINAL SCORE (MUSIC AND/OR LYRICS) WRITTEN FOR THE THEATRE:
Mitch Leigh and Joe Darion, *Man of La Mancha*

ACTOR IN A LEADING ROLE IN A PLAY: Hal Holbrook, *Mark Twain Tonight!*

ACTRESS IN A LEADING ROLE IN A PLAY: Rosemary Harris, *The Lion in Winter*

ACTOR IN A LEADING ROLE IN A MUSICAL: Richard Kiley, *Man of La Mancha*

ACTRESS IN A LEADING ROLE IN A MUSICAL: Angela Lansbury, *Mame*

ACTOR IN A FEATURED ROLE IN A PLAY: Patrick Magee, *Marat/Sade*

ACTRESS IN A FEATURED ROLE IN A PLAY: Zoe Caldwell, *Slapstick Tragedy*

ACTOR IN A FEATURED ROLE IN A MUSICAL: Frankie Michaels, *Mame*

ACTRESS IN A FEATURED ROLE IN A MUSICAL: Beatrice Arthur, *Mame*

SCENIC DESIGN: Howard Bay, *Man of La Mancha*

COSTUME DESIGN: Gunilla Palmstierna-Weiss, *Marat/Sade*

DIRECTION OF A PLAY: Peter Brook, *Marat/Sade*

DIRECTION OF A MUSICAL:
Albert Marre, *Man of La Mancha*

CHOREOGRAPHY: Bob Fosse, *Sweet Charity*

SPECIAL TONY AWARD: Helen Menken

Jerry Herman with two Mames: Angela Lansbury and Ginger Rogers

**JULIE TAYMOR:** Peter Brook's *A Midsummer Night's Dream* was extremely inspiring for me. I was probably about fifteen years old, and we drove all the way from Oberlin on a bus overnight to see it.

**ROSEMARY HARRIS:** The Tony Award is such a lovely pat on the back. It's the cherry on top of the cake. Everybody wants to have a Tony if possible! It's a wonderful institution. Everybody seems to know the Tony, even people who are not very *au fait* about the theatre.

It was a big surprise to me when they asked me to do *The Lion in Winter*. They said, "Do you think you can play somebody past childbearing?" I wasn't even married, but I said, "Of course I can," They said, "The part's yours." I read it, and I absolutely fell in love with it. It was everything that one wanted. It was comedy and tragedy. To play opposite Robert Preston was wonderful. And then of course it was the first straight part Christopher Walken ever played. He'd been a chorus boy before that. The show didn't run for very long. Stanley Kauffmann was a temporary critic for the *New York Times*; he was normally the film critic. Walter Kerr was the critic for the *Herald Tribune*, and he gave it a wonderful review. He said, "Put on your wind cheaters. There's a great gale blowing down at the Ambassador. This is the best play I've seen in a decade." If that had been the *Times* review, we would have run for quite a long time. But because Stanley Kauffmann didn't like it at all—he said he didn't like the modern language—we struggled. It was terribly sad. Poor Jim Goldman (the playwright) was devastated. We struggled along for about three months. Jim and I gave up part of our salaries to see if we could keep it going. I think we were getting $1,500 a week, and we both gave up $1,000 a week. Robert Preston, lovely Pres, said, "You're fools. I've been there, done that. It doesn't help." And sadly, he was right.

It was summertime when the Tonys came around. It was very exciting to be nominated. The ceremony was at the Rainbow Room at teatime. My show had closed, so nobody really quite knew why I was there. They made room for me at a table. I was sitting there with these other ladies eating cake and having tea, and then they said, "The winner is Rosemary Harris." The ladies at my table looked at me and said, "Oh! That's who you are." I got up and accepted my award, and it was lovely. I was as surprised as anybody!

My Tony Award is in a little white box. It's a flat round disk, which is what you now see on top of a pedestal when someone gets a Tony. That white box is now brown spotted with age, I'm afraid. On the back of the medallion where it has your name, mine is unique because the engraver got rather carried away and added an extra R to the word *star*.

**ANGELA LANSBURY:** I love the theatre, and my mother Moyna Macgill was a successful actress in London before World War II, so it was through her that I became drawn to the theatre and to acting. It was director Moss Hart who once famously wrote that "The world of the theatre is as closed a tribe and as removed from other civilian worlds as a gypsy encampment, and those who enter it are spoiled for anything else and are tainted with its insidious lure for the rest of their lives." I certainly was caught by the lure and became spoiled for anything else, and I am tremendously grateful and consider myself blessed to have been a part of the "tribe" all these years. It is a great honor to be recognized by one's colleagues and peers and given a Tony Award. However, I have always felt a little conflicted, because the other nominees were so talented and equally deserving. It always heightened the honor to be nominated among other such gifted actors. And, on a lighter note, it goes to show what can happen if one hangs in there long enough.

There are so many wonderful memories from the Tonys, it's impossible to pick a favorite. Winning my first Tony for *Mame* is high on the list, and of course when that lightning struck four more times, it was always amazing. Then, there was all the fun I had hosting the telecast several times, rubbing elbows, and performing with so many wonderful people in the business. However, my really favorite memories are from the times I sat in the dark theatre with my daughter Dierdre or my son Anthony beside me, as we listened while the nominees' names were being read out wondering—as one always does—whether it could possibly happen again. It was at those times, knowing no matter which way the pendulum swung, that they would always be there to love and support me and everything would be just fine. Having them with me was a great joy.

Presenter Barbra Streisand with (L to R) Joe Masteroff, John Kander, Fred Ebb, and Harold Prince, the team behind *Cabaret*

# WINNERS ○ 1967

**PLAY:** *The Homecoming*, Harold Pinter
Produced by Alexander H. Cohen

**MUSICAL:** *Cabaret*
Produced by Harold Prince in association with Ruth Mitchell

**ORIGINAL SCORE (MUSIC AND/OR LYRICS) WRITTEN FOR THE THEATRE:**
John Kander and Fred Ebb, *Cabaret*

**ACTOR IN A LEADING ROLE IN A PLAY:** Paul Rogers, *The Homecoming*

**ACTRESS IN A LEADING ROLE IN A PLAY:** Beryl Reid, *The Killing of Sister George*

**ACTOR IN A LEADING ROLE IN A MUSICAL:** Robert Preston, *I Do! I Do!*

**ACTRESS IN A LEADING ROLE IN A MUSICAL:** Barbara Harris, *The Apple Tree*

**ACTOR IN A FEATURED ROLE IN A PLAY:** Ian Holm, *The Homecoming*

**ACTRESS IN A FEATURED ROLE IN A PLAY:** Marian Seldes, *A Delicate Balance*

**ACTOR IN A FEATURED ROLE IN A MUSICAL:** Joel Grey, *Cabaret*

**ACTRESS IN A FEATURED ROLE IN A MUSICAL:** Peg Murray, *Cabaret*

**SCENIC DESIGN:** Boris Aronson, *Cabaret*

**COSTUME DESIGN:** Patricia Zipprodt, *Cabaret*

**DIRECTION OF A PLAY:** Peter Hall, *The Homecoming*

**DIRECTION OF A MUSICAL:** Harold Prince, *Cabaret*

**CHOREOGRAPHY:** Ron Field, *Cabaret*

Harold Pinter

**JOHN KANDER:** I grew up in Kansas City, Missouri, and started playing piano when I was four. I had a family which encouraged music; it was always in the house. When I was seven or eight, I saw musical theatre on the stage. At the same time, I started listening to the Met broadcasts. The fact that you could tell a story in music dazzled me, and it's stayed that way.

When I started working on *Cabaret* I listened to a lot of German jazz and vaudeville music. I have this ridiculous feeling that if you sit down at the keyboard and put your hands on the keys, they will do something. Mine usually do! Having done the listening and the background research and knowing what we were going for in terms of what the opening moment was, I put my hands on the keyboard the opening vamp for "Willkommen" came out. My hands knew more than I did! Most of the time Fred Ebb and I would do the very first moment first, because it would tell us what the piece was going to be stylistically. That opening vamp is *Cabaret* all capsulized. It opened the doors for the rest of the score.

You don't know what you're going to say when you open your mouth to speak. You know what you want to convey, but you don't know what the words are going to be. You don't think about sentence structure. You go straight from the thought to the words. That's what happens when I work. What I hear in my head comes out of the piano.

Sometimes you get praise and rewards for work that isn't very good, and you get slammed for a piece you know deep inside of you is excellent. The first time you get a Tony Award, it's a major moment. You don't know what to do with it inside, but you feel very good! As careers go on and you become clearer about what it is that you like and don't like about your work, the meaning of the reward changes.

**JOEL GREY:** I was on the very first televised Tony Awards. We opened the whole show with a performance of "Willkommen," as a matter of fact.

When Hal Prince was in the service during the war, he had seen a little guy in Germany who became the inspiration for my character. He was a real-life emcee, and looked kind of crazy; he was all painted up. Hal called me at a point when I was ready to quit the theatre. I had children and responsibilities, and there was no work. So, when Hal called, I said it was a bad time. He said, "Not anymore. There's a part in my new show that I'd like you to play."

I'd seen a number of second-rate vaudevillians over the years and had always been revolted by them. I took all that revulsion and poured it right into the emcee.

What a thrill and what a surprise to win the Tony for that role. I remember hearing my name, and then just running towards the stage. In 1967, the ceremony was very different from what it is now. It was very homey then. It was in a smaller theater, and the only people there were theatre people.

*Cabaret* was a hit from opening night. Then the movie followed. It's pretty rare that the person who does a role on Broadway gets to recreate it in the film, so that was certainly wonderful. Winning awards for both was the great big cherry on top of the whole delicious sundae.

Maurice Chevalier and
Audrey Hepburn

# WINNERS ◎ 1968

**PLAY:** *Rosencrantz and Guildenstern Are Dead*, Tom Stoppard
Produced by David Merrick Arts Foundation

**MUSICAL:** *Hallelujah, Baby!*
Produced by Albert Selden, Hal James, Jane C. Nusbaum, Harry Rigby

**ORIGINAL SCORE (MUSIC AND/OR LYRICS) WRITTEN FOR THE THEATRE:**
Jule Styne, Betty Comden, and Adolph Green, *Hallelujah, Baby!*

**ACTOR IN A LEADING ROLE IN A PLAY:** Martin Balsam,
*You Know I Can't Hear You When the Water's Running*

**ACTRESS IN A LEADING ROLE IN A PLAY:** Zoe Caldwell, *The Prime of Miss Jean Brodie*

**ACTOR IN A LEADING ROLE IN A MUSICAL:** Robert Goulet, *The Happy Time*

**ACTRESS IN A LEADING ROLE IN A MUSICAL:** Patricia Routledge,
*Darling of the Day*; Leslie Uggams, *Hallelujah, Baby!*

**ACTOR IN A FEATURED ROLE IN A PLAY:** James Patterson, *The Birthday Party*

**ACTRESS IN A FEATURED ROLE IN A PLAY:** Zena Walker, *Joe Egg*

**ACTOR IN A FEATURED ROLE IN A MUSICAL:** Hiram Sherman, *How Now, Dow Jones*

**ACTRESS IN A FEATURED ROLE IN A MUSICAL:** Lillian Hayman, *Hallelujah, Baby!*

**SCENIC DESIGN:** Desmond Heeley, *Rosencrantz and Guildenstern Are Dead*

**COSTUME DESIGN:** Desmond Heeley, *Rosencrantz and Guildenstern Are Dead*

**DIRECTION OF A PLAY:** Mike Nichols, *Plaza Suite*

**DIRECTION OF A MUSICAL:** Gower Champion, *The Happy Time*

**CHOREOGRAPHY:** Gower Champion, *The Happy Time*

**SPECIAL TONY AWARD:** Audrey Hepburn; Carol Channing;
Pearl Bailey; David Merrick; Maurice Chevalier;
APA-Phoenix Theatre; Marlene Dietrich

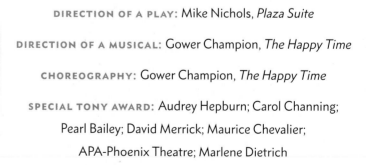

Jerry Herman and two of his Dollys: Pearl Bailey and Carol Channing

**TOM STOPPARD:** The first time I was nominated for a Tony was in the season of 1967. In those days nobody made such a fuss about the Tonys. I didn't have to be there for it, I just waited for a phone call to tell me whether *Rosencrantz and Guildenstern Are Dead* had won it or not. At the time my wife and I were living in a flat, and we were house hunting. I remember we said, "If it wins, we can buy the carpet." And it did win so we bought it.

**LESLIE UGGAMS:** Having won a Tony Award for *Hallelujah, Baby!* means so much more to me than my own personal or professional recognition. The fact that such a groundbreaking musical could have even made it to Broadway in the first place makes it a genuine part of history.

When we opened in April of 1967, there was so much tumult in America and around the world. Young people were filling the streets in protest of the Vietnam War, and civil rights leaders were marching against racial injustice. Progress was being made with the appointment of Thurgood Marshall as the first Black justice on the Supreme Court, and state laws against interracial marriage were finally struck down by SCOTUS. But ongoing backlash to the Civil Rights Act of 1964 and the Voting Rights Act of 1965 ultimately culminated in the assassination of Dr. Martin Luther King Jr. on April 4, 1968. So, consider just how powerful it was for our boundary-pushing musical to win not one, not two, but five Tony Awards, including Best Musical, just seventeen days later. It was truly surreal.

So many of the themes in *Hallelujah, Baby!* were still being played out in our culture at the time. Just as Georgina and company were struggling to overcome segregation, economic oppression, and racial and gender stereotypes, a new generation of Americans were fighting the same battles. But would audiences, and the industry, accept a new musical that embraced these challenges in such a unique way? Well, we got our answer. Yes, yes, they would!

For me, that Tony Award is a constant reminder that art can not only reflect the times but also encourage us to *change* them. It seems that some strides need to be made over and over. *Hallelujah, Baby!* is in some ways a chronicle of that very message—that change comes slowly, over decades and generations. But change *does* come. It must.

*Hallelujah, Baby!* was more than just a show *of* its time. It was also *ahead* of it. To this day I'm grateful to have that little statue on my shelf to remind me of how important Georgina's journey was and *still* is. Onward!

Patricia Routledge, Robert Goulet, Leslie Uggams, Martin Balsam, and Zoe Caldwell

# WINNERS ◎ 1969

**PLAY:** *The Great White Hope*, Howard Sackler
Produced by Herman Levin

**MUSICAL:** *1776*
Produced by Stuart Ostrow

**ACTOR IN A LEADING ROLE IN A PLAY:** James Earl Jones, *The Great White Hope*

**ACTRESS IN A LEADING ROLE IN A PLAY:** Julie Harris, *Forty Carats*

**ACTOR IN A LEADING ROLE IN A MUSICAL:** Jerry Orbach, *Promises, Promises*

**ACTRESS IN A LEADING ROLE IN A MUSICAL:** Angela Lansbury, *Dear World*

**ACTOR IN A FEATURED ROLE IN A PLAY:** Al Pacino, *Does a Tiger Wear a Necktie?*

**ACTRESS IN A FEATURED ROLE IN A PLAY:** Jane Alexander, *The Great White Hope*

**ACTOR IN A FEATURED ROLE IN A MUSICAL:** Ronald Holgate, *1776*

**ACTRESS IN A FEATURED ROLE IN A MUSICAL:** Marian Mercer, *Promises, Promises*

**SCENIC DESIGN:** Boris Aronson, *Zorba*

**COSTUME DESIGN:** Louden Sainthill, *Canterbury Tales*

**DIRECTION OF A PLAY:** Peter Dews, *Hadrian VII*

**DIRECTION OF A MUSICAL:** Peter Hunt, *1776*

**CHOREOGRAPHY:** Joe Layton, *George M!*

**SPECIAL TONY AWARD:** The National Theatre Company of Great Britain;
The Negro Ensemble Company; Rex Harrison;
Leonard Bernstein; Carol Burnett

Lead actor winners (L to R) James Earl Jones, Julie Harris, Angela Lansbury, and Jerry Orbach

Al Pacino and
Jane Alexander

**CAROL BURNETT:** My dream was to work on Broadway, and to be given a special Tony Award was a true honor and surprise. I had only done two shows on Broadway at that point. I was not like Bernadette Peters or Patti LuPone, but I got my start on Broadway and have returned many times since then. I am so grateful to have a Tony Award.

**JANE ALEXANDER:** *The Great White Hope* had been given an NEA $25,000 grant to be developed at Arena Stage, where I was a member of the company. I was given the role of Ellie Bachman. It was a huge script, about two hundred pages. We were a cast of sixty-three actors playing over two hundred roles. Most of the actors were Black, which was exciting. This was at the height of the Black Power movement. There were a lot of firsts associated with that play, including James Earl and I being the first interracial couple to be in a bed together. Being a part of the show was an amazing experience. When the first preview went up in October of 1968, there was dead silence at the curtain call, and then humungous applause, a standing ovation. We knew then we had a hit.

Our director, Ed Sherin, had seen James Earl Jones in plays in New York and just couldn't get him out of his mind. He knew he was the right person to play Jack Jefferson. He got him a trainer six months before the show to get him into the shape he needed to be in to play a professional boxer.

The reviews were outstanding, and James Earl and I were contracted for a year. He was already contracted to do the film, but the next day after I won the Tony my agent got a call asking me to be in the film too. We left after that first-year commitment to do the film, and Yaphet Kotto and Maria Tucci took over.

Winning that Tony Award changed everything. James Earl and I both won Tony Awards, and we both got Oscar nominations for the movie. And then we were set for our careers for the next thirty or forty years.

Ed Sherin helped develop the play, and his direction was so outstanding. It meant everything. It was shocking when he was left out of the nominations. So, when we got up there to accept our awards, Howard Sackler, Jimmy, and I mentioned him a lot.

I can't believe I've been nominated for a Tony Award eight times. It's wonderful and deeply satisfying to know that I'm part of the community in that way.

# ACCEPTANCE SPEECHES THROUGH THE YEARS

*I just have to thank the lord, and I still believe in him after four years in New York.* **CLEAVON LITTLE (1970)**

Henry Fonda and Jane Fonda

**HENRY FONDA (1979):** I guess this is for being a survivor. I probably will never get a better chance to thank all the people who have been a part of my life in the theatre over the last fifty-four years. It's been a wonderful life. You can be sure I'm very grateful. I've never been wildly happy about being me. I never really liked myself. But in the theatre, I was given chances to pretend that I was Mister Roberts, Clarence Darrow, and Justice Dan Snow. You got to be sure I'm grateful. And my thanks to the American Theatre Wing for this opportunity to tell you thank you very much.

**FRANCES STERNHAGEN (1974):** I wish that I could really share this with all of the people that I've ever worked with who are as good as I am and who haven't had the luck and the recognition. There are so many.

**JEFFERSON MAYS (2004):** In 1906 Antoinette Perry was described by a New York critic as being the sweetest, most piquant ingenue on Broadway, and I think Charlotte von Mahlsdorf would have loved to have been remembered in a similar fashion.

**DIAHANN CARROLL (1962):** I really wanted this. If you think I'm not going to talk about Richard Rodgers, you're crazy. I wanted to be on Broadway for seven and a half years, and he put me there. I would like to go and do other things, but I will never forget, because this man knocked on my door. He called me. And I love him.

**LARRY KRAMER (2011):** To gay people everywhere, whom I love so. *The Normal Heart* is our history. I could not have written it had not so many of us so needlessly died. Learn from it and carry on the fight. Let them know that we are a very special people, an exceptional people, and that our day will come.

**IAN HOLM (1967):** Ladies and gentlemen, this means that I can take home to England with me two very valuable objects from the United States. One brand-new all-American son, Barnaby, born February the twentieth, New York City, 1967, and now one brand-new all-American award, Tony, born twenty-sixth of March, 1967.

**NORBERT LEO BUTZ (2005):** I first and foremost want to thank God, because there is no way that somebody with my name from South St. Louis, Missouri, ends up at Radio City Music Hall holding one of these without some divine intervention.

**DOUGLAS TURNER WARD (1969):** Finally, I accept it on behalf of all of the men and women who preceded us with an idea about theatre of this orientation and who never received the means or encouragement to fulfill their ambition.

> I'd like to thank Francis Coppola for hiring Raul Julia, which rendered him unavailable for the part. **KEVIN KLINE (1981)**

**ORIN WOLF (2018):** Ten years ago I was captivated by Eran Kolirin's deceptively simple film about love and hope and faith, and watching David Yazbek and Itamar Moses and Dave Cromer and our entire team mount this thing onstage has been one of the greatest and one of the most rewarding experiences in my life. In *The Band's Visit*, music gives people hope and makes borders disappear. Although the characters are strangers to each other with great political divides, our show offers a message of unity in a world that more and more seems bent on amplifying our differences. In the end we are all far more alike than different, and I am so proud to be a part of a community that chooses to support that message. I have been blessed with so many great friends in this industry, I have come up in this industry and had so many wonderful mentors, but I want to shout out to one special one: Hal Prince, who has been dear to my heart and dear to this project. And I want to thank everyone who sacrificed and gave selflessly to make this show a reality.

**CARMEN PAVLOVIC (2020):** On a historic moment, historic night such as this, it feels a little odd to me to be talking about one show as Best Musical. I feel that every show of last season deserves to be thought of as the Best Musical. The shows that opened, the shows that closed not to return, the shows that nearly opened, and of course the shows that paused and were fortunate enough to be reborn. Best Musical is all of those shows. Best is what we've had to find in ourselves as we've walked this unimaginable journey and carried our shows across a desert. Best is what we know we need to become as we reimagine the Broadway of the future.

**NOEL COWARD (1970):** This is my first award, so please be kind. I would like to say to you that I have been in the theatre for sixty years, and the most rewarding thing in the world is to be appreciated by one's own people. Often when I have given a performance of incredible brilliance,

civilians have come round, and I have said to my few pro friends who were skittering about "Stay where you are." Because what I like is praise from my peers and tonight makes me think of the greatest tenderness and affection of an old friend of mine, Antoinette Perry, who was—as we see—the greatest theatre enthusiast that I've ever known. And I'm so proud to be here and receive this. And thank you all so much.

**JESSIE MUELLER (2014):** Carole King… You have taught me so much. You teach me so much every night I get to go up onstage and try to get through what you went through and come out of it with kindness, love, and forgiveness and a pure heart. You're just such an amazing woman. And I'm proud to be up here representing the amazing women that all the women in this category represented this year.

*Jessie Mueller and Carole King*

> I'm very pleased about this but I really should give credit to the man who designed the scenery. **JO MIELZINER (1970)**

# the 1970s

René Auberjonois

# WINNERS ◎ 1970

PLAY: *Borstal Boy*, Frank McMahon
Produced by Michael McAloney, Burton C. Kaiser

MUSICAL: *Applause*
Produced by Joseph Kipness, Lawrence Kasha

ACTOR IN A LEADING ROLE IN A PLAY: Fritz Weaver, *Child's Play*

ACTRESS IN A LEADING ROLE IN A PLAY: Tammy Grimes, *Private Lives* (revival)

ACTOR IN A LEADING ROLE IN A MUSICAL: Cleavon Little, *Purlie*

ACTRESS IN A LEADING ROLE IN A MUSICAL: Lauren Bacall, *Applause*

ACTOR IN A FEATURED ROLE IN A PLAY: Ken Howard, *Child's Play*

ACTRESS IN A FEATURED ROLE IN A PLAY: Blythe Danner, *Butterflies Are Free*

ACTOR IN A FEATURED ROLE IN A MUSICAL: René Auberjonois, *Coco*

ACTRESS IN A FEATURED ROLE IN A MUSICAL: Melba Moore, *Purlie*

SCENIC DESIGN: Jo Mielziner, *Child's Play*

COSTUME DESIGN: Cecil Beaton, *Coco*

LIGHTING DESIGN: Jo Mielziner, *Child's Play*

DIRECTION OF A PLAY: Joseph Hardy,
*Child's Play*

DIRECTION OF A MUSICAL: Ron Field, *Applause*

CHOREOGRAPHY: Ron Field, *Applause*

SPECIAL TONY AWARD: Noel Coward; Alfred
Lunt and Lynn Fontanne; New York Shakespeare
Festival; Barbra Streisand

Patricia Neal (Tony winner 1947), Jimmy Stewart, and winners
Tammy Grimes, and Joseph Hardy

**MELBA MOORE:** I never knew that theatre was going to be a part of my career. I wasn't an actor. Galt MacDermot was recording his album of the music of *Hair* with Jim Rado and Gerome Ragni. I was one of the singers in the recording session. They were still casting the musical at that point and told everyone at the session that if we came to sing for the director and the producer, they would find a part for us. I was the only one that went and was hired to be in the original cast of *Hair*. After a year and a half one of the women in the company suggested that I learn how to audition for Broadway so I could continue to work. She told me it was good practice to audition and to go out for a new show called *Purlie*. I went trying to learn how to audition, but I got the role!

I had one song in the show, which was the title song, "Purlie." It kept stopping the show, so Gary Geld and Peter Udell wrote "I Got Love" especially for me. I got to sing it at the Tony Awards. My fellow actors became like my family. I really learned to act doing *Purlie*. It was wonderful. My job was to laugh! Cleavon Little was hilarious and a great actor.

When I first read the script and saw the racial issues it dealt with, it seemed old. Then I realized that most of the audiences were white, and it would be a different experience for them than it was for me. What was happening on Broadway at that time was incredible and unbelievable at the same time. Doors and the heavens were opening up for Black people in theatre. Down the street was *Hello, Dolly!* But this time instead of Carol Channing or Barbra Streisand, it was starring Pearl Bailey, and her leading man was Cab Calloway.

When I performed on the Tony Awards it was shocking because all the lights were on. It was for TV! I looked out in the audience and saw Rex Harrison and all these stars that I'd only seen in the movies. They're all there looking at me! My category came up soon after my performance, so I was still backstage. Jack Cassidy announced it. Melissa Hart

Melba Moore (*Purlie*) in costume

was also nominated, and her name came right before mine as he read the nominees. Then he said, "And the winner is Melissa Moore." I figure that wasn't me, so I started to see how to get out of there. But then I heard the whole audience yelling, "Melba Moore!" I didn't realize why they were calling my name. Somebody helped me back onto the stage. When I got my Tony Award I was standing there like a deer in the headlights in stunned amazement. I hadn't prepared anything because I had enough to worry about with performing the number. I just said, "I don't know what to say, just thank you," and I turned, and I left.

That win changed my career instantly. I was visible, in the newspapers all the time. I was invited to do everybody's TV show—Ed Sullivan, Flip Wilson, Mike Douglas, Carol Burnett, Bea Arthur. Everyone who had a special invited me on. I even got my own show with Clifton Davis. I really became a star overnight. The Tony Award gave me a brand-new life.

Producer Alexander H. Cohen
with Maureen Stapleton

# WINNERS ◎ 1971

PLAY: *Sleuth*, Anthony Shaffer
Produced by Helen Bonfils, Morton Gottlieb, Michael White

MUSICAL: *Company*
Produced by Harold Prince

BOOK OF A MUSICAL: George Furth, *Company*

ORIGINAL SCORE (MUSIC AND/OR LYRICS) WRITTEN
FOR THE THEATRE: Stephen Sondheim, *Company*

ACTOR IN A LEADING ROLE IN A PLAY: Brian Bedford, *The School for Wives*

ACTRESS IN A LEADING ROLE IN A PLAY: Maureen Stapleton, *The Gingerbread Lady*

ACTOR IN A LEADING ROLE IN A MUSICAL: Hal Linden, *The Rothschilds*

ACTRESS IN A LEADING ROLE IN A MUSICAL: Helen Gallagher, *No, No, Nanette*

ACTOR IN A FEATURED ROLE IN A PLAY: Paul Sand, *Story Theatre*

ACTRESS IN A FEATURED ROLE IN A PLAY: Rae Allen, *And Miss Reardon Drinks a Little*

ACTOR IN A FEATURED ROLE IN A MUSICAL: Keene Curtis, *The Rothschilds*

ACTRESS IN A FEATURED ROLE IN A MUSICAL:
Patsy Kelly, *No, No, Nanette*

SCENIC DESIGN: Boris Aronson, *Company*

COSTUME DESIGN: Raoul Pène Du Bois, *No, No, Nanette*

LIGHTING DESIGN: R.H. Poindexter, *Story Theatre*

DIRECTION OF A PLAY: Peter Brook, *A Midsummer Night's Dream*

DIRECTION OF A MUSICAL: Harold Prince, *Company*

CHOREOGRAPHY: Donald Saddler, *No, No, Nanette*

SPECIAL TONY AWARD: Elliot Norton; Ingram Ash;
*Playbill*; Roger L. Stevens

Stephen Sondheim

Rae Allen, Hal Linden, Helen Gallagher, Patsy Kelly, Maureen Stapleton, and Brian Bedford

**DANNY BURSTEIN:** When I was a student at Queens College, I was cast in the role of Franklin Shepard in *Merrily We Roll Along*. It had just closed on Broadway three months before. I couldn't figure out Frank; he's such a shit! How do you play that? Somebody at school said, "You should ask Stephen Sondheim." I said, "Well yes, and I should ask Shakespeare about *Hamlet*." But he told me that he had Sondheim's address. I wrote him a letter telling him I was playing Frank in *Merrily* and asked him all these questions. Within the week, I got a letter back saying, "Danny, all those questions would have to be answered in a letter the size of *War and Peace*. Here's my number. Give me a call. We'll talk about it and figure it out." Three weeks later, I walked into his townhouse in Turtle Bay. James Lapine was just leaving. They were writing *Sunday in the Park*. I sat down. He went upstairs and came back with a huge carafe of wine and plopped it down in front of us with two glasses, and said, "Okay, what do you want to know?" And for the next three hours we just talked theatre.

**HAL LINDEN:** Winning the Tony was one of the most memorable moments in my life, but growing up, I had no intention of being an actor. I was a musician and a singer. I was in a band, and I was known as the singing saxophone player. I never had any interest in the theatre until I was in the army. I got involved with soldier shows. When I got out, I went to the American Theatre Wing with my GI Bill to study theatre. I did my first ever scene there with Bobby Morse.

*The Rothschilds* was about my thirteenth or fourteenth Broadway show, although they didn't all make it to Broadway. Some of them closed in Pittsburgh. I even closed one in rehearsal! There is no question that winning the Tony for that show changed my career. It led to *Barney Miller*. The producer had seen the show and decided I was the right choice to star in the show.

I dedicated my Tony to all the understudies on Broadway. I had been an understudy for years. I understudied Alan Alda, I understudied Robert Alda. I literally understudied everybody and his father! You do all of that work, and most of the time I never got to go on. When I won I said, "Keep the faith. It could happen." And it did. It started a whole career.

# WINNERS ⟳ 1972

PLAY: *Sticks and Bones*, David Rabe Produced by New York Shakespeare Festival—Joseph Papp

MUSICAL: *Two Gentlemen of Verona* Produced by New York Shakespeare Festival—Joseph Papp

BOOK OF A MUSICAL: John Guare and Mel Shapiro, *Two Gentlemen of Verona*

ORIGINAL SCORE (MUSIC AND/OR LYRICS) WRITTEN FOR THE THEATRE:
Stephen Sondheim, *Follies*

ACTOR IN A LEADING ROLE IN A PLAY: Cliff Gorman, *Lenny*

ACTRESS IN A LEADING ROLE IN A PLAY: Sada Thompson, *Twigs*

ACTOR IN A LEADING ROLE IN A MUSICAL: Phil Silvers, *A Funny Thing Happened on the Way to the Forum*

ACTRESS IN A LEADING ROLE IN A MUSICAL: Alexis Smith, *Follies*

ACTOR IN A FEATURED ROLE IN A PLAY: Vincent Gardenia,
*The Prisoner of Second Avenue*

ACTRESS IN A FEATURED ROLE IN A PLAY: Elizabeth Wilson, *Sticks and Bones*

ACTOR IN A FEATURED ROLE IN A MUSICAL: Larry Blyden,
*A Funny Thing Happened on the Way to the Forum*

ACTRESS IN A FEATURED ROLE IN A MUSICAL:
Linda Hopkins, *Inner City*

SCENIC DESIGN: Boris Aronson, *Follies*

COSTUME DESIGN: Florence Klotz, *Follies*

LIGHTING DESIGN: Tharon Musser, *Follies*

DIRECTION OF A PLAY: Mike Nichols, *The Prisoner
of Second Avenue*

DIRECTION OF A MUSICAL: Harold Prince and
Michael Bennett, *Follies*

CHOREOGRAPHY: Michael Bennett, *Follies*

SPECIAL TONY AWARD: The Theatre Guild—American Theatre Society;
*Fiddler on the Roof*; Ethel Merman; Richard Rodgers

Harold Prince, Alexis Smith,
and Stephen Sondheim

**NATHAN LANE:** As a publicity stunt the 1972 revival of *A Funny Thing Happened on the Way to the Forum*, starring the glorious Phil Silvers, Sgt. Bilko himself, had a free Fourth of July matinee. It was a blazing hot July day. I went with a few friends from high school and we got on a long line that went down the block to Eighth Avenue from the entrance to the Lunt-Fontanne Theatre. When we finally got to the front, I was let in and then they closed the doors, leaving my friends outside. They had reached capacity, and I was placed in standing room. When Phil Silvers made his first entrance the audience went nuts. He was, without question, the greatest Pseudolus I've ever seen, better than Zero, better than me, better than anybody. Well, it was written for him, but he turned it down originally. He was brilliant, so delightful, and lots of appropriate ad-libbing. During the House of Marcus Lycus scene, one of the beautiful courtesans ended her dance by throwing herself across his lap. She had tassels hanging from her blouse and little cymbals on her fingers. He gently swatted the tassels and played her cymbals. The audience roared with laughter. The young actor playing Hero interrupted him with the next line of dialogue and Silvers said, "Can't you see I'm working here?!" Then he turned to the audience and said, "So young. So anxious!" and then went back to playing with the tassels. When he finished with the bit he turned to Hero and said, "You were saying, dear boy?" It was musical comedy heaven. They always say when they talk about *Forum* that everyone who has played Pseudolus has won the Tony Award. First Zero Mostel, then Phil Silvers, then yours truly. For one, it proves what a great part it is. It also calls upon a lot of the performer. Singing, dancing, acting, physical comedy, you name it. Anyway, there was a little bit of a feeling that if I didn't win, I really wasn't cutting the mustard. But thankfully I got lucky and it all worked out.

Lead acting winners (L to R) Phil Silvers, Sada Thompson, Alexis Smith, and Cliff Gorman

**DAVID RABE:** I don't recall paying much attention to the Tonys as I grew up in Iowa, not until I was about to graduate

from high school. But once I was in college my interest in writing and theatre grew and the Tonys became a compelling event. Broadway was a place of mythical accomplishment. I finally made my way east over vacation my junior year. The money I'd saved was barely enough. I traveled by train and stayed in a dive hotel. The first play I saw was *A Taste of Honey* by Shelagh Delaney with Joan Plowright and Angela Lansbury. They were luminaries, and the play was incandescent. To this day it remains one of my favorite plays, a youthful judgment confirmed by a recent Off-Broadway production. I saw *Becket* with Laurence Olivier and Anthony Quinn. My seats were high up, always, of course, and I saw *Toys in the Attic* with Robert Loggia. But nothing compared to *A Taste of Honey*. I went east after college and lived near Philadelphia, where I saw Broadway tryouts. I remember Arthur Miller's *The Price* and one by Elaine May staring Mike Nichols with a memorable speech about gossip at the office water cooler. I traveled to New York infrequently, but saw a matinee of *Who's Afraid of Virginia Woolf?* Then came the army, which took me off and returned me, and I began writing plays, one of them *Sticks and Bones*. When Joe Papp wanted to move *Sticks and Bones* from the Public to Broadway, I was reluctant. The play was controversial. The actors at times said they needed combat pay to do it because there was sometimes a very hostile vibe coming from a part of the audience. The character of David struggles with coming back from the Vietnam War, which was still going on at the time. Ultimately, I think the play is about racism as much as it is about the war. The characters were named Ozzie, Harriet, David, and Rick. The use of that metaphor suggested something in the heart of the country that was poisoned and dangerous. Then came the Tony nominations for Liz Wilson, Tom Aldredge, Jeff Bleckner, and for the play. Liz won. There was a Pinter play, a Robert Bolt play, a Neil Simon play. It seemed impossible that I could win. But there I was, shocked and grateful, with Joe Papp at my side.

Ethel Merman on the 1972 broadcast of the Tony Awards

# WINNERS ◎ 1973

PLAY: *That Championship Season*, Jason Miller
Produced by New York Shakespeare Festival—Joseph Papp

MUSICAL: *A Little Night Music*
Produced by Harold Prince

BOOK OF A MUSICAL: Hugh Wheeler, *A Little Night Music*

ORIGINAL SCORE (MUSIC AND/OR LYRICS) WRITTEN FOR THE THEATRE:
Stephen Sondheim, *A Little Night Music*

ACTOR IN A LEADING ROLE IN A PLAY: Alan Bates, *Butley*

ACTRESS IN A LEADING ROLE IN A PLAY: Julie Harris, *The Last of Mrs. Lincoln*

ACTOR IN A LEADING ROLE IN A MUSICAL: Ben Vereen, *Pippin*

ACTRESS IN A LEADING ROLE IN A MUSICAL: Glynis Johns, *A Little Night Music*

ACTOR IN A FEATURED ROLE IN A PLAY: John Lithgow, *The Changing Room*

ACTRESS IN A FEATURED ROLE IN A PLAY: Leora Dana, *The Last of Mrs. Lincoln*

ACTOR IN A FEATURED ROLE IN A MUSICAL: George S. Irving, *Irene*

ACTRESS IN A FEATURED ROLE IN A MUSICAL: Patricia Elliott, *A Little Night Music*

SCENIC DESIGN: Tony Walton, *Pippin*

COSTUME DESIGN: Florence Klotz, *A Little Night Music*

LIGHTING DESIGN: Jules Fisher, *Pippin*

DIRECTION OF A PLAY: A.J. Antoon,
*That Championship Season*

DIRECTION OF A MUSICAL: Bob Fosse, *Pippin*

CHOREOGRAPHY: Bob Fosse, *Pippin*

SPECIAL TONY AWARD: John Lindsay; Actors Fund
of America; Shubert Organization

Ruth Mitchell, Stephen Sondheim, Hugh Wheeler, Florence Klotz, Patricia
Elliott, Harold Prince, and Glynis Johns from *A Little Night Music*

**JULES FISHER:** The Tony is meaningful to me because it means that my peers have said that work was good. I don't like to say *best* or *better*. Everyone's work is different. When I receive an award, it's because I did something that didn't look like anyone else's.

It's important to try to get into the mind of the director. The script is on a page. Everyone reads the same words, although it can be interpreted differently. I'm trying to find out what the director wants to communicate. We use light as a media, like paint, to help tell that story. Ideally the audience doesn't realize that they're more moved emotionally, even manipulated by the artistic crafting of light. They don't see the behavior of the light, but it causes them to appreciate the story more.

Today's technology gives lighting designers great power over splitting time, in shades of color, in repetition. We can repeat something so complicated that you could never do before. You couldn't expect a human to do it exactly the same way every night. However, that doesn't mean the lighting is better. Jo Mielziner did *Death of a Salesman* in 1949 with very few pieces of lighting equipment, very low-level technology—technology that hadn't changed for sixty years.

*Pippin* was the first time I worked with Bob Fosse. He took a show and made it an entertainment. He liked black, so the set was black, basically. The designers who worked with him were always told, "You can do anything you want, but leave the stage completely open for me to dance upon." With *Pippin* he asked for unusual effects that neither he nor I had even seen before. For example, he wanted to see dancers' hands and only hands ethereally floating in space. After Ben Vereen came out he was occasionally surrounded by hands that appeared out of nowhere. It was a challenge. He had no idea how to do it. I worked with our brilliant set designer Tony Walton to find a way to get the lights in a position that could light the actors' hands but fell nowhere else. You didn't see the light; you only saw their hands. It was a great technical and artistic challenge. *Pippin* was thrilling for me because not only did I get to work with Bob, who I had not known, but also to be able to make magical moments throughout the evening.

**PEGGY EISENHAUER:** I was influenced by Jules Fisher as a youngster, and then as an assistant. Jules had a most famous career before I ever came onto the scene. Our partnership is at the center of my creativity. It's unique in lighting design to create with a partner—someone that can continually bring visual and dramatic concepts to the conversation, and compound the interpretation of the director's vision.

*Pippin* was a seminal experience for me, coincidentally. As a kid I had a friend whose dad took us to see *Pippin*. I was already interested in theatre and lighting, and I was already aware of who Jules was. At one moment of the show Ben Vereen popped out from the stage left proscenium in an explosive bright purple spotlight—*POW!* That was a very visceral moment for me, and that's when I knew I wanted to pursue lighting design.

# WINNERS ◎ 1974

Janie Sell and Tommy Tune

**PLAY:** *The River Niger*, Joseph A. Walker
Produced by Negro Ensemble Co., Inc.

**MUSICAL:** *Raisin*
Produced by Robert Nemiroff

**BOOK OF A MUSICAL:** Hugh Wheeler, *Candide*

**ORIGINAL SCORE (MUSIC AND/OR LYRICS) WRITTEN FOR THE THEATRE:**
Frederick Loewe (music), Alan Jay Lerner (lyrics), *Gigi*

**ACTOR IN A LEADING ROLE IN A PLAY:** Michael Moriarty, *Find Your Way Home*

**ACTRESS IN A LEADING ROLE IN A PLAY:** Colleen Dewhurst,
*A Moon for the Misbegotten*

**ACTOR IN A LEADING ROLE IN A MUSICAL:** Christopher Plummer, *Cyrano*

**ACTRESS IN A LEADING ROLE IN A MUSICAL:** Virginia Capers, *Raisin*

**ACTOR IN A FEATURED ROLE IN A PLAY:** Ed Flanders, *A Moon for the Misbegotten*

**ACTRESS IN A FEATURED ROLE IN A PLAY:** Frances Sternhagen, *The Good Doctor*

**ACTOR IN A FEATURED ROLE IN A MUSICAL:** Tommy Tune, *Seesaw*

**ACTRESS IN A FEATURED ROLE IN A MUSICAL:** Janie Sell, *Over Here!*

**SCENIC DESIGN:** Franne and Eugene Lee, *Candide*

**COSTUME DESIGN:** Franne Lee, *Candide*

**LIGHTING DESIGN:** Jules Fisher, *Ulysses in Nighttown*

**DIRECTION OF A PLAY:** José Quintero, *A Moon for the Misbegotten*

**DIRECTION OF A MUSICAL:** Harold Prince, *Candide*

**CHOREOGRAPHY:** Michael Bennett, *Seesaw*

**SPECIAL TONY AWARD:** Liza Minnelli; Bette Midler; Peter Cook and
Dudley Moore; *A Moon for the Misbegotten*; *Candide*; Actors' Equity Association; Theatre
Development Fund; John F. Wharton; Harold Friedlander

Lead acting winners (L to R) Christopher Plummer, Virginia Capers, Colleen Dewhurst, and Michael Moriarty

**EUGENE LEE:** For me, the set does two things: it solves the story, and it solves the space. And by "solves," I mean it delivers the information and situations to the audience. I always say, "Scenery is overrated," but what isn't overrated is the relationship of the audience to the actors and, consequently, the story.

It's tough to think about awards and not lose your head a little bit, so I prefer to not think about them at all. But what winning a Tony represents; recognition by an industry and peer group full of talent and creativity, certainly feels like an honor and I'm very proud to be a part of it. Also, the award itself is very heavy!

**FRANNE LEE:** I had very little money to work with when we did *Candide*. Everything was begged and borrowed. I used fabric from old fabric stores in lower Manhattan. I even used an old tablecloth to make one of the costumes. I was a scrapper, and I loved it. It's not about how much you spend; it's more about how people feel when they look at your costumes. When I design, I think about what a character has in their closet. What would they wear in the rain? How would they dress for a ball? I think it makes it more meaningful and real, and I think it's more fun that way.

# WINNERS ◎ 1975

Lead acting winners (L to R)
John Cullum, Ellen Burstyn,
John Kani, Angela Lansbury,
and Winston Ntshona

**PLAY:** *Equus*, Peter Shaffer
Produced by Kermit Bloomgarden, Doris Cole Abrahams

**MUSICAL:** *The Wiz*
Produced by Ken Harper

**BOOK OF A MUSICAL:** James Lee Barrett,
Peter Udell, and Philip Rose, *Shenandoah*

**ORIGINAL SCORE (MUSIC AND/OR LYRICS) WRITTEN FOR THE THEATRE:**
Charlie Smalls, *The Wiz*

**ACTOR IN A LEADING ROLE IN A PLAY:** John Kani and Winston Ntshona,
*Sizwe Banzi Is Dead/The Island*

**ACTRESS IN A LEADING ROLE IN A PLAY:** Ellen Burstyn, *Same Time, Next Year*

**ACTOR IN A LEADING ROLE IN A MUSICAL:** John Cullum, *Shenandoah*

**ACTRESS IN A LEADING ROLE IN A MUSICAL:** Angela Lansbury, *Gypsy*

**ACTOR IN A FEATURED ROLE IN A PLAY:** Frank Langella, *Seascape*

**ACTRESS IN A FEATURED ROLE IN A PLAY:** Rita Moreno, *The Ritz*

**ACTOR IN A FEATURED ROLE IN A MUSICAL:** Ted Ross, *The Wiz*

**ACTRESS IN A FEATURED ROLE IN A MUSICAL:** Dee Dee Bridgewater, *The Wiz*

**SCENIC DESIGN:** Carl Toms, *Sherlock Holmes*

**COSTUME DESIGN:** Geoffrey Holder, *The Wiz*

**LIGHTING DESIGN:** Neil Peter Jampolis, *Sherlock Holmes*

**DIRECTION OF A PLAY:** John Dexter, *Equus*

**DIRECTION OF A MUSICAL:** Geoffrey Holder, *The Wiz*

**CHOREOGRAPHY:** George Faison, *The Wiz*

**SPECIAL TONY AWARD:** Al Hirschfeld; Neil Simon

Hinton Battle in costume as the Scarecrow in *The Wiz*,
costume by Geoffrey Holder

Geoffrey Holder

**HINTON BATTLE:** When I was fifteen years old, I was cast in the chorus of *The Wiz*. The show was in a pre-Broadway tryout in Detroit. The actor who was playing the Scarecrow, Stu Gilliam, was a very famous comedian at the time. He walked out after the first act of a performance. The stage manager came to me and asked if I wanted to go on in his place. I wasn't the understudy and didn't know the role, but I agreed to do it. I went into his dressing room and started getting into costume, and wig, and makeup. I had about twenty minutes. Geoffrey Holder was walking back and forth saying, "More glitter, darling." The stage manager was briefing me on the blocking. Stephanie Mills said she would help guide me. When I got onstage, I didn't know the lines. I kicked my leg, did a double turn, a triple turn, fell into a split and shook my head. The next thing I knew I got a call from 20th Century Fox, and they offered me the role. They rewrote the character to make him much younger. That was my debut on Broadway.

**GEORGE FAISON:** So many of us were at the beginning of our careers when we did *The Wiz*. Dee Dee Bridgewater, Hinton Battle, Phylicia Rashad. I cast Phylicia as a munchkin! I am so grateful to all the dancers that participated and went on this incredible journey with me. The road to Broadway was full of potholes and obstacles. There were legendary fights in bars, falling in love and out of love, and the cutting of costumes, the threats of firing, the firings. It was a great time filled with drama. To survive it was something! Everybody poured everything they had into that show. Our life was on the line! We didn't know if the show was going to end on the road or if we'd make it to New York. I changed the choreography many times until it fit and until I could draw all of the colloquial language and interpret that into dance. My experience with Alvin Ailey and then leading my own company prepared me to take on that responsibility. The secret to the success of *The Wiz* was the rigor, the hard work, and the discipline.

**EMILIO SOSA:** I had the divine fortune to enter Grace Costumes, a maker of opera, ballet, and Broadway costumes, as a twenty-one-year-old fashion student with no theater experience. One summer day, during our traditional catered lunches, Geoffrey Holder walked into my life, and I have never been the same since. I allow myself to think the reason he was so generous to me was that he saw a little of himself in me, a man of color in an industry not always welcoming. Although, Geoffrey always held his head high and commanded respect from all those around him. During the many decades of friendship and collaborations, I slowly learned my craft under his caring but critical eye. He was a brilliant painter, and substituted fabric for paint to create brilliant designs that would "fool the eye"—one of his favorite quotes, which I find myself using all the time. Geoffrey's costume designs were a dialogue with the audience. His use of color was what fascinated me the most. "You must always add orange or pink to red. It make the dress sing," once again "fooling the eye." His connection to Grace Costumes came through *The Wiz*, the hit musical, which earned him two Tony Awards, Best Director and Best Costumes. Grace created all the iconic costumes.

I remember we were making a gown he designed for his wife and muse, Carmen de Lavallade. It was created from an African print with large portraits of Marcus Garvey throughout. On this day, we presented the finished gown. Once inside the workroom, he asks for the dress form to be spun around so he can see the gown move. It was stunning, both for its design and political statement, since it would be worn at a very posh event. As we waited for his reaction, he calls me over and asks for a clear sequin. I quickly go to the trim drawer, grab a handful, and hurry back. "Place a sequin in the center of Mr. Garvey's eye"—which I dutifully did. "Now come here," he beckoned in his iconic baritone voice. I stood next to him and watched as the dress moved—the sequin caught the light, giving the impression that the eye was moving. "Brava, Carmen is going to love it! Now let's eat." I have hundreds of small nuggets of his genius stuck to my brain, which I use every day. And all aren't about design. Most are about life, what it means to be a man of color in a world not willing to judge us by the content of our character. Yet his legacy is a road map for me and others to follow and expand on. Geoffrey Holder broke down barriers so I can walk through them. I am forever in his debt for changing my life.

**ELLEN BURSTYN:** Charles Grodin and I were a team on *Same Time, Next Year*. It was a very successful show. When the Tony nominees were announced, I heard them first, and it was everybody but Charles. I was the closest to him, so I decided it should be me to tell him the news. I went and knocked on his dressing room door and told him the nominees were announced. He looked at my face and he said, "And you were, and I wasn't?" And I said, "It's worse than that." He said, "Everybody was, and I wasn't?" It was just so painful. It was like a duet was played on the piano, and one got a Grammy and the other didn't. When I received mine, which I was, of course, very happy to get, I mentioned him and that I would share it with him. He was so wonderful in the show. We played off each other; it was a real duet.

**RITA MORENO:** I was on Broadway performing in *Last of the Red Hot Lovers* with James Coco. I used to regale Jimmy backstage with quotes from a Puerto Rican singer-dancer character of no talent whatsoever whom I had invented. He would roar at her attitude and accent.

One time, Jimmy gave a party and invited me and Terrence McNally, a good friend of his. That evening, Jimmy prevailed on me to perform Googie (as she came to be known) for Terrence.

I did bits of the player King speech from *Hamlet*, quotes from *Hiawatha*, and sang pieces of "Everything's Coming Up Roses"…all with a thick Puerto Rican accent and the shameless confidence that only someone who was clueless could conjure. Terrence almost went up in smoke! And when he bid good night at the end of the evening, he said to me, "I am definitely writing a play for this character, she's just outrageous."

Several months later, my agent called and told me that I was offered a play by Terrence McNally in which I would play the part of Googie Gomez. He told me that Terrence would not have anyone but me in the Broadway production, which made sense since she was my invention. At that point, he had already tried out the play, entitled *The Tubs*, at Yale, which starred Carmen de Lavallade (then a drama student there) as the character called Rita "Googie" Gomez. I was very jealous indeed.

Terrence never gave me the credit for Googie until many years later when I mentioned it in a press interview. However, what's really important where Googie is concerned is that Terrence really understood her the moment I sang "Everything's Coming Up Roses."

Googie was a scene stealing, outrageous, and funny gift from this wonderful playwright. I will be forever grateful to him.

Frank Langella and Rita Moreno

# WINNERS ◎ 1976

**PLAY:** *Travesties*, Tom Stoppard Produced by David Merrick, Doris Cole Abrahams, and Burry Fredrik in association with S. Spencer Davids and Eddie Kulukundis

**MUSICAL:** *A Chorus Line* Produced by Joseph Papp, New York Shakespeare Festival

**BOOK OF A MUSICAL:** James Kirkwood and Nicholas Dante, *A Chorus Line*

**ORIGINAL SCORE (MUSIC AND/OR LYRICS) WRITTEN FOR THE THEATRE:** Marvin Hamlisch (music), Edward Kleban (lyrics), *A Chorus Line*

**ACTOR IN A LEADING ROLE IN A PLAY:** John Wood, *Travesties*

**ACTRESS IN A LEADING ROLE IN A PLAY:** Irene Worth, *Sweet Bird of Youth*

**ACTOR IN A LEADING ROLE IN A MUSICAL:** George Rose, *My Fair Lady*

**ACTRESS IN A LEADING ROLE IN A MUSICAL:** Donna McKechnie, *A Chorus Line*

**ACTOR IN A FEATURED ROLE IN A PLAY:** Edward Herrmann, *Mrs. Warren's Profession*

**ACTRESS IN A FEATURED ROLE IN A PLAY:** Shirley Knight, *Kennedy's Children*

**ACTOR IN A FEATURED ROLE IN A MUSICAL:** Sammy Williams, *A Chorus Line*

**ACTRESS IN A FEATURED ROLE IN A MUSICAL:** Carole Bishop, *A Chorus Line*

**SCENIC DESIGN:** Boris Aronson, *Pacific Overtures*

**COSTUME DESIGN:** Florence Klotz, *Pacific Overtures*

**LIGHTING DESIGN:** Tharon Musser, *A Chorus Line*

**DIRECTION OF A PLAY:** Ellis Rabb, *The Royal Family*

**DIRECTION OF A MUSICAL:** Michael Bennett, *A Chorus Line*

**CHOREOGRAPHY:** Michael Bennett and Bob Avian, *A Chorus Line*

**REGIONAL THEATRE AWARD:** The Arena Stage, Washington, DC

**SPECIAL TONY AWARD:** George Abbott; Mathilde Pincus; Thomas H. Fitzgerald; Circle in the Square; Richard Burton

Featured acting winners (L to R) Edward Herrmann, Carole Bishop (now known as Kelly Bishop), Shirley Knight, and Sammy Williams

1976 ◦ 69

**HAL LINDEN:** I had a wonderful relationship with George Abbott. He was very open with his actors. You could make suggestions, although everyone called him Mr. Abbott, never George. He actually let me add a line. He took the bus to Philadelphia with the rest of the company, which tells you something about his character. I had a very small part in his show *The Education of H*Y*M*A*N K*A*P*L*A*N.* I felt like I needed an exit line, so I came up with one. He listened to my idea on the bus and told me to try it in front of an audience. I did, and the line got a laugh and applause. Three days later I saw him backstage. He walked right by me and said, "Keep it in."

He was a famous stickler. One day he was playing golf with his wife. He teed off and hit a golf ball and threw himself off balance and fell. His wife ran over and told him not to move, she was going to get help. She said, "Just lay there." From the ground George said, "That's lie there."

**PRISCILLA LOPEZ:** *A Chorus Line* started as a series of tape sessions Michael Bennett had with a group of Broadway dancers talking about their lives. He told us that he thought dancers had a story to tell. I was one of the dancers and part of the process there from the very beginning. Marvin Hamlisch and Edward Kleban took many of the shows' lyrics directly from those sessions. The song "Nothing" came from my experience at the High School of Performing Arts. My story of going "up a steep and very narrow stairway" to my dance class ended up in "At the Ballet." The monologue Kelly Bishop had as Sheila was her own story. The way *A Chorus Line* evolved created a new remarkable era in theatre. *A Chorus Line* affected a whole generation. I received a Tony nomination for the role of Diana Morales.

**NATASHA KATZ:** Tharon Musser was the first person to bring computerized lighting to Broadway with *A Chorus Line*. The lighting for *A Chorus Line* is extremely complex. Every person on that line had three lights on them. Tharon's light plot is extremely famous because of these thought lights. When the characters would have these thoughts, it would go into lavender light. In many ways it was the beginning of lighting really being able to tell a story and let us know what somebody was thinking, where to look, and what the emotion was at the moment.

**ROBIN WAGNER:** Tharon Musser was easily one of the finest lighting designers working on Broadway at the time. Everything she did was beautiful. She just had that quality of light in her hands like no one else ever did.

# WINNERS ◎ 1977

Barry Bostwick, Dorothy Loudon, and Al Pacino

**PLAY:** *The Shadow Box*, Michael Cristofer
Produced by Allan Francis, Ken Marsolais, Lester Osterman, Leonard Soloway

**MUSICAL:** *Annie*
Produced by Lewis Allen, Mike Nichols, Irwin Meyer, Stephen R. Friedman

**BOOK OF A MUSICAL:** Thomas Meehan, *Annie*

**ORIGINAL SCORE (MUSIC AND/OR LYRICS) WRITTEN FOR THE THEATRE:** Charles Strouse (music), Martin Charnin (lyrics), *Annie*

**REVIVAL:** *Porgy and Bess* Produced by Sherwin M. Goldman, Houston Grand Opera

**ACTOR IN A LEADING ROLE IN A PLAY:** Al Pacino, *The Basic Training of Pavlo Hummel*

**ACTRESS IN A LEADING ROLE IN A PLAY:** Julie Harris, *The Belle of Amherst*

**ACTOR IN A LEADING ROLE IN A MUSICAL:** Barry Bostwick, *The Robber Bridegroom*

**ACTRESS IN A LEADING ROLE IN A MUSICAL:** Dorothy Loudon, *Annie*

**ACTOR IN A FEATURED ROLE IN A PLAY:** Jonathan Pryce, *Comedians*

**ACTRESS IN A FEATURED ROLE IN A PLAY:** Trazana Beverley, *For Colored Girls Who Have Considered Suicide/When the Rainbow Is Enuf*

**ACTOR IN A FEATURED ROLE IN A MUSICAL:** Lenny Baker, *I Love My Wife*

**ACTRESS IN A FEATURED ROLE IN A MUSICAL:**
Delores Hall, *Your Arms Too Short to Box with God*

**SCENIC DESIGN:** David Mitchell, *Annie*

**COSTUME DESIGN:** Theoni V. Aldredge, *Annie*; Santo Loquasto, *The Cherry Orchard*

**LIGHTING DESIGN:** Jennifer Tipton, *The Cherry Orchard*

**DIRECTION OF A PLAY:** Gordon Davidson, *The Shadow Box*

**DIRECTION OF A MUSICAL:** Gene Saks, *I Love My Wife*

**CHOREOGRAPHY:** Peter Gennaro, *Annie*

**REGIONAL THEATRE AWARD:** Mark Taper Forum, Los Angeles, California

**SPECIAL TONY AWARD:** Cheryl Crawford; Lily Tomlin; Barry Manilow; Diana Ross; National Theatre for the Deaf; Equity Library Theatre

**SANTO LOQUASTO:** When I started working at the Public in the early seventies I got to work with Theoni V. Aldredge. Though she was a very successful Broadway designer, she remained devoted to Joe Papp, designing everything at the Public. She could really manufacture shows in the best sense of the word and had a great team of assistants. Theoni was amazing. She was very smart, and so charming. She handled directors like no one else. She instilled confidence, especially with small, naturalistic plays. She was the go-to costume designer for years, and quite a force. She designed big Broadway mega hits like *A Chorus Line, Annie, 42nd Street, Dreamgirls,* and *La Cage.* And there were movies. She won an Oscar for *The Great Gatsby.*

Diana Ross arriving at the Shubert Theater

# WINNERS ○ 1978

**PLAY:** *Da*, Hugh Leonard
Produced by Lester Osterman, Marilyn Strauss, Marc Howard

**MUSICAL:** *Ain't Misbehavin'* Produced by Emanuel Azenberg,
Dasha Epstein, The Shubert Organization, Jane Gaynor, Ron Dante

**BOOK OF A MUSICAL:** Betty Comden and Adolph Green,
*On the Twentieth Century*

**ORIGINAL SCORE (MUSIC AND/OR LYRICS) WRITTEN FOR THE THEATRE:** Cy Coleman
(music), Betty Comden and Adolph Green (lyrics), *On the Twentieth Century*

**REVIVAL:** *Dracula*
Produced by Jujamcyn Theaters, Elizabeth I. McCann, John Wulp, Victor Lurie,
Nelle Nugent, Max Weitzenhoffer

**ACTOR IN A LEADING ROLE IN A PLAY:** Barnard Hughes, *Da*

**ACTRESS IN A LEADING ROLE IN A PLAY:** Jessica Tandy, *The Gin Game*

**ACTOR IN A LEADING ROLE IN A MUSICAL:** John Cullum, *On the Twentieth Century*

**ACTRESS IN A LEADING ROLE IN A MUSICAL:** Liza Minnelli, *The Act*

**ACTOR IN A FEATURED ROLE IN A PLAY:** Lester Rawlins, *Da*

**ACTRESS IN A FEATURED ROLE IN A PLAY:** Ann Wedgeworth, *Chapter Two*

**ACTOR IN A FEATURED ROLE IN A MUSICAL:** Kevin Kline, *On the Twentieth Century*

**ACTRESS IN A FEATURED ROLE IN A MUSICAL:** Nell Carter, *Ain't Misbehavin'*

**SCENIC DESIGN:** Robin Wagner, *On the Twentieth Century*

**COSTUME DESIGN:** Edward Gorey, *Dracula*

**LIGHTING DESIGN:** Jules Fisher, *Dancin'*

**DIRECTION OF A PLAY:** Melvin Bernhardt, *Da*

**DIRECTION OF A MUSICAL:** Richard Maltby Jr., *Ain't Misbehavin'*

**CHOREOGRAPHY:** Bob Fosse, *Dancin'*

**REGIONAL THEATRE AWARD:** The Long Wharf Theatre, New Haven, Connecticut

**SPECIAL TONY AWARD:** Irving Berlin; Charles Moss and Stan Dragoti

Lead acting winners (L to R)
Barnard Hughes, Liza
Minnelli, Jessica Tandy, and
John Cullum

Ann Wedgeworth

**ROBIN WAGNER:** There was a piece of music written for *On the Twentieth Century* that was meant for dance, but as it turned out there was really no dancing going on. Hal Prince and I started talking about what to do, and I suggested using it to have Imogene Coca make her journey on the train. It was quite remarkable musically. Cy Coleman was able to add the effects of the train—the steam, the sounds—all in music. We had Imogene on the front of the train coming downstage, then it turned around and she was on the back of it when it was going up stage. Then, at the final part the curtain closed, and we had a miniature train go across the stage. I knew we had something at that point because the audience started to applaud! I was so surprised. Then we added an airplane up above as a finale for that sequence, which was the history of transportation.

Robin Wagner's design for *On the 20th Century*

Frank Langella as Dracula, costume by Edward Gorey

# WINNERS ◎ 1979

**PLAY:** *The Elephant Man*, Bernard Pomerance
Produced by Richmond Crinkley, Elizabeth I. McCann, Nelle Nugent

**MUSICAL:** *Sweeney Todd*
Produced by Richard Barr, Charles Woodward, Robert Fryer, Mary Lea Johnson, Martin Richards

**BOOK OF A MUSICAL:** Hugh Wheeler, *Sweeney Todd*

**ORIGINAL SCORE (MUSIC AND/OR LYRICS) WRITTEN FOR THE THEATRE:**
Stephen Sondheim, *Sweeney Todd*

**ACTOR IN A LEADING ROLE IN A PLAY:** Tom Conti, *Whose Life Is It Anyway?*

**ACTRESS IN A LEADING ROLE IN A PLAY:** Constance Cummings, *Wings*;
Carole Shelley, *The Elephant Man*

**ACTOR IN A LEADING ROLE IN A MUSICAL:** Len Cariou, *Sweeney Todd*

**ACTRESS IN A LEADING ROLE IN A MUSICAL:** Angela Lansbury, *Sweeney Todd*

**ACTOR IN A FEATURED ROLE IN A PLAY:** Michael Gough, *Bedroom Farce*

**ACTRESS IN A FEATURED ROLE IN A PLAY:** Joan Hickson, *Bedroom Farce*

**ACTOR IN A FEATURED ROLE IN A MUSICAL:**
Henderson Forsythe,
*The Best Little Whorehouse in Texas*

Angela Lansbury, Len Cariou, Tom Conti, and Carole Shelley

ACTRESS IN A FEATURED ROLE IN A MUSICAL:
Carlin Glynn, *The Best Little Whorehouse in Texas*

SCENIC DESIGN: Eugene Lee, *Sweeney Todd*

COSTUME DESIGN: Franne Lee, *Sweeney Todd*

LIGHTING DESIGN: Roger Morgan, *The Crucifer of Blood*

DIRECTION OF A PLAY: Jack Hofsiss, *The Elephant Man*

DIRECTION OF A MUSICAL: Harold Prince, *Sweeney Todd*

CHOREOGRAPHY: Michael Bennett and Bob Avian, *Ballroom*

REGIONAL THEATRE AWARD: American Conservatory
Theater, San Francisco, California

SPECIAL TONY AWARD: Richard Rodgers;
Henry Fonda; Walter F. Diehl; Eugene O'Neill
Memorial Theatre Center

Jack Hofsiss, Richard Rodgers, and Harold Prince

**FRANNE LEE:** I saw *Sweeney Todd* as over the top, much in the same way an opera is over the top. I thought my design should be based on political cartoons. I did a lot of research, and even though the show takes place in England, I really latched on to these German cartoons from the turn of the century. Mrs. Lovett's hair came right out of those cartoons.

Sweeney came from the bowels; he was a fugitive and a murderer. I liked the idea of him being like a fisherman from that period. He wore two layers of pants, his regular pants and then the rubber ones that went over them. I saw him as someone who found his clothes on the street. His clothes were ill fitting; his pants were held up by suspenders. Mrs. Lovett was a poor pie maker; she didn't have very much. Her skirt was made from a fabric that was similar to the lining of a Victorian skirt. She didn't have any money for shoes, so she wore slippers. The people that lived during that period who were poor were very poor. I wanted to capture that feeling, and through the costumes show the class difference between them and the judge and Johanna. As Sweeney Todd and Mrs. Lovett started to become prosperous, their clothes got better.

# ACCEPTANCE SPEECHES THROUGH THE YEARS

I must say this is a sneaky way to get back on television.

**JACKIE GLEASON (1960)**

**HENDERSON FORSYTHE (1979):** It's so great to work and play in the theatre. In our profession play and work are the same thing. To get the laughs, to sense the tears, to feel the electrics from an audience and on top of that to get paid for it, and on top of that to receive an award for doing what I love most in all the world to do, it's almost too much for one person. But don't mistake me, I'm going to keep this trophy and I'll keep on acting as long as I possibly can, and I hope I keep on getting paid for it.

Henderson Forsythe and Carlin Glynn

**HELEN HAYES (1980):** I think it's customary, and I know it's becoming at moments like this to speak with becoming humility, but I'm not going to do that. I don't feel a bit humble. I feel proud as a lord and ten feet tall. There's a verse in Proverbs that goes something like this: Length of days in the right hand, and in the left hand riches and honors. That's me. I can't buy anything with my riches, and I wouldn't want to part with any of them anyway, because they're my memories, mostly of the theatre, because that's where I lived most of my life. Memories of plays that I've been so proud to be a part of. Of actors and actresses that I've worked with or watched from the front who inspired me to go on and try to be better and better. Of the wonderful people that are drawn to our world like the man for whom this award has been named. Lawrence Langner, a lawyer who came to the theatre with a lot of big dreams and never quit till he made them all realities. Yes, these are my memories. And as for honors, well this stands high above them all because it comes to me from my own people.

**VIOLA DAVIS (2010):** I don't believe in luck or happenstance. I absolutely believe in the presence of God in my life. I was born into circumstances where I couldn't see it with my eyes, I couldn't touch it with my hands, and so I had to believe it in my heart.

It seems almost too much to receive a prize for doing a job that was so very pleasant. **CECIL BEATON (1960)**

**ARIELLE TEPPER MADOVER (2010):** I believe with all my heart that it is our duty as actors, directors, designers, and fellow producers to do just what Rothko did. To inspire, engage, and foster new artists to fall in love with our craft and make it their own.

> I have to, of course, thank Lorraine Hansberry, who actually built the neighborhood of Clybourne Park. We just moved in and depressed the property values. **BRUCE NORRIS (2012)**

**JORDAN ROTH (2012):** There are those rare people who can look at the world and see things the rest of us don't see until they show us. These are the writers. There are the special few who can take that vision and turn it back into a world. These are the directors, the designers. There are fearless beings who can live in that world and show us who we are. These are our actors. There are dedicated people who know why that world matters so very much. Crew, theater staff, producers, investors, managers, marketers. And then there are the people who step forward and say show me this world. Open me, change me. These are our audiences. And when all of these people come together and say yes, there is theatre.

**JONATHAN PRYCE (1977):** I'd like to be able to say I didn't expect to win this, but to fly from London and get dressed up like this means I can't say "I was just passing, so I dropped in."

**DOROTHY LOUDON (1977):** I had a feeling if I ever got up here, I could work this room.

**AL PACINO (1977):** The theatre gave me a chance to be in movies, and movies gave me a chance to come back to the theatre, and I'm grateful to both.

**MELVIN BERNHARDT (1978):** Can we get in tight on this? I hate to direct someone else's show, but my mother in Buffalo always sits close, and I want her to see this.

**KENNY LEON (2020):** Breonna Taylor, Breonna Taylor, Breonna Taylor. George Floyd, George Floyd, We will never ever forget you. We opened *A Soldier's Play* the same week that we lost Kobe Bryant and his beautiful daughter Gigi. All lives are precious. All lives are precious. I'm a graduate of a historically Black college, CAU in Atlanta, Georgia, and I want to say to all those students present, past, and those yet to come, yes you can. But what I want to say to you and all of those at home and the people in the room, we can do

Bruce Norris and Jordan Roth

better. Charles Fuller wrote this play. Wait a minute. No diss to Shakespeare, no diss to Ibsen, to Chekhov, to Shaw. They're all at the table. But the table got to be bigger. We need the late, great Melvin Van Peebles sitting at the table. We need Ntozake [Shange] sitting at the table. We need our young people to learn about all of our amazing writers in this land that we are standing on tonight, this Native American land. So we need to hear all of the stories. When we hear all of the stories, we are better!

**HELEN GALLAGHER (1971):** This award is to all of us that have stuck in a business maybe long after anybody wanted us. Stuck because we didn't know what else to do— no imagination. Stuck because we had to stick. It's for us that stick.

**IVO VAN HOVE (2016):** I came here for the first time when I was twenty mainly to see David Bowie in *The Elephant Man* at the Booth Theatre. And one of those days I was sitting on a bench and a woman came to me. She asked, "What do you want to be?" I said, "I want to be a theatre director." And she grabbed a piece of paper and a pen, and she asked me to sign that because, she said, "You never know." And indeed, you never know. She's watching now, and she's now thinking, *See? I was right.*

**PHIL SILVERS (1972):** It is assumed my children and their mother—my five girls—are watching in Los Angeles, and tomorrow when I call them I'm sure they'll be happy, and then will want to know, was David Cassidy there?

**TONY WALTON (1973):** The whole experience of *Pippin* was such a treat that this seems somehow like cheating. I do receive it very gratefully, but I won't be surprised if at midnight it starts rolling back towards Boris Aronson's house.

**JOHN CAIRD (1982):** There are two theatre capitals in the world, London and New York, and I don't think any of us felt that we had properly completed the job on *Nicholas Nickleby* until we had played it on both sides of the Atlantic, and we'd like to thank you all for giving us such a wonderful time while we were over here.

**DAVID ZIPPEL (1990):** When I found out I was doing a musical with Cy Coleman, Larry Gelbart, Michael Blakemore, and Robin Wagner, I thought, "My God I'm the only one on this team I've never heard of." Thank you for this award. Now I've heard of me.

Some of you may be right, I may not deserve this honor, but I don't deserve arthritis either, and I have that. And I got this! **CHARLES DURNING (1990)**

**GREGORY HINES (1992):** It's very hard for me to just say thank you to George Wolfe. Because George Wolfe encouraged me to try things that I didn't have in my heart to try. He asked me to go in places that I was unsure of and not to go with what had always worked for me. I so appreciate that from George. I appreciate George's courage in trying to bring to the American musical stage a musical dealing with African American issues and themes that doesn't find us happy and dancing all the time. Where we try to say something about the condition. Where we try to say some things that we don't see on the stage.

**CAROLE (KELLY) BISHOP (1976):** I've played in this theater several times in the chorus, and I am again. I've

done Tony Awards here too in the chorus, and this is one of those dreams and it's come true. And I have to accept this along with the rest of the cast because it's impossible without them. I'll keep it at my house though.

**MICHAEL BENNETT (1976):** I only wanted one thing: to be a Broadway director. And I am. And I wanted one moment, and I have it. And I thank you.

**MARVIN HAMLISCH (1976):** The people who really win this award are the people who love the theatre and who love writing for it. So, I'm sharing this award with really all the music writers for the theatre, 'cause I'm glad to be one of you.

I feel this a great, great, great honor this evening, and I'm very proud also to accept it on behalf of a play that I feel has created some history for us as women. And women of all colors, by the way. **TRAZANA BEVERLEY (1977)**

**JOHN CAMERON MITCHELL (2015):** Thank you, American Theatre Wing, for recognizing this strange little show that Stephen Trask and I created with the help of Peter Askin and David Binder so many years ago when *trans* was a weird word and punk rock

was nowhere close to Broadway. People say, "Oh, everything's been done. Nothing is new." I say, turn off the internet. Combine all the things that you love in the world. Take some time, and you might come up with something special that's lasting.

# the 19 80s

# WINNERS ○ 1980

Richard Kiley and
Vivian Matalon

Tim Rice and Andrew
Lloyd Webber

Lead acting winners (L to R)
Patti LuPone, Jim Dale, Phyllis
Frelich, and John Rubinstein

**PLAY:** *Children of a Lesser God*, Mark Medoff
Produced by Emanuel Azenberg, The Shubert Organization, Dasha Epstein, Ron Dante

**MUSICAL:** *Evita* Produced by Robert Stigwood

**BOOK OF A MUSICAL:** Tim Rice, *Evita*

**ORIGINAL SCORE (MUSIC AND/OR LYRICS) WRITTEN FOR THE THEATRE:**
Andrew Lloyd Webber (music), Tim Rice (lyrics), *Evita*

**REVIVAL:** *Morning's at Seven*
Produced by Elizabeth I. McCann, Nelle Nugent, Ray Larson

**ACTOR IN A LEADING ROLE IN A PLAY:** John Rubinstein, *Children of a Lesser God*

**ACTRESS IN A LEADING ROLE IN A PLAY:** Phyllis Frelich, *Children of a Lesser God*

**ACTOR IN A LEADING ROLE IN A MUSICAL:** Jim Dale, *Barnum*

**ACTRESS IN A LEADING ROLE IN A MUSICAL:** Patti LuPone, *Evita*

**ACTOR IN A FEATURED ROLE IN A PLAY:** Daniel Rounds, *Morning's at Seven*

**ACTRESS IN A FEATURED ROLE IN A PLAY:** Dinah Manoff, *I Ought to Be in Pictures*

**ACTOR IN A FEATURED ROLE IN A MUSICAL:** Mandy Patinkin, *Evita*

**ACTRESS IN A FEATURED ROLE IN A MUSICAL:** Priscilla Lopez,
*A Day in Hollywood/A Night in the Ukraine*

**SCENIC DESIGN:** John Lee Beatty, *Talley's Folley*; David Mitchell, *Barnum*

**COSTUME DESIGN:** Theoni V. Aldredge, *Barnum*

**LIGHTING DESIGN:** David Hersey, *Evita*

**DIRECTION OF A PLAY:** Vivian Matalon, *Morning's at Seven*

**DIRECTION OF A MUSICAL:** Harold Prince, *Evita*

**CHOREOGRAPHY:** Tommy Tune and Thommie Walsh,
*A Day in Hollywood/A Night in the Ukraine*

**REGIONAL THEATRE AWARD:** Actor's Theatre of Louisville, Kentucky

**SPECIAL TONY AWARD:** Helen Hayes; Mary Tyler Moore; Goodspeed Opera House;
Richard Fitzgerald; Hobe Morrison

**DANNY BURSTEIN:** Jim Dale is one of my true theatrical heroes. I love him so much. I've seen everything he's done. He embodies so much about what theatre mentors are supposed to do. They give back to younger actors, and that's what he's done for me. And I do it now for others.

Jim and I were nominated for Tonys opposite each other one year. For a kid growing up in Queens, to have been nominated in a category with Jim Dale, with one of my heroes, was thrill enough. Sitting there as a kid, watching him do his shows, I thought he was the most talented person I'd ever seen in my life. And to think that we were in a category together! I'm forever proud just to be associated in some way with all the people that I've been nominated with. But when you get to be nominated with your heroes that's especially great.

**JOHN LEE BEATTY:** I tied for the Tony with David Mitchell, who designed *Barnum*. It was always a miracle back then (when plays and musicals were not in separate categories) when a play would win for Best Scenic Design. This was the year of *Barnum*, which was an event. I was a young man on the way up, and David was a big established star designer. It was like the design world's equivalent of when Barbra Streisand and Katharine Hepburn tied for the Best Actress Oscar!

When they announced my name, I ran down the aisle, and then I heard there was a tie and there was someone else coming down. It was such a blur. I thanked my parents on national television. Can you imagine how many brownie points I got at home? They deserved thanks for putting up with the mess I made all through childhood making scenery, filling the garage and sometimes covering the dining room table.

In 1980 it was the Alexander Cohen Tony Awards. The Tony you won was a television prop, which was made out of wood. If you looked at it closely it wasn't the world's greatest prop. Of course, it didn't have your name on it. They only had a small number of them. When you won you stood there with your Tony Award, you went offstage, and someone grabbed it from you because they had to run it around behind the curtain and put it back on the rack on the other side, so they had enough to give out later. You never see it again! There was this gauntlet of people, including stagehands, who were congratulating you and pushing you down this line of about twenty people to a stage door—this was at the Mark Hellinger—and all of a sudden, I was outside in the empty street. What just happened?! Because I'm a set designer, it wasn't like there were flashbulbs going off. I'm not Liza Minnelli or Patti LuPone (who won that year)! They put me in a bar next door. I think one person took my picture and someone asked me what the name of my local paper was back in the small town in California I came from. I ended up sitting there for two hours talking with Tisa Farrow, Mia Farrow's sister. I called my good WASP mother—it was a delayed broadcast—and told her I won. She started to cry and caught herself and said, "Excuse me." She added that she would have to tell my father so he could watch.

**PATTI LuPONE:** My original dream was to be a rocker, but I knew I had a Broadway voice. Every time I sang rock I sounded like Ethel Merman. I knew instinctively that I would end up on the Broadway musical stage—even at a young age, I knew that was my destiny.

The whole experience of *Evita* was incredibly difficult. It's almost an impossible role to sing. It's knocked several singers out. It's a brutal score if you sing it in those keys. There was certainly no guarantee I was going to win the Tony, especially because it was such a controversial musical, but when I did it was an incredible relief because of the amount of work that went into it. I appreciated that the nominators and the voters recognized how difficult a role it was. My applause used to dip after Mandy Patinkin's. Mandy was the Greek chorus, and very likable, and Evita was extremely controversial. She was a Nazi sympathizer. It was difficult every night to go out there and play knowing the audience wasn't quite sure what to make of me, Patti. I was only playing a part! It's you in that curtain call. So, winning the Tony was sort of a vindication and a validation and a very big relief.

Mandy and I became incredibly close because we both were going through a wacky time. It wasn't a happy time at all. The show was raked over the coals by the critics. It was the audience that made *Evita* a hit. I had Peronistas and anti-Peronistas showing up saying, "You have her to a tee." There was an adoration and a mystification of this woman that I experienced during the run. What really put the show over the top was the commercial. People all over the country saw it.

**PRISCILLA LOPEZ:** VCRs had just been invented and I got one. There was a festival of all the Marx Brothers films. I recorded it and watched all the movies. Not long after that my husband told me that I missed a call saying

Featured Actors in a Musical winners Priscilla Lopez and Mandy Patinkin

that Tommy Tune was doing a show about the Marx Brothers and wanted me to audition. Talk about unbelievable timing! He told me to guess what part I was up for. I said, "Margaret Dumont?" No…The only other thing I could think of was the ingenue. No again. Then I slowly realized it was Harpo! I was a wreck at my first audition because I had been in L.A. for three years, and I hadn't been singing and dancing. Still, after the first go around I was asked to come back and prepare a mime. I decided I would come back *as* Harpo Marx. I went to Brooklyn and got my father's pants, checkered shirt, and raincoat, and Jonathan Tunick lent me a horn. I went to 14th Street and bought this blond curly-haired wig and a hat. From watching all the films I knew all of Harpo's shtick. I did all of it at the audition. When I finished I jumped off the edge of the stage, ran up the aisle, and jumped into the lap of Dick Vosburgh, who was the writer, and kissed him as Harpo would have done. That got me the job. Vosburgh was obsessed with the Marx Brothers and recognized that I knew Harpo inside out.

For my performance in *A Day in Hollywood/A Night in the Ukraine* my colleagues and peers who shared my love and respect for theatre bestowed upon me the honor of "Best Featured Actress in a Musical Tony Award 1981." *Yes!!!*

# WINNERS ◎ 1981

**PLAY:** *Amadeus*, Peter Shaffer
Produced by The Shubert Organization, Elizabeth I. McCann, Nelle Nugent, Roger S. Berlind

**MUSICAL:** *42nd Street* Produced by David Merrick

**BOOK OF A MUSICAL:** Peter Stone, *Woman of the Year*

**ORIGINAL SCORE (MUSIC AND/OR LYRICS) WRITTEN FOR THE THEATRE:**
John Kander (music), Fred Ebb (lyrics), *Woman of the Year*

**REVIVAL:** *The Pirates of Penzance*
Produced by Joseph Papp, The New York Shakespeare Festival

**ACTOR IN A LEADING ROLE IN A PLAY:** Ian McKellen, *Amadeus*

**ACTRESS IN A LEADING ROLE IN A PLAY:** Jane Lapotaire, *Piaf*

**ACTOR IN A LEADING ROLE IN A MUSICAL:** Kevin Kline, *The Pirates of Penzance*

**ACTRESS IN A LEADING ROLE IN A MUSICAL:** Lauren Bacall, *Woman of the Year*

**ACTOR IN A FEATURED ROLE IN A PLAY:** Brian Backer, *The Floating Light Bulb*

**ACTRESS IN A FEATURED ROLE IN A PLAY:** Swoosie Kurtz, *Fifth of July*

**ACTOR IN A FEATURED ROLE IN A MUSICAL:** Hinton Battle, *Sophisticated Ladies*

**ACTRESS IN A FEATURED ROLE IN A MUSICAL:** Marilyn Cooper, *Woman of the Year*

**SCENIC DESIGN:** John Bury, *Amadeus*

**COSTUME DESIGN:** Willa Kim, *Sophisticated Ladies*

**LIGHTING DESIGN:** John Bury, *Amadeus*

**DIRECTION OF A PLAY:** Peter Hall, *Amadeus*

**DIRECTION OF A MUSICAL:** Wilford Leach,
*The Pirates of Penzance*

**CHOREOGRAPHY:** Gower Champion, *42nd Street*

**REGIONAL THEATRE AWARD:** Trinity Square Repertory
Company, Providence, Rhode Island

**SPECIAL TONY AWARD:** Lena Horne

Lead acting winners (L to R) Kevin Kline, Jane Lapotaire, Lauren Bacall, and Ian McKellen

ROBIN WAGNER: During rehearsal for *42nd Street* one day, Gower Champion said to me, "I think I put a piece of everything I've done in my life in this show." Of course, the show went on to be a huge success. And Gower died on opening night. I was at the hospital with him when he died. It was about three in the afternoon. I was there with his son and David Merrick. Merrick didn't want anyone at the show to know until after that night's performance. As the cast was happily taking their curtain call, David came onstage in front of the audience. He stopped the applause and said, "This is a tragic night." The audience laughed, thinking this was a joke. He continued to tell them that Gower had died. There were gasps from the cast and the audience. Jerry Orbach called for the curtain to be closed and said good night to the audience.

Lena Horne, Elizabeth Taylor, Ben Vereen, and Jane Lapotaire

MATTHEW BRODERICK: When I was a teenager, I watched Brian Backer win a Tony Award. I remember thinking that now he owned the world. That was the first time I realized somebody my age could have one of those. That made a significant impression on me.

# WINNERS ◎ 1982

**PLAY:** *The Life and Adventures of Nicholas Nickleby*, David Edgar

Produced by James M. Nederlander, The Shubert Organization, Elizabeth I. McCann, Nelle Nugent

**MUSICAL:** *Nine*

Produced by Michel Stuart, Harvey J. Klaris, Roger S. Berlind, James M. Nederlander,
Francine LeFrak, Kenneth D. Greenblatt

**BOOK OF A MUSICAL:** Tom Eyen, *Dreamgirls*

**ORIGINAL SCORE (MUSIC AND/OR LYRICS) WRITTEN FOR THE THEATRE:**
Maury Yeston, *Nine*

**REVIVAL:** *Othello*

Produced by Barry and Fran Weissler, CBS Video Enterprises

**ACTOR IN A LEADING ROLE IN A PLAY:** Roger Rees, *The Life and
Adventures of Nicholas Nickleby*

**ACTRESS IN A LEADING ROLE IN A PLAY:** Zoe Caldwell, *Medea*

**ACTOR IN A LEADING ROLE IN A MUSICAL:** Ben Harney, *Dreamgirls*

**ACTRESS IN A LEADING ROLE IN A MUSICAL:** Jennifer Holliday, *Dreamgirls*

**ACTOR IN A FEATURED ROLE IN A PLAY:** Zakes Mokae, *"Master Harold"...and the Boys*

**ACTRESS IN A FEATURED ROLE IN A PLAY:** Amanda Plummer, *Agnes of God*

Presenter James Earl Jones and Best Featured Actor in
a Play Zakes Mokae

**ACTOR IN A FEATURED ROLE IN A MUSICAL:** Cleavant Derricks, *Dreamgirls*

**ACTRESS IN A FEATURED ROLE IN A MUSICAL:** Liliane Montevecchi, *Nine*

**SCENIC DESIGN:** John Napier and Dermot Hayes,
*The Life and Adventures of Nicholas Nickleby*

**COSTUME DESIGN:** William Ivey Long, *Nine*

**LIGHTING DESIGN:** Tharon Musser, *Dreamgirls*

**DIRECTION OF A PLAY:** Trevor Nunn and John Caird,
*The Life and Adventures of Nicholas Nickleby*

**DIRECTION OF A MUSICAL:** Tommy Tune, *Nine*

**CHOREOGRAPHY:** Michael Bennett and Michael Peters, *Dreamgirls*

**REGIONAL THEATRE AWARD:** The Guthrie Theatre,
Minneapolis, Minnesota

**SPECIAL TONY AWARD:** The Actors' Fund of America; Warner Communications;
Radio City Music Hall

---

**CLEAVANT DERRICKS:** I knew *Dreamgirls* was going to be a hit on opening night. I had never seen an audience react like that. People were screaming, and they gave us a standing ovation that did not stop for the longest time. Within weeks we were sold out for the next six months.

Michael Bennett called Ben Harney and me into his office one day. He told us he thought we were both going to be nominated for Tony Awards. Michael Bennett said that if he put us both in the same category, we would split the vote and probably both lose. He was going to put Ben in as Best Actor and me as Featured Actor. He thought that would give us the best chance of winning. I didn't believe him, but it was good to know that he thought highly of my work. That was his plan, but then Obba Babatundé was also nominated! In the end Michael was right. Ben Harney and I both won Tonys for *Dreamgirls*.

I'm so appreciative to have a Tony Award. There's no better way for an actor to go down in history. In theatre you are out there on that stage every night, and you have to deliver. To win a Tony Award, for me, is the epitome for an actor in the world of theatre. I am so appreciative of being recognized for an achievement in my life that I never dreamed would happen.

**JENNIFER HOLLIDAY:** I made my Broadway debut in *Your Arms Too Short to Box with God*. Someone suggested to Michael Bennett that he go and see me. He was producing *Dreamgirls* at that point, but not yet directing. Nell Carter was originally cast as Effie, but she got the TV show *Gimme a Break!* and they needed to replace her. Michael came to see a matinee and asked me and my castmate Cleavant Derricks if we'd be interested in being part of a workshop. I didn't know who he was; of course, Cleavant did. I was already doing eight shows a week, so I didn't know if I was interested. Cleavant told me it was a good idea, and so I agreed. Sheryl Lee Ralph and Loretta Devine had already been working on the show for a couple of years. It was originally a vehicle for Sheryl Lee Ralph; Tom Eyen wrote it for her.

When I first started working with Michael Bennett, I was so new to theatre. I had only done that one show, which was more of a revue. He didn't want me to work with an acting coach. Instead, he gave me all these Barbra Streisand VHS tapes. He wanted me to watch them to learn how to tell a story through song. Of course, she had this amazing, beautiful voice, but what I took away was how long she held those notes. That fascinated me. I copied her. I would practice and practice holding notes the way she did. I asked Michael if I

Musical acting winners (L to R) Ben Harney, Jennifer Holliday, Liliane Montevecchi, and Cleavant Derricks

could put that in "And I Am Telling You I'm Not Going." I wanted to slow the song down and hold a note. He gave me the go-ahead to try it. It just worked. I also added the gospel funk feel to the section where Effie sings "tear down the mountains." That came from me being raised in the church. Those are my two major contributions to that song.

I had the opportunity to perform "And I Am Telling You" on the Tony broadcast. I felt I had to do a great performance to make Michael proud and show him that he had taught me.

I feel honored and blessed to have a Tony. There are so many others that haven't been recognized who are also deserving. I always want to show that I'm worthy of being a Tony Award winner, but I also don't think I won because I'm more special than anybody else. Things just happen. I would not have been able to bring Effie to life in that way or win a Tony had Michael Bennett not taught and nurtured me.

# WINNERS ◎ 1983

**PLAY:** *Torch Song Trilogy*, Harvey Fierstein

Produced by Kenneth Waissman, Martin Markinson, Lawrence Lane, John Glines, BetMar, Donald Tick

**MUSICAL:** *Cats*

Produced by Cameron Mackintosh; The Really Useful Company, Inc.;
David Geffen; The Shubert Organization

**BOOK OF A MUSICAL:** T. S. Eliot, *Cats*

**ORIGINAL SCORE (MUSIC AND/OR LYRICS) WRITTEN FOR THE THEATRE:**
Andrew Lloyd Webber (music), T. S. Eliot (lyrics), *Cats*

**REVIVAL:** *On Your Toes*

Produced by Alfred de Liagre Jr., Roger L. Stevens, John Mauceri, Donald R. Seawell, André Pastoria

**ACTOR IN A LEADING ROLE IN A PLAY:** Harvey Fierstein, *Torch Song Trilogy*

**ACTRESS IN A LEADING ROLE IN A PLAY:** Jessica Tandy, *Foxfire*

**ACTOR IN A LEADING ROLE IN A MUSICAL:** Tommy Tune, *My One and Only*

**ACTRESS IN A LEADING ROLE IN A MUSICAL:** Natalia Makarova, *On Your Toes*

**ACTOR IN A FEATURED ROLE IN A PLAY:** Matthew Broderick, *Brighton Beach Memoirs*

**ACTRESS IN A FEATURED ROLE IN A PLAY:** Judith Ivey, *Steaming*

**ACTOR IN A FEATURED ROLE IN A MUSICAL:** Charles Honi Coles, *My One and Only*

**ACTRESS IN A FEATURED ROLE IN A MUSICAL:** Betty Buckley, *Cats*

**SCENIC DESIGN:** Ming Cho Lee, *K2*    **COSTUME DESIGN:** John Napier, *Cats*

**LIGHTING DESIGN:** David Hersey, *Cats*

**DIRECTION OF A PLAY:** Gene Saks, *Brighton Beach Memoirs*

**DIRECTION OF A MUSICAL:** Trevor Nunn, *Cats*

**CHOREOGRAPHY:** Tommy Tune and Thommie Walsh, *My One and Only*

**REGIONAL THEATRE AWARD:** Oregon Shakespeare Festival Association

Betty Buckley as Grizabella in *Cats*

**DEREK McLANE:** Ming Cho Lee was an artist in the truest sense of the word. He did not have a commercial career, and he didn't seem to be particularly interested in commercial projects. He was interested in the art of the design, and he was often very hard on himself. As a student of Ming's, it was interesting to hear him talk about his own work, because he was weirdly objective. He would talk about things that he had done well without false humility, but he was also ruthless with himself about the things he didn't feel like he had figured out successfully. The way he held his own work to account at such a high level, without sentimentality, was inspiring.

Ming's work was distinctive. There was such a strong style and exquisite level of taste to it that any of us who studied with him, whether or not we wanted to design in his style, were in awe of the level of talent and execution of his work. That carried over very much to how he was as a teacher. He was not sentimental with any of his students. He was blunt, he didn't offer false praise, and when you designed something that wasn't very good, he told you in no uncertain terms. It felt as though he cared so deeply about each student's success that it was as if he was personally pained when they did not do well. It was amazing how overjoyed he was when you did something that was good, and he let everybody know about it. He was a super teacher, like none that I have ever had anywhere else in my life.

He designed and won the Tony Award for *K2* when I was his student. That set was not like many of his other sets, in that it was astonishingly realistic. It was an enormous cliff of ice, rendered in such a lifelike way, you felt there was actually a mountain in the theatre. Ming had them take the floor of the theater out, so the mountain started below the stage and continued out of sight above, framed only by the proscenium. When the curtain went up at the start of the play, you didn't see any actors. You just heard the sound of ice axes and occasional conversation. Slowly and eventually the actors came into view from below the stage, as they were climbing this mountain. It was unbelievable. It was such a singular set that defined our image of that show, so muscular that it is now impossible to imagine how that play could have existed without that design.

**JOE MANTELLO:** *Torch Song Trilogy* winning Best Play and [producer] John Glines thanking his lover was a hugely profound moment for me growing up as a closeted kid in the Midwest. To witness that and sense change occurring—I think it was the first time someone had acknowledged their lover in an acceptance speech—was like a beacon in the distance promising that things were going to be okay.

**HARVEY FIERSTEIN:** My life and my career is just a series of mistakes and opportunities. Life does not change if you say no, only if you say yes. *Torch Song Trilogy* got to Broadway because I wanted the show to close. We had done it Off-Off-Broadway, and then moved it Off-Broadway to the Actors Playhouse. [John] Glines rebuilt the Actors Playhouse for the show. I came out of the subway one day and there was a line from our box office around the block. I felt stuck. The theater had maybe 120 seats, and we were selling out. They kept begging me to move it to Broadway, and I said no. Every producer who wanted to move it wanted me to take out the backroom scene, which for me is the heart of the show. I refused to move it unless that scene stayed. Finally, Ken Waissman and his partners Betty Lee Hunt and Maria Pucci wanted to bring it to the Little Theatre with that scene included. I said yes because I figured it would never close Off-Broadway, but on Broadway, how many people really want to watch somebody get fucked for ten minutes? I figured this way I would have a Broadway credit. We opened and then ran for five years.

The fact that *Torch Song* won for Best Play and I won for Best Actor was and still is a very unreal kind of thing. We opened in June and played a whole year before the Tonys came around again. Broadway was different at that time. Half of the theaters were closed. Betty Lee Hunt came up with the idea that instead of a closed theatre, there should be signs that said "See a Broadway show for the fun of it." Half of the theaters had that sign. The shows that were playing then were for real New York theatre people. Some of the other shows that season were *Equus*, *'night, Mother*, *K2*, *Plenty*. The musicals were *Pirates of Penzance* and *Barnum*. Broadway was a different world, a more insular world, and I became part of that. This was the moment when they tore down Broadway theaters like the Hayes and the Morosco. I certainly didn't think that this gay play that had been around for a year already was going to garner any real interest. There were plays that just opened; we all know how that works. When the Tonys happened I was not prepared because I never thought it was a possibility. I was just really excited sitting there with my boyfriend, and then came the wins. Our producer John Glines got up and thanked his lover and partner, and then the next night Johnny Carson thanked his partner, Doc Severinsen. A culture war had been fought and won.

The world has changed since then. Not because we were the first openly gay people; we weren't. Not because we were the first openly gay show; there had been openly gay shows before. We were the first to make money, which is all-important in America. Nothing else matters. Theatre is a commercial venture. If you can't make money off it, you ain't going to see it, and if you make money off it, you're going to see lots of it. All of a sudden that door was now open.

The Tony becomes a defining part of you. It means you're part of the club, you belong.

**MATTHEW BRODERICK:** It was shocking when I won the Tony. It was for playing Eugene Morris Jerome, which was such a good part. It almost felt like I was cheating a little bit. But I was extremely excited to get it. What made it even more special was that Harvey Fierstein won that year too. Harvey had given me my first real role when he cast me in the Off-Broadway production of *Torch Song Trilogy*. I loved that play. I remember the audition. I really enjoyed meeting Harvey. I had never heard a voice like that or seen a human being like that. I was unable to move to Broadway with the show because I was hired for Neil Simon's new play *Brighton Beach Memoirs*. When they hired me (maybe the fifth callback?), they said Neil Simon was also doing a movie and that I could fit that in before I started working on the play. It was hard to leave *Torch Song* right before the Broadway transfer, but I was very happy to be making my first movie and making

Tommy Tune, Harvey Fierstein, and Matthew Broderick

my own Broadway debut. I was very scared to tell Harvey, but he was not upset about it. Almost too much not upset about it! He was very kind and told me, "We've always known we wouldn't have you forever. Of course, you have to take the other job."

I grew up thinking Neil Simon was a way of writing. I didn't think he was an actual human being until I saw him at the audition for *Brighton Beach Memoirs*. They said, "This is Neil Simon," and I thought, "Oh, it's a bald man with glasses." But a very charming man.

I was very happy doing *Brighton Beach Memoirs*, but I had some tragedy in my life at the same time. My dad had been sick, and he died days after the first table readthrough of *Brighton Beach*. When the Tonys were coming up, my mom's friend, the director Vivian Matalon, wanted to help me with my Tony speech because I was so young. We went to lunch and basically wrote it out. He was very strict about what should be in and out, so he had a lot to do with that speech. I was glad for that help. I knew I was going to mention my father, and I didn't want to do that on the fly because I didn't know what would have happened to me. I wanted to be dignified, but mostly I just wanted to dedicate it to my father.

# WINNERS ◯ 1984

**PLAY:** *The Real Thing*, Tom Stoppard

Produced by Emanuel Azenberg, The Shubert Organization, Icarus
Productions, Byron Goldman, Ivan Bloch, Roger Berlind, Michael Codron

**MUSICAL:** *La Cage aux Folles*

Produced by Allan Carr, Kenneth D. Greenblatt, Marvin A. Krauss,
Stewart F. Lane, James M. Nederlander, Martin Richards, Barry Brown, Fritz Holt

**BOOK OF A MUSICAL:** Harvey Fierstein, *La Cage aux Folles*

**ORIGINAL SCORE (MUSIC AND/OR LYRICS) WRITTEN FOR THE THEATRE:**

Jerry Herman, *La Cage aux Folles*

**REVIVAL:** *Death of a Salesman* Produced by Robert Whitehead, Roger L. Stevens

**ACTOR IN A LEADING ROLE IN A PLAY:** Jeremy Irons, *The Real Thing*

**ACTRESS IN A LEADING ROLE IN A PLAY:** Glenn Close, *The Real Thing*

**ACTOR IN A LEADING ROLE IN A MUSICAL:** George Hearn, *La Cage aux Folles*

**ACTRESS IN A LEADING ROLE IN A MUSICAL:** Chita Rivera, *The Rink*

**ACTOR IN A FEATURED ROLE IN A PLAY:** Joe Mantegna, *Glengarry Glen Ross*

**ACTRESS IN A FEATURED ROLE IN A PLAY:** Christine Baranski, *The Real Thing*

**ACTOR IN A FEATURED ROLE IN A MUSICAL:** Hinton Battle, *The Tap Dance Kid*

**ACTRESS IN A FEATURED ROLE IN A MUSICAL:** Lila Kedrova, *Zorba*

**SCENIC DESIGN:** Tony Straiges, *Sunday in the Park with George*

**COSTUME DESIGN:** Theoni V. Aldredge, *La Cage aux Folles*

**LIGHTING DESIGN:** Richard Nelson, *Sunday in the Park with George*

**DIRECTION OF A PLAY:** Mike Nichols, *The Real Thing*

**DIRECTION OF A MUSICAL:** Arthur Laurents, *La Cage aux Folles*

**CHOREOGRAPHY:** Danny Daniels, *The Tap Dance Kid*

**REGIONAL THEATRE AWARD:** Old Globe Theatre, San Diego, California

**SPECIAL TONY AWARD:** *La Tragedie de Carmen*; Peter Feller;
*A Chorus Line*; Al Hirschfeld

Al Hirschfeld

**CHITA RIVERA:** I was so excited to do *The Rink*. First of all, it was Kander and Ebb. And it was Liza. She and I had always wanted to work together. When Freddy and John asked me to do it, I said, "Liza and I always wanted to play girlfriends." And there was this silence on the other end. Freddy said, "Well, it's not exactly girlfriends. It's mother and daughter!"

My mother had just passed away, and I was wearing black. When they announced my name as the winner for *The Rink*, I stood up and I felt my mother. I turned around and I embraced Liza and I walked, and my mother walked with me. That was a gift.

**HINTON BATTLE:** Vivian Matalon was the director of the *Tap Dance Kid*. He wasn't sure that I could carry the role of Dipsey, so I had to audition. It was a tough audition. They were matching up people. There were three Dipseys, three different Wills, three Emmas. I'd never auditioned like that before for theatre. The three Dipseys were all very different in age and type and everything. You don't know what they're looking for. Vivian was giving notes and making adjustments. It was a tedious, long audition. But I won out!

**HARVEY FIERSTEIN:** To me *La Cage* is the story of a man who has to keep his son from his first marriage and his new wife from killing each other. The drag and the gay and all that are our circumstances; the colorings of it, but it's a human story about human beings. That's what I write about.

Working with Jerry Herman was like working with Auntie Mame. He lived in a townhouse in the East 60s. Jerry was very into real estate and rehabbing, so he had decorated his house all in beige. You would ring the doorbell, and the houseboy answered and ushered you in up four flights of stairs to the studio. The walls of this room were covered with eight-foot-tall sheets of *Mame* and *Dolly*, *Milk and Honey* and *Dear World*. It was just a little intimidating! The very first time I was there he sang the opening of a musical number from *Torch Song*. He wrote this song, which became "A Little More Mascara" from *La Cage*. It was very thrilling. Jerry and I very much became the parents of *La Cage*. We never had a fight. We discussed everything and never did anything unless we were in total agreement.

**GLENN CLOSE:** *The Real Thing* was one of the great highlights of my career. I would go to rehearsal and at one desk would be Tom Stoppard and at the other desk was Mike Nichols, two bona fide geniuses. Those two wonderful men had a big influence on me. It was an honor to be in the American premiere of a Tom Stoppard play. And what a cast! Jeremy Irons and Christine Baranski and Peter Gallagher. Cynthia Nixon was fifteen, and she was in our show and *Hurlyburly* at the same time! I was incredibly proud of our show. We swept the Tonys that year. There's nothing better when you and your colleagues all win, because you're very much part of a collaborative team. To have the entire team recognized is beyond thrilling.

Lead acting winners (L to R) Jeremy Irons, Glenn Close, Chita Rivera, and George Hearn

# WINNERS ◎ 1985

Roger Miller and wife, Mary Arnold

PLAY: *Biloxi Blues*, Neil Simon

Produced by Emanuel Azenberg, the Center Theater Group/
Ahmanson Theatre, Los Angeles

MUSICAL: *Big River*

Produced by Rocco Landesman, Heidi Landesman, Rick Steiner,
M. Anthony Fisher, Dodger Productions

BOOK OF A MUSICAL: William Hauptman, *Big River*

ORIGINAL SCORE (MUSIC AND/OR LYRICS) WRITTEN FOR THE THEATRE:

Roger Miller, *Big River*

REVIVAL: *Joe Egg*

Produced by The Shubert Organization, Emanuel Azenberg, Roger Berlind,
Ivan Bloch, MTM Enterprises, Inc.

ACTOR IN A LEADING ROLE IN A PLAY: Derek Jacobi, *Much Ado About Nothing*

ACTRESS IN A LEADING ROLE IN A PLAY: Stockard Channing, *Joe Egg*

ACTOR IN A FEATURED ROLE IN A PLAY: Barry Miller, *Biloxi Blues*

ACTRESS IN A FEATURED ROLE IN A PLAY: Judith Ivey, *Hurlyburly*

ACTOR IN A FEATURED ROLE IN A MUSICAL: Ron Richardson, *Big River*

ACTRESS IN A FEATURED ROLE IN A MUSICAL: Leilani Jones, *Grind*

SCENIC DESIGN: Heidi Landesman, *Big River*

COSTUME DESIGN: Florence Klotz, *Grind*

LIGHTING DESIGN: Richard Riddell, *Big River*

DIRECTION OF A PLAY: Gene Saks, *Biloxi Blues*

DIRECTION OF A MUSICAL: Des McAnuff, *Big River*

REGIONAL THEATRE AWARD: Steppenwolf Theatre Company, Chicago, Illinois

SPECIAL TONY AWARD: Yul Brynner; New York State Council on the Arts

Gene Saks

Ron Richardson, Yul Brynner, and Jackie Gleason

**DES McANUFF:** Rocco Landesman gave me a script to develop called *Big River* by Bill Hauptman. There was no composer. Bill had done a fantastic job of adapting it. I think I came in at the right moment because there was no score. I thought of Randy Newman and some other people, but Rocco was absolutely focused like a missile on Roger Miller. He was right. Roger thematically accompanied the novel and never tried to compete with it. You could never get him to write a song for a place in the piece. Ninety percent of the songs were written for other reasons. "Leavin's Not the Only Way to Go" was written for Willie Nelson breaking up with his wife. The first song he wrote was called "Hand for the Hog." It was inspired by a Pap Finn line to Judge Thatcher where he says, "You see this hand? Well, this is the hand of a hog." It had nothing to do with applause for pigs. I had to figure out that Tom Sawyer could sing that in

a fantasy sequence when Huck is going back to the island to escape with Jim. It was an unbelievable amount of work, but it was worth it. Roger always said, "Des, I don't need to interfere with this book. I'm just going to work in between the cracks."

Ron Richardson was such a lovely man. He was a singer first and foremost and a new actor. He was great to work with and direct. I give notes out on four-by-five pads, so I can tear them off immediately and give them to the actors. There's no translation process. I would give hundreds of notes. Ron kept every one of those notes and papered his dressing room with them. I was so thrilled when he won the Tony. It's such a tragedy that we lost him. God knows the world we'd be living in without the scourge of AIDS. We lost so many great artists, so many brilliant people.

**MICHAEL DAVID:** The Tonys are Broadway's once-a-year megaphone. One of the few times there is national attention on this foolhardy thing we do.

The thing that I like most about the Tony Award for Best Musical or Play or Revival is that it recognizes everyone offstage, onstage, and backstage. Most of these artists and artisans are unseen and untold. When there's this rare acknowledgment from your peers for the work, we welcome them all onstage for that nod they rarely get.

I suppose having a Tony is a wonderful confirmation that this foolish thing I've chosen to do for most of the years in my lifetime is worthy; having a dozen, even better. I'm proud to have them on behalf of everyone.

**STOCKARD CHANNING:** It took four years for *Joe Egg* to get to Broadway. It started at Williamstown and the Long Wharf, where I did it with Richard Dreyfuss. I was going through many changes in my life, both personally and professionally, and this was a new chapter. The show was met with great acclaim. It was frustrating because Richard Dreyfuss wasn't able to continue with it, so we thought that was the end. However, Jim Dale came on, and the show lifted. Jim and I did the show in an auditorium at the Fashion Institute of Technology, which was a challenge! It was not an easy birth getting that show to Broadway! It was four years of my life that was extremely complex and important. It wasn't just another play. I was so in love with the show and very proud of it. That was a beautiful time.

*Joe Egg* is a tricky show to do. The first act is basically like a vaudeville routine, and you have to get that tone right. The crazy things that the main characters do together are just covering the depths of their pain, and in my character's case, the maddening belief that her child is going to grow and survive. That's what eventually ends their marriage. It's heartbreaking, because if you do your job right, the audience falls in love with the two of you. It's about a marriage. It's an extraordinarily written piece.

Stockard Channing

# WINNERS ◎ 1986

**PLAY:** *I'm Not Rappaport*, Herb Gardner Produced by James Walsh, Lewis Allen, Martin Heinfling

**MUSICAL:** *The Mystery of Edwin Drood* Produced by Joseph Papp

**BOOK OF A MUSICAL:** Rupert Holmes, *The Mystery of Edwin Drood*

**ORIGINAL SCORE (MUSIC AND/OR LYRICS) WRITTEN FOR THE THEATRE:** Rupert Holmes, *The Mystery of Edwin Drood*

**REVIVAL:** *Sweet Charity*
Produced by Jerome Minskoff, James M. Nederlander, Arthur Rubin, Joseph Harris

**ACTOR IN A LEADING ROLE IN A PLAY:** Judd Hirsch, *I'm Not Rappaport*

**ACTRESS IN A LEADING ROLE IN A PLAY:** Lily Tomlin, *The Search for Signs of Intelligent Life in the Universe*

**ACTOR IN A LEADING ROLE IN A MUSICAL:** George Rose, *The Mystery of Edwin Drood*

**ACTRESS IN A LEADING ROLE IN A MUSICAL:** Bernadette Peters, *Song & Dance*

**ACTOR IN A FEATURED ROLE IN A PLAY:** John Mahoney, *The House of Blue Leaves*

**ACTRESS IN A FEATURED ROLE IN A PLAY:** Swoosie Kurtz, *The House of Blue Leaves*

**ACTOR IN A FEATURED ROLE IN A MUSICAL:** Michael Rupert, *Sweet Charity*

**ACTRESS IN A FEATURED ROLE IN A MUSICAL:** Bebe Neuwirth, *Sweet Charity*

**SCENIC DESIGN:** Tony Walton, *The House of Blue Leaves*

**COSTUME DESIGN:** Patricia Zipprodt, *Sweet Charity*

**LIGHTING DESIGN:** Pat Collins, *I'm Not Rappaport*

**DIRECTION OF A PLAY:**
Jerry Zaks, *The House of Blue Leaves*

**DIRECTION OF A MUSICAL:** Wilford Leach, *The Mystery of Edwin Drood*

**CHOREOGRAPHY:** Bob Fosse, *Big Deal*

**REGIONAL THEATRE AWARD:** American Repertory Theater, Cambridge, Massachusetts

Swoosie Kurtz

**JOHN LEE BEATTY:** It was fun going to the Tonys with Tony Walton. You could smuggle food in back then, so we used to share sandwiches and rum and cokes and cookies. Tony was so funny. One year he said, "Oh, John, you and I aren't going to win this year, so why don't we just have a good time?" I said, "How do you know, Tony? You're so wonderful." He said, "Look, I can show you how." He would watch the camera work and he'd say, "You see the camera work on this number is better than the camera work on that one. They think this one's going to win." And it did! He'd been there so often and of course had so many. He was just cynical enough and funny enough to be perfect company.

Tony could always bring up glamour, even in the most unlikely circumstances. You wouldn't think of *House of Blue Leaves* as glamorous, but he made it so.

**JERRY ZAKS:** Really great actors like John Mahoney by virtue of their inherent talent, credibility, and homework will automatically bring 80 percent of the work into the rehearsal room. My job is to make suggestions and give performance notes that will hopefully translate into the best possible performance that they can give.

**BERNADETTE PETERS:** It's exciting to have the opportunity to originate a role on Broadway. When I first heard about *Song & Dance*, I thought I was hearing wrong. I said, "What do you mean, throughout the whole first act there's just one character? What are you saying? There's no one else onstage?!" I had to do the entire first act by myself. I love a challenge. I decided I had to do this one. I figured out how to talk to people that are not actually there. You create people. I was singing to specific people in my character's life and made it all come alive. I dealt with the emotionality of the songs and what my character was going through internally.

Don Black, the lyricist, was there, which was great. Richard Maltby Jr. was the director, and it was his job to figure out not only where I would go but also what could change from scene to scene. It's different when there's just one person onstage. I had one outfit because I couldn't leave the stage to change.

I had one little moment in Act 2, which was the dance section. It was fun not to have to sit out the entire act and be part of the cast. It was a great cast of young dancers and we all became friends.

Of course when you do a show like that you have no social life. You're giving it all every night, and the next day I would take a singing lesson to put my voice back in alignment for the show that night. It was quite an undertaking, but it was fun.

Lead acting winners (L to R) George Rose, Lily Tomlin, Bernadette Peters, and Judd Hirsch

Lead acting winners (L to R) Robert Lindsay, Maryann Plunkett, Linda Lavin, and James Earl Jones

# WINNERS ◎ 1987

**PLAY:** *Fences*, August Wilson
Produced by Carole Shorenstein Hays, The Yale Repertory Theatre

**MUSICAL:** *Les Misérables* Produced by Cameron Mackintosh

**BOOK OF A MUSICAL:** Alain Boublil and Claude-Michel Schönberg, *Les Miserables*

**ORIGINAL SCORE (MUSIC AND/OR LYRICS) WRITTEN FOR THE THEATRE:** Claude-Michel Schönberg (music), Herbert Kretzmer and Alain Boublil (lyrics), *Les Misérables*

**REVIVAL OF A PLAY:** *All My Sons*
Produced by Jay H. Fuchs, Steven Warnick, Charles Patsos

**ACTOR IN A LEADING ROLE IN A PLAY:** James Earl Jones, *Fences*

**ACTRESS IN A LEADING ROLE IN A PLAY:** Linda Lavin, *Broadway Bound*

**ACTOR IN A LEADING ROLE IN A MUSICAL:** Robert Lindsay, *Me and My Girl*

**ACTRESS IN A LEADING ROLE IN A MUSICAL:** Maryann Plunkett, *Me and My Girl*

**ACTOR IN A FEATURED ROLE IN A PLAY:** John Randolph, *Broadway Bound*

**ACTRESS IN A FEATURED ROLE IN A PLAY:** Mary Alice, *Fences*

**ACTOR IN A FEATURED ROLE IN A MUSICAL:** Michael Maguire, *Les Misérables*

**ACTRESS IN A FEATURED ROLE IN A MUSICAL:** Frances Ruffelle, *Les Misérables*

**SCENIC DESIGN:** John Napier, *Les Misérables*

**COSTUME DESIGN:** John Napier, *Starlight Express*

**LIGHTING DESIGN:** David Hersey, *Les Misérables*

**DIRECTION OF A PLAY:** Lloyd Richards, *Fences*

**DIRECTION OF A MUSICAL:** Trevor Nunn and John Caird, *Les Misérables*

**CHOREOGRAPHY:** Gillian Gregory, *Me and My Girl*

**REGIONAL THEATRE AWARD:** San Francisco Mime Troupe

**SPECIAL TONY AWARD:** George Abbott; Jackie Mason

Producers Jay H. Fuchs and Steven Warnick (*All My Sons*)

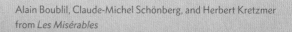

Alain Boublil, Claude-Michel Schönberg, and Herbert Kretzmer from *Les Misérables*

**RUBEN SANTIAGO-HUDSON:** August Wilson was like a big brother to me. The first time I auditioned for him, he wrote a note that said, "Same music I have. Same song." He showed it to me years later. He was talking about my cadence and delivery, my stories. That meant so much to me that I'm still repeating it.

August Wilson was an amazing writer. His plays bring Black life into the center of the world and make people realize we're all the same. I think there's a hunger and a need and a curiosity about Black people and the way we do things when white people aren't there. August was unabashedly proud to show that. I think that curiosity will help a lot of us escape ignorance. We may do things a certain way that may be foreign to some, but they are equally powerful and important. August was a keeper of culture. He excavated the things that have been hidden and destroyed and forgotten and beaten out of Black people. His plays restore what's been erased from our hearts and souls, and builds us back up by saying, "That's worthy. You're worthy." In the end I think you find out that we all want the same thing: peace, justice, and equality. The sad part is that we're always fighting for it.

August Wilson

Tevor Nunn, Gwen Verdon, and Bob Fosse

**KENNY LEON:** The first show I saw on Broadway was *Fences* with James Earl Jones. That was the first time I knew theatre was more than just stories. I saw that it was cultural and social. I sat there and watched this young (at the time) playwright August Wilson's production, and it reminded me of growing up in Tallahassee, Florida, and of my culture. It hit me that if we dig into specifics of our cultural history, we can be a gift to the whole community. At that point in my life, I was a National Endowment for the Arts Theatre Communications Group director fellow. I was chosen as one of only six in the country. Through that program I got a group of people together to go to New York to see the show. Afterwards I led a discussion about race in America. I got to meet August Wilson then, and he gave me permission to do any of his plays in the future. A year later I was able to direct *Joe Turner's Come and Gone*. There wasn't a published draft of it yet, but he gave me permission to do it.

I love August Wilson's offstage characters in all of his plays. I can see them. When you can create real people who are not even onstage, you have done something truly amazing.

August would always say that people would come up to him to tell him what they liked and what they didn't like about his plays. He would always say, "Where were they when the page was blank?" I always think of that. It starts when the page is blank. I can imagine August with the blank page coming up with characters like Hambone, Aunt Ester, Floyd, Memphis, and Holloway. All those people in all those plays, that's a community. That's a representation of Africans in America. August is our country's greatest playwright.

Angela Lansbury presenting George Abbott with his special Tony award just weeks before his 100th birthday

Double winner John Napier (set of *Les Misérables* and costumes for *Starlight Express*) and presenter Lynn Redgrave

Lloyd Richards

Featured actors in a musical Frances Ruffelle and Michael Maguire from *Les Misérables*

James Earl Jones and Mary Alice

# WINNERS ◯ 1988

John Mahoney, L. Scott Caldwell, B.D. Wong, and Amy Irving

**PLAY:** *M. Butterfly*, David Henry Hwang
Produced by Stuart Ostrow, David Geffen

**MUSICAL:** *The Phantom of the Opera*
Produced by Cameron Mackintosh, The Really Useful Theatre Company, Inc.

**BOOK OF A MUSICAL:** James Lapine, *Into the Woods*

**ORIGINAL SCORE (MUSIC AND/OR LYRICS) WRITTEN FOR THE THEATRE:**
Stephen Sondheim, *Into the Woods*

**REVIVAL OF A PLAY:** *Anything Goes*
Produced by Lincoln Center Theater, Gregory Mosher, Bernard Gersten

**ACTOR IN A LEADING ROLE IN A PLAY:** Ron Silver, *Speed the Plow*

**ACTRESS IN A LEADING ROLE IN A PLAY:** Joan Allen, *Burn This*

**ACTOR IN A LEADING ROLE IN A MUSICAL:** Michael Crawford,
*The Phantom of the Opera*

Madonna with costar Ron Silver (*Speed the Plow*)

**ACTRESS IN A LEADING ROLE IN A MUSICAL:** Joanna Gleason, *Into the Woods*

**ACTOR IN A FEATURED ROLE IN A PLAY:** B.D. Wong, *M. Butterfly*

**ACTRESS IN A FEATURED ROLE IN A PLAY:** L. Scott Caldwell,
*Joe Turner's Come and Gone*

**ACTOR IN A FEATURED ROLE IN A MUSICAL:** Bill McCutcheon, *Anything Goes*

**ACTRESS IN A FEATURED ROLE IN A MUSICAL:** Judy Kaye, *The Phantom of the Opera*

**SCENIC DESIGN:** Maria Björnson, *The Phantom of the Opera*

**COSTUME DESIGN:** Maria Björnson, *The Phantom of the Opera*

**LIGHTING DESIGN:** Andrew Bridge, *The Phantom of the Opera*

**DIRECTION OF A PLAY:** John Dexter, *M. Butterfly*

**DIRECTION OF A MUSICAL:** Harold Prince, *The Phantom of the Opera*

**CHOREOGRAPHY:** Michael Smuin, *Anything Goes*

**REGIONAL THEATRE AWARD:** South Coast Repertory of Costa Mesa, California

**SPECIAL TONY AWARD:** Brooklyn Academy of Music

Mandy Patinkin, Lee Remick, Stephen Sondheim, and James Lapine

**DAVID HENRY HWANG:** To be the first Asian American playwright produced on Broadway and then have the play run for a couple of years and subsequently all over the world was certainly unprecedented. *M. Butterfly* was considered sort of strange at the time and radical. I give a lot of credit to the producers. Stuart Ostrow had only done musicals like *1776* and *Pippin*. He took this huge chance on me. I was a twenty-nine-year-old Asian American playwright with no Broadway credentials. His co-producer was David Geffen. We originally opened in Washington, DC, at the National Theater and didn't get good reviews. We were hemorrhaging money. Geffen wanted to close the show, so Stuart mortgaged his house to get us to New York. The show went to the Eugene O'Neill Theatre at a time when Rocco Landesman had just been hired to run Jujamcyn. Broadway was struggling, and Rocco rolled the dice on booking and investing in *M. Butterfly*.

It's a great thrill and honor to be the first AAPI playwright to be produced on the Great White Way. Asian Americans have always been stereotyped as perpetual foreigners. One can have been in this country for several generations, and people will still compliment you on speaking English so well. Recently we've seen AAPIs scapegoated for the pandemic and targeted during the current spike in anti-Asian violence. Broadway is such a quintessentially American institution, so to become part of that legacy is heartening. It also comes with a certain burden. Anytime

David Henry Hwang, B.D. Wong, and Stuart Ostrow from *M. Butterfly*

a group hasn't been represented in any medium, and you become the first visible person, you're supposed to represent everyone of your community, your race, etc. Nobody can do that because none of these communities is homogeneous. There are a wide range of experiences. You can only speak in your own voice and hope you represent as many people as possible.

The Tonys are probably the only theatre brand which is a household name in America. Winning a Tony, for me, means that I am part of an American institution that's about as mainstream as you can get. You can do work on Broadway that is challenging and provocative and moves the needle. To be able to write something that was from my heart and risky and win a Tony for it was transformative. It affirmed my belief in playwriting as an art form, where you say what you want to say and see what happens. Sometimes people are going to like your work and sometimes they won't. I was lucky that *M. Butterfly* touched a chord. Thanks to Broadway, it became, as Stuart Ostrow would say, "A shot heard around the world."

**ANDREW LLOYD WEBBER:** *Phantom of the Opera* is the best example in my career where there was a real collaboration with the director and myself about how we really kept the action of the show moving. We never let the penny drop.

**BERNADETTE PETERS:** It is a privilege to sing Stephen Sondheim's music and his words. He crafted his songs so carefully, thinking of it from every angle and choosing the best one. His songs are a blueprint for what's going on with a character. He writes so specifically that if you're holding a note, there's a reason. All you have to do is follow the map of his music. The great part about working with him is that it was like Shakespeare was there and you could ask him what he meant when he wrote certain things. I loved getting his notes when he came backstage. If I had a suggestion, he'd take it seriously. If he disagreed, he would explain exactly why. He would always go so deep with every character that he wrote. I loved playing Desiree in *A Little Night Music* and Sally in *Follies*. One day he said to me, "Congratulations. You look crazy!"

# WINNERS ◯ 1989

**PLAY:** *The Heidi Chronicles*, Wendy Wasserstein
Produced by The Shubert Organization, Suntory International Corp.,
James Walsh, Playwrights Horizons

**MUSICAL:** *Jerome Robbins' Broadway*
Produced by The Shubert Organization, Roger Berlind, Suntory International Corp.,
Byron Goldman, Emanuel Azenberg

**REVIVAL:** *Our Town*
Produced by Lincoln Center Theatre, Gregory Mosher, Bernard Gersten

**ACTOR IN A LEADING ROLE IN A PLAY:** Philip Bosco, *Lend Me a Tenor*

**ACTRESS IN A LEADING ROLE IN A PLAY:** Pauline Collins, *Shirley Valentine*

**ACTOR IN A LEADING ROLE IN A MUSICAL:** Jason Alexander, *Jerome Robbins' Broadway*

**ACTRESS IN A LEADING ROLE IN A MUSICAL:** Ruth Brown, *Black and Blue*

**ACTOR IN A FEATURED ROLE IN A PLAY:** Boyd Gaines, *The Heidi Chronicles*

**ACTRESS IN A FEATURED ROLE IN A PLAY:** Christine Baranski, *Rumors*

**ACTOR IN A FEATURED ROLE IN A MUSICAL:** Scott Wise, *Jerome Robbins' Broadway*

**ACTRESS IN A FEATURED ROLE IN A MUSICAL:** Debbie Shapiro,
*Jerome Robbins' Broadway*

**SCENIC DESIGN:** Santo Loquasto, *Cafe Crown*

**COSTUME DESIGN:** Claudio Segovio and Hector Orezzoli, *Black and Blue*

**LIGHTING DESIGN:** Jennifer Tipton, *Jerome Robbins' Broadway*

**DIRECTION OF A PLAY:** Jerry Zaks, *Lend Me a Tenor*

**DIRECTION OF A MUSICAL:** Jerome Robbins,
*Jerome Robbins' Broadway*

**CHOREOGRAPHY:** Cholly Atkins, Henry LeTang, Frankie Manning,
and Fayard Nicholas, *Black and Blue*

**REGIONAL THEATRE AWARD:** Hartford Stage Company, Hartford, Connecticut

Jerry Zaks and Tony Walton

**SANTO LOQUASTO:** Working in the theatre as a designer was my dream growing up. I was a classic stagestruck kid. My mother enrolled me in children's theatre in Pennsylvania, but it was the scenery and the craft of it that drew my attention. Costumes went hand in hand with scenery. Even now I think of myself as a set designer more than a costume designer. Growing up going to the library, there was a series of books in the theatre section called Fireside Books. They published successful current Broadway plays. In those books there were always photographs of the scenery. I pored over the work of Jo Mielziner and the great designers of the fifties into the sixties.

One of the benefits of working in New York is that I occasionally got to know and collaborate with other wonderful set designers like Desmond Heeley, Tony Walton, Derek McLane, Ming Cho Lee, and Eugene Lee. Working with first-rate amazing designers was fantastic. And that happened because I was brought on as a costume designer, and I got to see what other set designers did and how they did it. These experiences have been invaluable.

When I was in grad school I would work load-ins at the Shubert Theatre in New Haven. Not only did I make fifty bucks a show, but more importantly I got to see the scenery and work of Oliver Smith and Boris Aronson up close. When *Zorba* was trying out, I ushered as well so I could watch repeatedly, witnessing the changes and seeing the production take shape.

Presenter Nell Carter (center) with the choreographers of *Black and Blue* (L to R) Cholly Atkins, Frankie Manning, Fayard Nicholas, and Henry LeTang

**SAVION GLOVER:** It was a wonderful experience working on *Black and Blue*. I got to be in the same space where Frankie Manning, Cholly Atkins, Henry LeTang, and Fayard Nicholas were choreographing. I was amongst giants. These men are the creators of the reason why I exist.

**JASON ALEXANDER:** I'm always so impressed by the performances at the Tony Awards. It's not always the big production numbers that get me as much as when someone who's doing their big number does it for the Tonys without benefit of any momentum of the show behind them. They deliver this incredibly connected, moving, powerful performance from out of nowhere.

When I was about twelve or thirteen was when I knew I wanted to be an actor. When I would stand in the bathroom with a toothbrush and imagine what award I would be getting, it was the Tony. I only imagined or dreamed about a career in the theatre and in New York. Hal Prince and Stephen Sondheim were like Christ and Moses. It's unimaginable that you're going to get the opportunity to work with either of them, let alone both of them.

I turned down the chance to audition for *Jerome Robbins' Broadway* three times. My dear friend Manny Azenberg described the show to me as a revue of Jerome Robbins's greatest Broadway dances. Well, already I don't get through the door because I can't dance that kind of material. It's so beyond my skill set. Manny said I would be the emcee, the glue. But that didn't feel like it was really an actor's role. I could only imagine it as a kind of host or narrator and I didn't think that would be interesting to do, especially for all the months I'd have to rehearse and perform it, so I kept saying no. Manny had done me a favor when we worked on *Broadway Bound* together. I had gotten a pilot, which he let me out of my contract a month early to do. So now, he called in the favor. I said, "You can't make me do a Broadway show!" He said, "No. That's not the favor. The favor is, you have to meet him and audition for him. Then if you don't want to do it, you don't want to do it." I walked in the door to meet Jerome Robbins for the first time, and the first thing out of his mouth was, "Why the fuck am I having so much trouble getting you to audition for my show?" My response was "With all due respect,

Lead acting winners (L to R) Philip Bosco, Pauline Collins, Ruth Brown, and Jason Alexander

Mr. Robbins, I don't want to be in your show. Please don't misunderstand me. I'm going to be the first person on line to buy a ticket. I can't wait to see it. It's the most thrilling thing I've ever heard of. But I'm incapable of dancing your material, and Manny keeps telling me 'emcee.'" He said, "Manny has it wrong." He asked if I knew *Fiddler on the Roof*. I said, "I'm a Jew from New Jersey. The only reason my mother let me be an actor is because she dreamed one day I'd be Tevye." He had me sing "Sunrise, Sunset." I was twenty-eight then, so I'd been rehearsing that role for twenty-six years. I sang it and looked over at Jerry at the end of the song. He had a tear rolling down his face. He explained to me that he knew the numbers he wanted the show to do, but he didn't know what made it an evening. He didn't know how to put these ideas together. I had done some writing during *Broadway Bound* that both Neil Simon and Manny adored. Manny sold Jerry on the idea that I could write the connective material and somehow perform it. Jerry also knew that he wanted an actor to play Tevye for the *Fiddler* section, and Pseudolus for the *Forum* section, etc. All these character roles. He said, "If you will help me, if you will collaborate with me and help me create this show, you'll be creating your own part. I give you my word, if you're not happy as an actor on opening night, I will let you leave the next day, no matter what your contract says." Knowing that I had aspirations to direct, and this opportunity was coming from one of the greatest, if not the greatest director of the twentieth century, I decided there were worse things I could do than sit at his heels for a couple of months and try to learn something. Thinking it would do nothing for me as an actor, I took the gig.

The Tony is, and all awards are, a marker of who you are, where you are at a moment in time. At that moment in time, in that season of Broadway, I was lucky enough to be in a really terrific piece with a really terrific role that happened to play to my strengths and talents. Hundreds of actors could have done that role, but I was the one that had it. And because I didn't screw it up it sparkled in a certain way at that moment to the point where the community singled me out. That's a great thing, but it's a snapshot of who and where and what you are in a moment. I'm so proud to have it, and it's so deeply meaningful to me, but not in the way that I thought it would be when I was twelve.

# ACCEPTANCE SPEECHES THROUGH THE YEARS

**JOANNA GLEASON (1988):** To James and Stephen, who for the past two years have treated me really like a collaborator on this project, and though you think I've felt like a baker's wife, I've really felt for two years like Cinderella at the ball. Thank you for the slipper.

Nell Carter, Bill McCutcheon, and Jim Dale

**MICHAEL CRAWFORD (1988):** There are so many ups and downs in this business. Well, the time I've had here in New York, there have been so many wonderful things that have happened to me. I know about the law of averages. I must be due to be knocked down by a truck any day now.

Ron Silver, Joanna Gleason, Michael Crawford, and Joan Allen

**THOMAS KAIL (2016):** Lin gave us a gift. My job was to try to deliver that gift. My job was to try to honor the work that Andy and Alex put forth. Where I was inspired by their humanity, which is greater than their talent. It's the only thing perhaps greater than their talent. And Lin. Oh, dear Lin. I exist to try to build, to interpret. To take what you have given and to bring honor to that. When I don't have the words, you do. When I don't know where to go, I look on the page, and it is always there. The answer is always with the writer. So let's continue to tell stories. What we've seen this season is that there are stories to be told and there are people that want to hear them. Keep telling the stories. I'm so proud to be a part of this Broadway community. I'm so proud to work in the theatre. And I thank you very much.

**RON RIFKIN (1998):** In 1984 I went into the coat business. I gave up acting and I thought that I would never step on a stage again. Somehow, I managed to keep dreaming. I never dreamed that I would be in a musical on Broadway, much less receiving an award for it.

**LEA SALONGA (1991):** This can't be for real. I remember watching these on TV when I was a little girl in Manila, and this can't be real. I'd like to first thank God for all of his blessings. I'd also like to thank Actors' Equity for giving me the chance to come here to the United States....This also goes to everybody back home who dreams of winning a Tony. Well, I got one, and the dream can come true for someone else too.

**PATRICIA ZIPPRODT (1986):** I would especially like to thank all the people who work and make the costume come to life. The sewers, the drapers, the Barbara Materas, the shoemakers, the wig makers, the hat makers, the dyers, the painters, the shoppers—because we all know that no one has ever gone onstage wearing a sketch, and without all these people we wouldn't be able to execute our craft.

**HERB GARDNER (1986):** This is ample evidence that there is life after Frank Rich.

**MARY TYLER MOORE (1980):** This will symbolize for me forever the absolute joy in creative risk taking. It's the essence of live theatre, and I am so very proud to be now a part of that community. My deepest thanks to Manny Azenberg for inviting me, and to all of you for this very warm welcome. I love the neighborhood.

Mary Tyler Moore and Ann Miller

**JONATHAN TUNICK (1997):** This is the first Tony ever given to an orchestrator, and it's a great privilege to be the first orchestrator to receive one. I know that my fellow nominees will want to join me in thanking the American Theatre Wing for recognizing our profession and for—if you'll pardon the expression—welcoming us aboard. We orchestrators have a little secret. Actually, we have a lot of little secrets. But we know that only music that's well written can be well orchestrated.

**PETER STONE (1997):** I want to thank PBS for having this extra hour, thereby allowing playwrights and directors almost as much respect as actors and producers.

Brian Dennehy with Arthur Miller

**ARTHUR MILLER (1999):** I'd like to share a hope with you that I have nursed for a long time: *Iceman, Streetcar, Salesman.* If big plays like these arrived in a contemporary producer's mail, they would be unlikely to show up on a Broadway stage. The Broadway economy would make them too expensive and too risky to produce commercially, new and untried as they were. Which of course is how they were produced originally. So let us seize this fleeting moment to hope that a new determination and a fresh resolve will inspire the powers that be to change what needs changing so that a new generation of fiercely ambitious playwrights will come again; will once again find welcome for their big, world-challenging plays somewhere west of London, somewhere east of the Hudson River.

**NEIL SIMON (1985):** I have always dreamed naturally of winning a Tony. I just didn't think I would have to dream through twenty-two plays to get it. But it was well worth the sleep....Matthew Broderick, I hope you go on playing me till you're ninety.

**RUPERT HOLMES (1986):** God, I hope my home video-tape recorder is working right now.

**GEORGE ROSE (1986):** Sometimes a show comes along that makes you really glad you became an actor, and you realize that certainly in no other profession in the world are fun and work and play and music and laughter all so sweetly and so generously comingled.

# the 19 90s

# WINNERS ○ 1990

**PLAY:** *The Grapes of Wrath*, Frank Galati Produced by The Shubert Organization, Steppenwolf Theater Co., Suntory International Corp, Jujamcyn Theaters

**MUSICAL:** *City of Angels* Produced by Nick Vanoff, Roger Berlind, Jujamcyn Theaters, Suntory International Corp., The Shubert Organization

**BOOK OF A MUSICAL:** Larry Gelbart, *City of Angels*

**ORIGINAL SCORE (MUSIC AND/OR LYRICS) WRITTEN FOR THE THEATRE:** Cy Coleman (music), David Zippel (lyrics), *City of Angels*

**REVIVAL:** *Gypsy* Produced by Barry and Fran Weissler, Kathy Levin, Barry Brown

**ACTOR IN A LEADING ROLE IN A PLAY:** Robert Morse, *Tru*

**ACTRESS IN A LEADING ROLE IN A PLAY:** Maggie Smith, *Lettice and Lovage*

**ACTOR IN A LEADING ROLE IN A MUSICAL:** James Naughton, *City of Angels*

**ACTRESS IN A LEADING ROLE IN A MUSICAL:** Tyne Daly, *Gypsy*

**ACTOR IN A FEATURED ROLE IN A PLAY:** Charles Durning, *Cat on a Hot Tin Roof*

**ACTRESS IN A FEATURED ROLE IN A PLAY:** Margaret Tyzack, *Lettice and Lovage*

**ACTOR IN A FEATURED ROLE IN A MUSICAL:** Michael Jeter, *Grand Hotel, the Musical*

**ACTRESS IN A FEATURED ROLE IN A MUSICAL:** Randy Graff, *City of Angels*

**SCENIC DESIGN:** Robin Wagner, *City of Angels*

**COSTUME DESIGN:** Santo Loquasto, *Grand Hotel, the Musical*

**LIGHTING DESIGN:** Jules Fisher, *Grand Hotel, the Musical*

**DIRECTION OF A PLAY:** Frank Galati, *The Grapes of Wrath*

**DIRECTION OF A MUSICAL:** Tommy Tune, *Grand Hotel, the Musical*

**CHOREOGRAPHY:** Tommy Tune, *Grand Hotel, the Musical*

**REGIONAL THEATRE AWARD:** Seattle Repertory Theatre

**TONY HONOR:** Alfred Drake

Steppenwolf Theatre's Randall Arney and Stephen Eich with Frank Galati (center)

Lead acting winners (L to R) James Naughton, Maggie Smith, Tyne Daly, and Robert Morse

**MICHAEL MAYER:** I remember watching the Tonys as a young adult and becoming increasingly fixated on Tommy Tune. There was *Nine*, *My One and Only*, *Grand Hotel*, and *Will Rogers Follies*. All so different and each so accomplished. I had only known him as a dancer and choreographer, but it blew my mind that he also won Tonys for directing. He was an inspiration.

Even though I'm not a choreographer, his aesthetic and artistry was extremely important to me as I was becoming a director myself.

**NATASHA KATZ:** Jules Fisher's lighting for *Grand Hotel* was a big turning point for me. There was a fluidity to the lighting, and his color saturation was something that I'd never seen before.

Featured acting winners (L to R) Margaret Tyzack, Michael Jeter, Randy Graff, and Charles Durning

Robin Wagner, Jules Fisher, and Santo Loquasto

Design winners Willa Kim, Jules Fisher, and Heidi Landesman

# WINNERS ◎ 1991

PLAY: *Lost in Yonkers*, Neil Simon
Produced by Emanuel Azenberg

MUSICAL: *The Will Rogers Follies*
Produced by Pierre Cossette, Martin Richards, Sam Crothers,
James M. Nederlander, Stewart F. Lane, Max Weitzenhoffer, Japan Satellite Broadcasting, Inc.

BOOK OF A MUSICAL: Marsha Norman, *The Secret Garden*

ORIGINAL SCORE (MUSIC AND/OR LYRICS) WRITTEN FOR THE THEATRE:
Cy Coleman (music), Betty Comden and Adolph Green (lyrics), *The Will Rogers Follies*

REVIVAL: *Fiddler on the Roof*
Produced by Barry and Fran Weissler, Pace Theatrical Group

ACTOR IN A LEADING ROLE IN A PLAY: Nigel Hawthorne, *Shadowlands*

ACTRESS IN A LEADING ROLE IN A PLAY: Mercedes Ruehl, *Lost in Yonkers*

ACTOR IN A LEADING ROLE IN A MUSICAL: Jonathan Pryce, *Miss Saigon*

ACTRESS IN A LEADING ROLE IN A MUSICAL: Lea Salonga, *Miss Saigon*

ACTOR IN A FEATURED ROLE IN A PLAY: Kevin Spacey, *Lost in Yonkers*

ACTRESS IN A FEATURED ROLE IN A PLAY: Irene Worth, *Lost in Yonkers*

ACTOR IN A FEATURED ROLE IN A MUSICAL: Hinton Battle, *Miss Saigon*

ACTRESS IN A FEATURED ROLE IN A MUSICAL: Daisy Eagan, *The Secret Garden*

SCENIC DESIGN: Heidi Landesman, *The Secret Garden*

COSTUME DESIGN: Willa Kim, *The Will Rogers Follies*

LIGHTING DESIGN: Jules Fisher, *The Will Rogers Follies*

DIRECTION OF A PLAY: Jerry Zaks, *Six Degrees of Separation*

DIRECTION OF A MUSICAL: Tommy Tune, *The Will Rogers Follies*

CHOREOGRAPHY: Tommy Tune, *The Will Rogers Follies*

REGIONAL THEATRE AWARD: Yale Repertory Theater,
New Haven, Connecticut

TONY HONOR: Father George Moore

*Miss Saigon*'s Jonathan Pryce, Hinton Battle, and Lea Salonga

Marsha Norman

Neil Simon

**NATHAN LANE:** Neil Simon was a theatrical hero of mine from an early age. When I was around eleven years old I joined a play of the month club called the Fireside Theatre, and the first play they sent me was *The Odd Couple*. I can remember hiding it in a geography book and reading it during a class and laughing my head off. Cut to 1987, I was broke and needed a job. The actor Mark Nelson, who was doing *Broadway Bound* on Broadway at the time, mentioned they were putting together a national tour and that I should audition for the role of the brother Stanley. I got myself an audition, went in to read, and got offered the part later that day. Neil had been at the audition, but I didn't actually meet him until opening night in Los Angeles. There was a knock at my dressing room door, and when I opened it Neil Simon was standing there. He was taller than I imagined, with the famous horn-rimmed glasses and a smile that said, "I know something you don't know and I'm probably going to write a play about it." I think he sensed my nervousness at meeting him, and he was very kind and complimentary, which put me at ease. He could be a tough customer if he wasn't happy with the way things were going, but he was always kind to me and I always tried to do my best for him.

When I was playing Nathan Detroit in *Guys and Dolls* for Jerry Zaks, he told me Neil had sent him a play about the writers room for Sid Caesar and that he wanted me to play one of the writers. We were going to do a reading of it, and at the last minute Jerry called me and said they couldn't find an actor to play Sid Caesar. "When we do the play we want a big guy, six-two, two hundred pounds, but for the purposes of the reading we'd like you to do it because you'll bring the right energy to it." So we did the reading and afterward they said now they couldn't imagine anyone else doing it. I said, "But don't you want some big hulking guy?" And Neil said, "What you lack in height, you make up for in anger!" It was a great experience to work with Neil Simon and really see him in action, especially during an out-of-town tryout. He was one of my heroes and I just wanted to make him happy and fulfill whatever he had written.

The real full circle came later when he asked me to play Oscar in the revival of *The Odd Couple*, and of course, later, when I was asked to speak at his memorial. It was all very emotional, remembering being an eleven-year-old and reading his play in my geography book and what he had meant to me. I couldn't tell you where the international date line is but I can tell you where every laugh in the poker game is.

Adolph Green, Betty Comden, and Cy Coleman with Tyne Daly looking on

**JASON ALEXANDER:** Neil (Simon) walked with the gods. He gave a great opening night gift. He would write all of his plays on a yellow legal pad in longhand. On opening night, he would give you a framed page from his handwritten script that your character was on and he'd write a note on it. You can only do that if you know you're Neil Simon! His note on mine was beautiful. It said, "Dear Jason, If Danny wasn't my brother, I would happily make you mine. Thank you for everything. Neil."

Eleven-year-old Daisy Eagan accepting the Tony Award for *The Secret Garden* with presenter Audrey Hepburn

**SUTTON FOSTER:** Watching the Tonys in 1991 was very pivotal for me. I was sixteen, and I remember watching Daisy Eagan win. My mind was blown that a kid could not only be on Broadway but win a Tony Award. *The Will Rogers Follies* performed on that same show. There was a line of eighteen girls who were all tall, who all could sing and dance and tap. They all had big teeth and big smiles. They looked like me. I was five foot nine; I was a dancer; I could sing; I had big teeth. I remember turning to my mom and saying, "I can do that." About a month later there was a national search for the tour of *The Will Rogers Follies* in Detroit, Michigan, which is where I was living. Because of the Tonys I knew the show. I had just turned seventeen, and you had to be eighteen to audition. My mom said to tell them I would be eighteen on my next birthday. I was flown to New York for a callback, and I was cast in the first national tour of *The Will Rogers Follies*. I spent my senior year of high school touring all over the country, all because I saw a representation of myself on the Tonys.

**HINTON BATTLE:** I was living in Los Angeles when my agent called to tell me that *Miss Saigon* was coming to America, and they wanted to see me. I didn't want to do it. I auditioned and was terrible. I didn't even learn the song. I wanted them to pass on me. I left thinking it was over, but my agent called to say they wanted to see me again. At this point I flew to New York and learned the song in my hotel room. When it came time for the audition, I sang the song and really went for it. At the end there was dead silence. Finally, they said, "Do you want the job or not?" I, of course, accepted!

I didn't know it, but Cameron (Mackintosh) had taken all the tickets to the Tonys after party because he wanted everyone to enter together. When I finally got there, they asked me for my ticket, which I didn't have. They turned me away. People were saying, "He just won a Tony!" It was chaos. I didn't get to go to the after party.

# WINNERS ◎ 1992

Judd Hirsch holding a Tony Award
and a message to his mother

**PLAY:** *Dancing at Lughnasa*, Brian Friel
Produced by Noel Pearson, Bill Kenwright, Joseph Harris

**MUSICAL:** *Crazy for You*
Produced by Roger Horchow, Elizabeth Williams

**BOOK OF A MUSICAL:** William Finn and James Lapine, *Falsettos*

**ORIGINAL SCORE (MUSIC AND/OR LYRICS) WRITTEN FOR THE THEATRE:**
William Finn, *Falsettos*

**REVIVAL:** *Guys and Dolls*

Produced by Dodger Productions, Roger Berlind, Jujamcyn Theaters/TV Asahi,
Kardana Productions, the John F. Kennedy Center for the Performing Arts

**ACTOR IN A LEADING ROLE IN A PLAY:** Judd Hirsch, *Conversations with My Father*

**ACTRESS IN A LEADING ROLE IN A PLAY:** Glenn Close, *Death and the Maiden*

**ACTOR IN A LEADING ROLE IN A MUSICAL:** Gregory Hines, *Jelly's Last Jam*

**ACTRESS IN A LEADING ROLE IN A MUSICAL:** Faith Prince, *Guys and Dolls*

**ACTOR IN A FEATURED ROLE IN A PLAY:** Laurence Fishburne, *Two Trains Running*

**ACTRESS IN A FEATURED ROLE IN A PLAY:** Brid Brennan, *Dancing at Lughnasa*

**ACTOR IN A FEATURED ROLE IN A MUSICAL:** Scott Waara, *The Most Happy Fella*

**ACTRESS IN A FEATURED ROLE IN A MUSICAL:** Tonya Pinkins, *Jelly's Last Jam*

**SCENIC DESIGN:** Tony Walton, *Guys and Dolls*

**COSTUME DESIGN:** William Ivey Long, *Crazy for You*

**LIGHTING DESIGN:** Jules Fisher, *Jelly's Last Jam*

**DIRECTION OF A PLAY:** Patrick Mason, *Dancing at Lughnasa*

**DIRECTION OF A MUSICAL:** Jerry Zaks, *Guys and Dolls*

**CHOREOGRAPHY:** Susan Stroman, *Crazy for You*

**REGIONAL THEATRE AWARD:** The Goodman Theatre of Chicago

**TONY HONOR:** *The Fantasticks*

Winner William Finn (center) with
Patti LuPone and Ron Silver

**JERRY ZAKS:** When you get it right, it's because of the talents of a large group of collaborators. Many smart decisions are made and magically it works. There is ignition between the stage and the audience. It's deeply spiritual and physical; you can feel it. The shows that I've won Tonys for did that.

My job begins with the material. If it's a comedy, it better make me laugh out loud. Otherwise, how can I expect an audience to laugh out loud? As you get through the rehearsal process the actors learn their roles, technical elements are added, and dress rehearsals follow. Finally, all that's been theoretical up to now gets thrown out the window because you have an audience. The audience tells you where they're interested, where they're not interested, where they find something funny, where they're bored or

Laurence Fishburne

impatient. Their reactions guide what I do next. They tell me what needs to be improved. It's a constant process of refining until opening night. And I can finally breathe.

**NATHAN LANE:** Tony Walton was one of the great talents and a true gentleman of the theatre. His design for the 1992 *Guys and Dolls* was so extraordinary, you had to really live up to those sets in a way. The show's subtitle is "A Musical Fable of Broadway" and his design took that very much to heart. It was tricky to find the right tone in early previews, you had to really take the stage and be as bold as Tony had been. You couldn't do the naturalistic small independent film version of *Guys and Dolls*. You had to come on and stake your claim or get lost in all that color and creativity.

**LAURENCE FISHBURNE:** I started my career with a play in 1971 at Woodie King's New Federal Theatre, and for the first four years of my career I did three other plays. I was also made a member of the Negro Ensemble Company at the age of fourteen.

Being on Broadway had always been a goal of mine. I wanted to have the opportunity to originate a role on Broadway in a drama written by an African American playwright, directed by an African American. There were very few, if any, straight black dramas on Broadway between 1975 and 1984. In 1984 we got *Ma Rainey's Black Bottom*. I was able to realize my goal with my performance in *Two Trains Running*. I was working with Lloyd Richards, August Wilson, and Roscoe Lee Browne. These three men were mentors, my teachers, and my fathers in many respects.

After I won the Tony, I bumped into August in the bowels of the Gershwin Theater. He had heard my acceptance speech and he said to me, "You've been holding out on me. You should be writing." I had been journaling for a while at that point, but two or three years later I started writing my first play, *Riff Raff*. Not only did August give me permission to be a writer, he also gave me a directive.

I learned so many things from Lloyd Richards, none of which were communicated verbally: his powers of observation, his leadership style, his sensitivity to everyone that was under his umbrella as a director. He had a very

paternal way about him in the best sense of that word. He was a great guide. He didn't direct you so much as he guided you. Like a good shepherd, he led from behind.

Being a Tony winner makes me a part of something bigger than myself. I'm grateful to have been able to make a small contribution to the American theatre. It was very gratifying after being an actor for twenty years to win a Tony for my Broadway debut. It was one of the most special events of my professional life.

**GLENN CLOSE:** It's people within the theatre community who nominate. A nomination means that you have been recognized by your peers. There is no greater honor. Theatre is where you really refine your craft as an actor. You get to perform eight times a week. With every performance, you have the chance to dig deeper, discover more—to refine, refine and refine.

**SUSAN STROMAN:** When I got up onstage to accept, I was thinking about my hometown in Delaware. I even thanked everyone in Delaware! When

Lead acting winners (L to R) Gregory Hines, Glenn Close, Faith Prince, and Judd Hirsch

you win that first Tony Award you take everybody you've ever met in your whole life up on that stage with you. They're all there on your shoulders. The people you've crossed paths with in your life that have been connected to the theatre or have taught you life lessons are the reason that you're able to get up on that stage. *Crazy for You* was very special because it is a joyous show. I think that idea of bringing so much joy to so many people added to the excitement of the award. Everything about that Tony Awards was joyous.

**SAVION GLOVER:** Gregory Hines taught me everything that I am, and I don't say that lightly. He was my teacher, my family, my mentor. He shared his professionalism, respect, wisdom, and so much more with me. He had a significant impact on me, and I learned so much from my experiences with Gregory.

Winners from *The Who's Tommy*: Pete Townshend, Wayne Cilento, and Des McAnuff

# WINNERS ◎ 1993

**PLAY:** *Angels in America: Millennium Approaches*, Tony Kushner

Produced by Jujamcyn Theaters, Mark Taper Forum/Gordon Davidson, Margo Lion, Susan Quint Gallin, Jon B. Platt, The Baruch-Frankel-Viertel Group, Frederick Zollo, Herb Alpert

**MUSICAL:** *Kiss of the Spider Woman—The Musical*

Produced by the Live Entertainment Corp. of Canada/Garth Drabinsky

**BOOK OF A MUSICAL:** Terrence McNally, *Kiss of the Spider Woman—The Musical*

**ORIGINAL SCORE (MUSIC AND/OR LYRICS) WRITTEN FOR THE THEATRE:**
John Kander (music), Fred Ebb (lyrics), *Kiss of the Spider Woman—The Musical*; Pete Townshend, *The Who's Tommy*

**REVIVAL:** *Anna Christie*

Produced by Roundabout Theater Co., Todd Haimes

**ACTOR IN A LEADING ROLE IN A PLAY:** Ron Leibman, *Angels in America: Millennium Approaches*

**ACTRESS IN A LEADING ROLE IN A PLAY:** Madeline Kahn, *The Sisters Rosensweig*

**ACTOR IN A LEADING ROLE IN A MUSICAL:**
Brent Carver, *Kiss of the Spider Woman—The Musical*

**ACTRESS IN A LEADING ROLE IN A MUSICAL:**
Chita Rivera, *Kiss of the Spider Woman—The Musical*

Presenter Bea Arthur with Featured Actress in a Musical winner Andrea Martin

Diahann Carroll, John Kander, Terrence McNally, Fred Ebb, Pete Townshend, and Marvin Hamlisch

Featured Actress in a Play winner
Debra Monk with presenter
Mercedes Ruehl

**ACTOR IN A FEATURED ROLE IN A PLAY:** Stephen Spinella,
*Angels in America: Millennium Approaches*

**ACTRESS IN A FEATURED ROLE IN A PLAY:**
Debra Monk, *Redwood Curtain*

**ACTOR IN A FEATURED ROLE IN A MUSICAL:** Anthony Crivello,
*Kiss of the Spider Woman—The Musical*

**ACTRESS IN A FEATURED ROLE IN A MUSICAL:**
Andrea Martin, *My Favorite Year*

**SCENIC DESIGN:** John Arnone, *The Who's Tommy*

**COSTUME DESIGN:** Florence Klotz, *Kiss of the Spider Woman—The Musical*

**LIGHTING DESIGN:** Chris Parry, *The Who's Tommy*

**DIRECTION OF A PLAY:** George C. Wolfe,
*Angels in America: Millennium Approaches*

**DIRECTION OF A MUSICAL:** Des McAnuff, *The Who's Tommy*

**CHOREOGRAPHY:** Wayne Cilento, *The Who's Tommy*

**REGIONAL THEATRE AWARD:** La Jolla Playhouse

**SPECIAL TONY AWARD:** *Oklahoma!*

**TONY HONOR:** IATSE; Broadway Cares/Equity Fights AIDS

Agnes de Mille representing
*Oklahoma!*'s special Tony Award, with
Wayne Cilento and Gregory Hines.
De Mille choreographed the original
production in 1943 and won Tony
awards for her choreography in 1947
(*Brigadoon*) and 1962 (*Kwamina*).

Design winners John Arnone, Florence
Klotz, and Chris Parry

1993 • 121

**CHITA RIVERA:** Kander and Ebb asked me to do *Kiss of the Spider Woman*, and I said yes. Anything they did I was on board for if they asked me. They really knew me and what I could do more than I did. Their material was superb.

**GEORGE C. WOLFE:** I remember seeing Tony Kushner's *Angels in America* at the Mark Taper in Los Angeles and being in awe of its language, its politics, its daring theatricality and dazzling wit. Its everything. Cut to a few months later, I get a call from producer/human being extraordinaire Margo Lion, letting me know that Tony wanted to talk to me about his play. I'd never read *Angels*, only seen the L.A. production, but he came over to my place on 95th Street, and we talked for a few hours,

maybe longer. A couple of days later Margo calls back, letting me know that Tony wanted me to direct *Angeles in America* on Broadway.

As much as I loved, loved working on Part One of *Angels*, *Millennium Approaches*, I loved even more working on Part Two, *Perestroika*, because Part Two was still finding itself. With Part One, a large part of my job was spent protecting the actors and myself, by keeping the hype and expectations, which were monumental, out of the rehearsal room, so that we could actually dig in and do the hard, messy, tough work necessary to make the material truly soar and take flight. With Part Two, I felt the need to do the same degree of protection for Tony as well, because he was still wrestling with the text.

Lead acting winners (L to R) Ron Leibman, Madeline Kahn, Chita Rivera, and Brent Carver

One of my favorite nights ever of working on any show; we were in previews with *Perestroika*, and the opening scene to Act 2, "The Epistle," was still finding itself. And so after the show, Tony, the stage managers, Ellen McLaughlin (who played the Angel), Stephen Spinella (Prior), Jeffrey Wright (Belize), and myself went to some bar or restaurant—it may have been Joe Allen's—and after commandeering three or four tables, we got to work, digging and cutting, offering up what we each thought was working about the scene and what was not. Tony then went home, and came back the next day with a new, I think, twenty-five-page version of the scene, which went into the show that night. Thrilling.

Direction of a Play winner George C. Wolfe with presenter Ellen Burstyn

**JANE ALEXANDER:** I remember how delicious Madeline Kahn was in *The Sisters Rosensweig*. I would just look over at her and think, *How the hell does she do that?* Her timing, the way she approached the role—I just adored her. We had one laugh in *The Sisters Rosensweig* that was the longest laugh I ever experienced. She could make the entire audience erupt with laughter.

*The Sisters Rosensweig*'s Jane Alexander, Wendy Wasserstein, and Madeline Kahn at a Tony Awards nominee luncheon.

Jarrod Emick

# WINNERS ◎ 1994

**PLAY:** *Angels in America: Perestroika*, Tony Kushner

Produced by Jujamcyn Theaters, Mark Taper Forum/Gordon Davidson, Artistic Director with Margo Lion, Susan Quint Gallin, Jon B. Platt, The Baruch-Frankel-Viertel Group, and Frederick Zollo, in association with The New York Shakespeare Festival, Mordecai/Cole Productions, Herb Alpert

**MUSICAL:** *Passion*

Produced by The Shubert Organization, Capital Cities/ABC, Roger Berlind, Scott Rudin, Lincoln Center Theater

**BOOK OF A MUSICAL:** James Lapine, *Passion*

**ORIGINAL SCORE (MUSIC AND/OR LYRICS) WRITTEN FOR THE THEATRE:**
Stephen Sondheim, *Passion*

**REVIVAL OF A PLAY:** *An Inspector Calls*

Produced by Noel Pearson, The Shubert Organization, Capital Cities/ABC, Joseph Harris

**REVIVAL OF A MUSICAL:** *Carousel*

Produced by Lincoln Center Theater, André Bishop, Bernard Gersten, The Royal National Theatre, Cameron Mackintosh, the Rodgers and Hammerstein Organization

**ACTOR IN A LEADING ROLE IN A PLAY:** Stephen Spinella,
*Angels in America: Perestroika*

**ACTRESS IN A LEADING ROLE IN A PLAY:** Diana Rigg, *Medea*

**ACTOR IN A LEADING ROLE IN A MUSICAL:**
Boyd Gaines, *She Loves Me*

**ACTRESS IN A LEADING ROLE IN A MUSICAL:**
Donna Murphy, *Passion*

Jane Greenwood and Ann Hould-Ward

Lead acting winners (L to R) Stephen Spinella, Diana Rigg, Donna Murphy, and Boyd Gaines

ACTOR IN A FEATURED ROLE IN A PLAY: Jeffrey Wright, *Angels in America: Perestroika*

ACTRESS IN A FEATURED ROLE IN A PLAY: Jane Adams, *An Inspector Calls*

ACTOR IN A FEATURED ROLE IN A MUSICAL: Jarrod Emick, *Damn Yankees*

ACTRESS IN A FEATURED ROLE IN A MUSICAL: Audra McDonald, *Carousel*

SCENIC DESIGN: Bob Crowley, *Carousel*

COSTUME DESIGN: Ann Hould-Ward, *Beauty and the Beast*

LIGHTING DESIGN: Rick Fisher, *An Inspector Calls*

DIRECTION OF A PLAY: Stephen Daldry, *An Inspector Calls*

DIRECTION OF A MUSICAL: Nicholas Hytner, *Carousel*

CHOREOGRAPHY: Sir Kenneth MacMillan, *Carousel*

SPECIAL TONY AWARD FOR LIFETIME ACHIEVEMENT IN THE THEATRE:
Jessica Tandy and Hume Cronyn

REGIONAL THEATRE AWARD: McCarter Theatre, Princeton, New Jersey

Nell Carter having fun with Audra McDonald

**DONNA MURPHY:** We're talking about my childhood dream of a life in the theatre not only coming true but being celebrated by my esteemed peers and colleagues. I will never forget my experiences of performing and being honored at the Tony Awards and will always carry immense gratitude and wonder for having become a small part of their remarkable history and legacy.

**NIKKI M. JAMES:** Seeing Audra McDonald, a woman of color, in a role that was not traditionally written for her to play and to be recognized with a Tony had a tremendous on impact on me as a young woman.

# WINNERS  1995

**PLAY:** *Love! Valour! Compassion!*, Terrence McNally
Produced by Manhattan Theatre Club, Lynne Meadow, Barry Grove, Jujamcyn Theatres

**MUSICAL:** *Sunset Boulevard*
Produced by The Really Useful Company

**BOOK OF A MUSICAL:** Don Black and Christopher Hampton, *Sunset Boulevard*

**ORIGINAL SCORE (MUSIC AND/OR LYRICS) WRITTEN FOR THE THEATRE:** Andrew Lloyd
Webber (music), Don Black and Christopher Hampton (lyrics), *Sunset Boulevard*

**REVIVAL OF A PLAY:** *The Heiress*
Produced by Lincoln Center Theater, André Bishop, Bernard Gersten

**REVIVAL OF A MUSICAL:** *Show Boat*
Produced by Livent (U.S.) Inc.

**ACTOR IN A LEADING ROLE IN A PLAY:** Ralph Fiennes, *Hamlet*

**ACTRESS IN A LEADING ROLE IN A PLAY:**
Cherry Jones, *The Heiress*

**ACTOR IN A LEADING ROLE IN A MUSICAL:**
Matthew Broderick, *How to Succeed in
Business without Really Trying!*

Frances Sternhagen                                                    John Glover

ACTRESS IN A LEADING ROLE IN A MUSICAL:
Glenn Close, *Sunset Boulevard*

ACTOR IN A FEATURED ROLE IN A PLAY:
John Glover, *Love! Valour! Compassion!*

ACTRESS IN A FEATURED ROLE IN A PLAY:
Frances Sternhagen, *The Heiress*

ACTOR IN A FEATURED ROLE IN A MUSICAL:
George Hearn, *Sunset Boulevard*

ACTRESS IN A FEATURED ROLE IN A MUSICAL:
Gretha Boston, *Show Boat*

SCENIC DESIGN: John Napier, *Sunset Boulevard*

COSTUME DESIGN: Florence Klotz, *Show Boat*

LIGHTING DESIGN: Andrew Bridge, *Sunset Boulevard*

DIRECTION OF A PLAY: Gerald Gutierrez, *The Heiress*

DIRECTION OF A MUSICAL: Harold Prince, *Show Boat*

CHOREOGRAPHY: Susan Stroman, *Show Boat*

SPECIAL TONY AWARD FOR LIFETIME ACHIEVEMENT IN THE THEATRE:
Carol Channing; Harvey Sabinson

REGIONAL THEATRE AWARD: Goodspeed Opera House

TONY HONOR: National Endowment for the Arts

Winner Gerald Gutierrez with
Sarah Jessica Parker

Lead acting winners (L to R) Matthew Broderick, Cherry Jones, Glenn Close, and Ralph Fiennes

**MATTHEW BRODERICK:** I always loved *How to Succeed…*and Robert Morse. I desperately wanted to do the show. I was originally going to do it with Gene Saks directing, so I found a singing teacher named Keith Davis. I worked with Keith, learning singing and enjoying every minute of it, and then I made Gene audition me because I didn't want to make a fool of myself. Gene approved, but it turned out we didn't have the rights. Another company had it, and Des McAnuff was directing. There was a period I was scared Des was going to do it with someone else, but I managed to weasel myself in!

It was great fun. I had never done anything like a musical, and Des was there the whole way to help me through, along with Ted Sperling, the musical director, and Wayne Cilento, the choreographer. The ensemble also gave me a lot of help. I found out later that people were worried because in rehearsal I wasn't singing out loud. It took me about two weeks for me to do that. Ted Sperling would be playing the piano and he would sing for me because I was still shy. I was very scared about the singing and the dancing. But I like the challenge of scary things, and I love musicals, and was very happy to be in one that I loved.

That show happened during a period in which everyone was concerned about the length of the Tony broadcast. They were quite hysterical about saving time. From rehearsal onward it seemed that everybody was screaming at me to go fast and to not talk for more than twenty-one seconds or they'd kill me. I didn't write a speech because there was so little time. I thought I'd just be spontaneous. The adrenaline when you're up there is hard to describe. You look out and you see Tommy Tune and everyone you've ever loved staring at you. The TV is on you. There a flashing thing saying, "Stop! Stop! Get off! Get off!" The two people I wanted to thank were my now wife, who had been my total savior through the whole thing, and Keith Davis, who taught me to sing. He was in his nineties and would have liked to hear his name on television. I was so nervous I got up there and completely forgot.

I enjoy presenting at the Tonys. If I'm doing it, it's usually because they've decided I have some friend who's been nominated. It's very fun to give one to somebody. I was so excited to give one to Robert Morse when he won for *Tru*. Jennifer Holliday gave me mine. I told her that years later, but she didn't seem to remember at all!

Working in theatre is getting to work among giants. It's a great honor. My father didn't get a Tony Award, so I'm aware that you don't always get an award even if you're as good as the person that won. There are so many wonderful actors, and the circumstances didn't line up for them to get one. But I'm extremely happy that I did.

**SUSAN STROMAN:** *Show Boat* with Hal Prince was wonderful because the estate allowed us to look at it in a new light. Hal was very much a part of changing the script. It was Hal's idea for me to use montages to propel the time forward. I worked with the wonderful costume designer Florence Klotz on how to do that. Eugene Lee, the set designer, gave me a great revolving door at the Palmer House. As people would pour out the lights would change, and the costumes would change, it was very clear that we were moving through time. Within those montages we showed elements of society that were changing through history. The greatest moments in the theatre are the ones where you collaborate so closely with the set designer, the costume designer, the director. Everyone's on the same page, and it takes every single department to make it happen.

I loved working with Hal Prince. He was a real theatre animal, which I am too. To be in his office, surrounded by all that memorabilia and all his accomplishments, and seeing him working on a new piece was thrilling for me. The best piece of advice I ever got from Hal was after you open a show, no matter what happens,

if you get good reviews or bad reviews, the next day you need to schedule that next meeting for that next show and new collaborators. I have now done that for the last twenty years. It keeps you going forward in your art. In the end it is about the creation of the piece and the collaboration. What happens afterwards you can't totally control. Hal was always about the work. His influence on me was huge. He gave me so much respect as a young female choreographer in a male-dominated business and so much support when I started to create my own work. He was always there with a supportive and kind word, cheering me on. He was my greatest champion. When Hal Prince believed in you, that belief gave you more strength. To this day I still feel him very much alive in my life, even though he is gone.

Susan Stroman

Bernadette Peters, Nathan Lane, and Liza Minnelli opening the show at the Majestic Theatre

# WINNERS ☉ 1996

**PLAY:** *Master Class*, Terrence McNally
Produced by Robert Whitehead, Lewis Allen, Spring Sirkin

**MUSICAL:** *Rent* Produced by Jeffrey Seller, Kevin McCollum,
Allan S. Gordon, The New York Theatre Workshop

**BOOK OF A MUSICAL:** Jonathan Larson, *Rent*

**ORIGINAL SCORE (MUSIC AND/OR LYRICS) WRITTEN FOR THE THEATRE:**
Jonathan Larson, *Rent*

**REVIVAL OF A PLAY:** *A Delicate Balance*
Produced by Lincoln Center Theater, André Bishop, Bernard Gersten

**REVIVAL OF A MUSICAL:** *The King and I*
Produced by Dodger Productions, The John F. Kennedy Center for the Performing Arts,
James M. Nederlander, Perseus Productions, John Frost, The Adelaide Festival Centre,
The Rodgers and Hammerstein Organization

**ACTOR IN A LEADING ROLE IN A PLAY:** George Grizzard, *A Delicate Balance*

**ACTRESS IN A LEADING ROLE IN A PLAY:** Zoe Caldwell, *Master Class*

**ACTOR IN A LEADING ROLE IN A MUSICAL:** Nathan Lane,
*A Funny Thing Happened on the Way to the Forum*

Lead acting winners (L to R) Donna Murphy, Nathan Lane, Zoe Caldwell, and George Grizzard

**ACTRESS IN A LEADING ROLE IN A MUSICAL:** Donna Murphy, *The King and I*

**ACTOR IN A FEATURED ROLE IN A PLAY:** Ruben Santiago-Hudson, *Seven Guitars*

**ACTRESS IN A FEATURED ROLE IN A PLAY:** Audra McDonald, *Master Class*

**ACTOR IN A FEATURED ROLE IN A MUSICAL:** Wilson Jermaine Heredia, *Rent*

**ACTRESS IN A FEATURED ROLE IN A MUSICAL:** Ann Duquesnay, *Bring in 'da Noise, Bring in 'da Funk*

**SCENIC DESIGN:** Brian Thomson, *The King and I*

**COSTUME DESIGN:** Roger Kirk, *The King and I*

**LIGHTING DESIGN:** Jules Fisher and Peggy Eisenhauer, *Bring in 'da Noise, Bring in 'da Funk*

**DIRECTION OF A PLAY:** Gerald Gutierrez, *A Delicate Balance*

**DIRECTION OF A MUSICAL:** George C. Wolfe, *Bring in 'da Noise, Bring in 'da Funk*

**CHOREOGRAPHY:** Savion Glover, *Bring in 'da Noise, Bring in 'da Funk*

**REGIONAL THEATRE AWARD:** Alley Theatre of Houston

Wilson Jermaine Heredia

Ruben Santiago-Hudson and Savion Glover

**RUBEN SANTIAGO-HUDSON:** It feels great to be acknowledged by your peers and people who love theatre. Always put it in perspective, though. I have no control over anything but what I put onstage. I have no control over the people putting their checkmarks by names of people that they relate to or respect or like. As a Tony voter myself, I try to be fair, but I also have personal feelings about things. I've been called out a few times, I've been in that number, so I feel pretty good about that. It's wonderful as a goal, but more importantly, you should always be striving for excellence.

When I started out and I became aware of the history of the Tonys, I had no hope of ever being there. But I think we've made some progress in that respect. People of color are now doing a wider range of things, but we still have to look at the percentages. What percent of the plays being done are produced by people of color? How many of the Tony voters are of color? Many times I'm the singular Black voice in the room at meetings.

**AUDRA McDONALD:** *Master Class* gave me the chance to learn how to become a solid actress. I learned so much from being onstage with Zoe Caldwell every night. She was a teacher, and she wanted me to learn and grow. She became a mentor and someone I turned to a great deal until her passing.

**GEORGE C. WOLFE:** I met Savion Glover while working on my first Broadway show, *Jelly's Last Jam*. He was a teenager. I was not. When I became producer of the Public Theatre, he was one of the first artists I invited to come down to Lafayette Street and play. He brought dancers into the room; I brought artists I'd worked with before or knew of: Ann Duquesnay, Reggie Gaines, Daryl Waters, and Zane Marks. I'd always wanted to explore the relationship between history and rhythm; how the Southern agrarian rhythms, i.e., slavery, affected Black American culture versus the Northern rhythms of industrialization. And so each morning we'd all meet in LuEsther Hall, and I'd give, for lack of better words, assignments: "Savion, create a Charleston that feels like the world is being hurled into madness." "Reggie, take us inside a party where we meet Harlem's elite." Everyone would then go off to their respective corners and start crafting dances, lyrics, music, prose, which were in turn layered on top of one another, and that's how *Bring in 'da Noise, Bring in 'da Funk* came into being.

Savion had learned to dance from old tap dancers, who had learned from even older tap dancers, so it was like collaborating with this living repository of history and rhythm. At the exact same time the show was being built, my mother was dying, so working on *Noise/Funk* became a creative refuge for me, the only place I felt safe at a time of deep sadness and uncertainty.

The defiance, heartache, fragility, and joy which is vibrantly and viscerally at the core of Black American culture was potently alive in the room while *Noise/Funk* was being birthed.

The preview process of working on a new play or musical, especially a musical, can be astonishingly brutal. It also happens to be one that I love. When I first moved to New York, I would go see shows in previews three or four times. I think I went to see Hal Prince's production of *Merrily We Roll Along* at least six times. Bob Fosse, Michael Bennett, Jerome Robbins, I'd go to all of their shows in previews, one because it was cheaper, and two, because I was studying them, processing the changes that were being made now that the final scene partner, i.e. the audience, had joined the journey. In addition to studying these master storytellers at work, I think I was also absorbing some of the required toughness necessary to survive performing open heart surgery on your work with over a thousand paying customers watching every night. Even so, regardless of how tough you think you are, nothing prepares you for looking up at the first preview of *Angels in America* and seeing Jerome Robbins in the audience. And just as the first preview is coming to an end and you think you've survived, the stage manager's headset shuts down, making it impossible for her to communicate with any of the crew, and so you hear the usually calm Mary Klinger shouting from the rear of the balcony, "Open the fucking ceiling so the angel can come through." Previews.

**SAVION GLOVER:** Being a Tony winner forever cements me in this Mount Rushmore of recognitions. It's like being president. If I die without a tombstone, I'll still have a Tony Award. I'm very honored and grateful to all who have made it possible for my name to be associated with the Tonys in any way. I am thankful for their contribution to my existence.

*Bring in 'da Noise, Bring in 'da Funk* was my story. I was living my life onstage, and that fueled not only my creativity but also my excitement for the show.

# WINNERS ◎ 1997

---

**PLAY:** *The Last Night of Ballyhoo*, Alfred Uhry
Produced by Jane Harmon, Nina Keneally, Liz Oliver

**MUSICAL:** *Titanic*
Produced by Dodger Endemol Theatricals, Richard S. Pechter, The John F. Kennedy Center

**BOOK OF A MUSICAL:** Peter Stone, *Titanic*

**ORIGINAL SCORE (MUSIC AND/OR LYRICS) WRITTEN FOR THE THEATRE:**
Maury Yeston, *Titanic*

**REVIVAL OF A PLAY:** *A Doll's House*
Produced by Bill Kenwright, Thelma Holt

**REVIVAL OF A MUSICAL:** *Chicago*
Produced by Barry and Fran Weissler, Kardana Productions, Inc.

**ACTOR IN A LEADING ROLE IN A PLAY:** Christopher Plummer, *Barrymore*

**ACTRESS IN A LEADING ROLE IN A PLAY:** Janet McTeer, *A Doll's House*

**ACTOR IN A LEADING ROLE IN A MUSICAL:** James Naughton, *Chicago*

**ACTRESS IN A LEADING ROLE IN A MUSICAL:** Bebe Neuwirth, *Chicago*

Lead Acting Winners (L to R) James Naughton, Bebe Neuwirth, Janet McTeer, and Christopher Plummer

Ann Reinking

ACTOR IN A FEATURED ROLE IN A PLAY: Owen Teale, *A Doll's House*

ACTRESS IN A FEATURED ROLE IN A PLAY: Lynne Thigpen, *An American Daughter*

ACTOR IN A FEATURED ROLE IN A MUSICAL: Chuck Cooper, *The Life*

ACTRESS IN A FEATURED ROLE IN A MUSICAL: Lillias White, *The Life*

SCENIC DESIGN: Stewart Laing, *Titanic*

COSTUME DESIGN: Judith Dolan, *Candide*

LIGHTING DESIGN: Ken Billington, *Chicago*

DIRECTION OF A PLAY: Anthony Page, *A Doll's House*

DIRECTION OF A MUSICAL: Walter Bobbie, *Chicago*

CHOREOGRAPHY: Ann Reinking, *Chicago*

ORCHESTRATIONS: Jonathan Tunick, *Titanic*

SPECIAL TONY AWARD FOR LIFETIME ACHIEVEMENT IN THE THEATRE:
Bernard B. Jacobs

REGIONAL THEATRE AWARD:
Berkeley Repertory Theatre

Ken Billington

Chuck Cooper

**LILLIAS WHITE:** It is such an honor to be recognized by my peers in this business. I feel like I belong to a special club, and they're very particular about who they invite to be in the club. The Tony is the highest honor that can be given to anyone in the theatre. It's special.

I was allowed to be myself as Sonja in *The Life*. I got to explore and create every night. I loved the cast and crew and the creators. One of the biggest gifts you can get in the theatre is to create a role, and especially when you get to do it with Cy Coleman, Ira Gasman, Michael Blakemore, and Joey McKneely.

Chuck Cooper is a gem to work with. He's in the moment and gives you the reality of that moment of the play. He's such a joy to work with. You look in his eyes and see the character come to life, which elevates myself and everyone around him. He is generous and kind. I love working with people like that.

# WINNERS ◎ 1998

Julie Taymor and Garry Hynes,
the first two women to win
Best Director in the same year

**PLAY:** *Art*, Yasmina Reza
Produced by David Pugh, Sean Connery, Joan Cullman

**MUSICAL:** *The Lion King*
Produced by Disney

**BOOK OF A MUSICAL:** Terrence McNally, *Ragtime*

**ORIGINAL SCORE (MUSIC AND/OR LYRICS) WRITTEN FOR THE THEATRE:**
Stephen Flaherty (music), Lynn Ahrens (lyrics), *Ragtime*

**REVIVAL OF A PLAY:** *A View from the Bridge*

Produced by Roundabout Theatre Company, Todd Haimes, Ellen Richard, Roger Berlind, James M.
Nederlander, Nathaniel Kramer, Elizabeth Ireland McCann, Roy Gabay, Old Ivy Productions

**REVIVAL OF A MUSICAL:** *Cabaret*

Produced by Roundabout Theatre Company, Todd Haimes, Ellen Richard

**ACTOR IN A LEADING ROLE IN A PLAY:** Anthony LaPaglia, *A View from the Bridge*

**ACTRESS IN A LEADING ROLE IN A PLAY:** Marie Mullen, *The Beauty Queen of Leenane*

**ACTOR IN A LEADING ROLE IN A MUSICAL:**
Alan Cumming, *Cabaret*

**ACTRESS IN A LEADING ROLE IN A MUSICAL:**
Natasha Richardson, *Cabaret*

**ACTOR IN A FEATURED ROLE IN A PLAY:**
Tom Murphy, *The Beauty Queen of Leenane*

**ACTRESS IN A FEATURED ROLE IN A PLAY:**
Anna Manahan, *The Beauty Queen of Leenane*

Garth Fagan

Nominee John Leguizamo and
winner Audra McDonald

ACTOR IN A FEATURED ROLE IN A MUSICAL:
Ron Rifkin, *Cabaret*

ACTRESS IN A FEATURED ROLE IN A MUSICAL:
Audra McDonald, *Ragtime*

SCENIC DESIGN: Richard Hudson, *The Lion King*

COSTUME DESIGN: Julie Taymor, *The Lion King*

LIGHTING DESIGN: Donald Holder, *The Lion King*

DIRECTION OF A PLAY: Garry Hynes, *The Beauty Queen of Leenane*

DIRECTION OF A MUSICAL: Julie Taymor, *The Lion King*

CHOREOGRAPHY: Garth Fagan, *The Lion King*

ORCHESTRATIONS: William David Brohn, *Ragtime*

REGIONAL THEATRE AWARD: Denver Center Theatre Company

SPECIAL TONY AWARD: Ben Edwards; Edward E. Colton

TONY HONOR: The International Theatre Institute
of the United States

Playwright Yasmina Reza (center)
with *Art* producers Joan Cullman
and Sean Connery

**JULIE TAYMOR:** I think in the beginning, people couldn't quite figure out what I do, how I could meld and mesh with Disney. Was I selling out, or did they not know what they were getting into? Tom Schumacher and Peter Schneider at Disney allowed me to do what I felt was needed. I wanted to make what was in the movie background and invisible, the foreground. In the theater you see the chorus's faces, you hear their voices; they are herds of animals, flocks of birds. You're aware of the human presence. The inspiration of *The Lion King* is from Africa, so it was important to me to make the presence of the African American artists and the Africans the forefront of this show. At that time the only shows that were fully African American were about racism. What was unique and new about *The Lion King* was that it transcended race and celebrated it at the same time.

We opened in Minneapolis, out of town. I remember the first public performance—the first preview, we were so utterly shocked by the audience's reaction. They started screaming, and you couldn't hear a thing. We were just weeping. When we finally opened in New York City we were aware that we had something special.

Julie Taymor (center) with Disney's Tom Schumacher and Peter Schneider

*The Lion King* goes back to the essence of what theatre is all about, which is to suspend your disbelief. When you see the strings, the rods, the humans in the legs of the elephant, the beauty of a dancer with three gazelles, they are brought back to their earliest experiences of make-believe.

The show has traveled the world, and the connection to real life—politically, socially, in every way—has been powerful.

**RACHEL CHAVKIN:** A huge part of my relationship to design was shaped by looking at Julie Taymor's work and fearing, "I'll never make something as beautiful as this," and being haunted by that. So when starting a new project I do a ton of visual research, to get me thinking out of the box—and because of my insecurities.

**ALAN CUMMING:** My approach to playing the Emcee in *Cabaret* was to read Christopher Isherwood's memoir, *Christopher and His Kind. Cabaret* was based on his novel *Goodbye to Berlin*. I wanted to make sure we represented the world of those seedy, dirty clubs properly. Those clubs were important; those were the first things Hitler shut down because they were antiestablishment and sexually and politically progressive. I thought of the Emcee as a rent boy who could sing. He was someone who hung around the clubs and eventually became the emcee. He's not actually a proper character; he's more of a symbol. He interacts with the audience more than he interacts with any of the other characters. There wasn't a character arc of him; it was about the character arc of the whole show and the sensibility of the show, where you want the audience to go so that at the end, they hopefully feel complicit in what's happened. It was exciting to be able to do that.

Playing the Emcee is very much about getting everybody so jazzed up and thinking this is the most fabulous place you could be, so when the nasty stuff starts to happen it happens insidiously and gradually. You're already invested in it, and you don't want to look away.

*Cabaret* opened at Henry Miller's Theatre. It was like the Kit Kat Club in that on weekends it was an actual club. The stage we performed on was the dance floor. I loved it. I would go into my dressing room, which was like having your own apartment in a club. I'd go there and have a sort of pregame with friends, and then go downstairs and dance on the stage.

When you win a Tony that becomes your prefix forever. I'm so proud of that show and how innovative it was. It really altered the landscape of Broadway. Actors performing in the band and playing instruments had never happened before. That's now de rigueur. The immersive quality of it was also fresh. The idea that the audience was in the club hadn't been done before. It was very ahead of its time in many ways. It was exciting to be part of something like that. Sexually, people hadn't seen anything like that on the Broadway stage. It was artistically very fulfilling because it challenged and provoked people for reasons that only enhanced the piece. That was my favorite thing about it.

Lead acting winners (L to R) Marie Mullen, Alan Cumming, Natasha Richardson, and Anthony LaPaglia

# WINNERS ◎ 1999

Co-orchestrators Douglas
Besterman and Ralph Burns
(*Fosse*)

**PLAY:** *Side Man*, Warren Leight

Produced by Weissberger Theater Group, Jay Harris,
Peter Manning, Roundabout Theatre Company, Todd Haimes,
Ellen Richard, Ron Kastner, James Cushing, Joan Stein

**MUSICAL:** *Fosse*

Produced by Livent (U.S.) Inc.

**BOOK OF A MUSICAL:** Alfred Uhry, *Parade*

**ORIGINAL SCORE (MUSIC AND/OR LYRICS) WRITTEN FOR THE THEATRE:** Jason Robert
Brown, *Parade*

**REVIVAL OF A PLAY:** *Death of a Salesman*

Produced by David Richenthal, Jujamcyn Theaters, Allan S. Gordon, Fox Theatricals,
Jerry Frankel, The Goodman Theatre

**REVIVAL OF A MUSICAL:** *Annie Get Your Gun*

Produced by Barry and Fran Weissler, Kardana, Michael Watt, Irving Welzer, Hal Luftig

**ACTOR IN A LEADING ROLE IN A PLAY:** Brian Dennehy, *Death of a Salesman*

**ACTRESS IN A LEADING ROLE IN A PLAY:** Judi Dench, *Amy's View*

**ACTOR IN A LEADING ROLE IN A MUSICAL:** Martin Short, *Little Me*

**ACTRESS IN A LEADING ROLE IN A MUSICAL:**
Bernadette Peters, *Annie Get Your Gun*

**ACTOR IN A FEATURED ROLE IN A PLAY:**
Frank Wood, *Side Man*

**ACTRESS IN A FEATURED ROLE IN A PLAY:**
Elizabeth Franz, *Death of a Salesman*

Uta Hagen

Lez Brotherston and
Matthew Bourne

Carol Burnett, Julie Andrews,
Judi Dench, and Isabelle
Stevenson

**ACTOR IN A FEATURED ROLE IN A MUSICAL:**
Roger Bart, *You're a Good Man, Charlie Brown*

**ACTRESS IN A FEATURED ROLE IN A MUSICAL:** Kristin Chenoweth,
*You're a Good Man, Charlie Brown*

**SCENIC DESIGN:** Richard Hoover, *Not About Nightingales*

**COSTUME DESIGN:** Lez Brotherston, *Swan Lake*

**LIGHTING DESIGN:** Andrew Bridge, *Fosse*

**DIRECTION OF A PLAY:** Robert Falls, *Death of a Salesman*

**DIRECTION OF A MUSICAL:** Matthew Bourne, *Swan Lake*

**CHOREOGRAPHY:** Matthew Bourne, *Swan Lake*

**ORCHESTRATIONS:** Ralph Burns and Douglas Besterman, *Fosse*

**SPECIAL TONY AWARD FOR LIFETIME ACHIEVEMENT IN THE THEATRE:**
Uta Hagen; Arthur Miller; Isabelle Stevenson

**REGIONAL THEATRE AWARD:** Crossroads Theatre Company, New Brunswick, New Jersey

**SPECIAL TONY AWARD:** *Fool Moon*

**MICHAEL MAYER:** The role of Sally Brown didn't exist in the original version of *You're a Good Man, Charlie Brown*. Kristin Chenoweth came in and auditioned for the role of Patty (an amalgam of several girls from *Peanuts*). I had seen Kristin in *Steel Pier* and thought she was special, but her audition for Patty was a game changer. I had a revelation: I should create the role of Sally Brown for Kristin! I called the producers and told them I wanted to make a big change. They arranged for me to meet with Charles Schulz. He loved the idea and said I could use any of his material that I wanted. I found all this great stuff for Sally Brown, in particular a strip about her arguing with her teaching about her bad grades. I brought this to Andrew Lippa, the musical supervisor, and he wrote "My New Philosophy." The rest is history.

**KRISTIN CHENOWETH:** I was offered the role of Winnie in *Annie Get Your Gun* with Bernadette Peters. I was encouraged to take that job because it was a for sure hit. At the same time, I had the opportunity to audition for Michael Mayer for *Charlie Brown*. My intuition told me to go. Michael said, "I don't know what I'm going to do yet. But you've got to do this show." I still wasn't sure what

to do. Then we talked on the phone, and he said, "You're getting an offer. You're not playing Lucy; you're playing another part. You have to trust me." It sounded shady, but I knew him, so it wasn't. In my gut I knew I should take this part. So, I turned down a for sure for a maybe. When we walked in the first day of rehearsals, Anthony Rapp sat down and there was a Charlie hat, Ilana sat down with Lucy, Stanley with Schroeder, B.D. Wong with Linus, Roger with Snoopy. And then there was Sally. I was so excited, and I knew it was perfect. I'm a little sister; I was not too far removed from who she was. Michael gave me the freedom to look through all of the Charles Schulz books. Out of town we tried different things to see what worked and what didn't. I had a director that trusted me and that I trusted.

Andrew Lippa wrote Sally's song "My New Philosophy." I didn't know how the song was going to go over. It's an acting piece as much as a song. We opened in Skokie, Illinois, our first audience. The song got a standing ovation. I was very grateful that I listened to my gut. *Annie Get Your Gun* went on and was a big hit. *Charlie Brown* struggled, but for me it was the right decision. Every time I have followed my

Featured Actress in a Muscial winner Kristin Chenoweth (center) with Swoosie Kurtz and Ben Stiller

gut it has served me well. Charles Schulz wrote me a letter, which said, "If I had put Sally into real life, it would be you." *Charlie Brown* was a life changer and a career changer.

Our cast performed on the Tony Awards immediately before they gave out the award for Best Featured Actress in a Musical. Just in case I won I didn't want to be dressed as Sally. I wanted to look like a person, a woman. I had about fifteen to twenty seconds to change. Ilana Levine helped me change wigs and throw on a dress. I said to her, "If I don't win, talk about all dressed up and no place to go," and we started laughing. Then I heard my name and she shoved me out there and screamed so loud for me. I think I was in shock. My dad, who loves Bernadette Peters as I do, was with me that night and we went to the Tony party. He got to meet Bernadette, so to him, I made it.

Sometimes I still can't believe I won. It means to me that whoever the people in charge are, they thought that performance deserved to be recognized. That, in and of itself, launched a career that I have been very happy doing. I love what I do. Being on a stage is like being in church for me, and I love church. That win meant a lot to me.

**MARTIN SHORT:** For an actor the Tony is the greatest award of all. In film, you can put a mediocre actor in *Hamlet*, and if the director is brilliant and the editor is astounding and everyone does enough takes, that actor can go on to win an Oscar. But that couldn't happen onstage. In the theatre, even with a great director, an actor's performance can't be rescued. At the end of the day, it's the actor up there alone proving his worth. That's why to win that Tony is the ultimate in satisfaction.

I love the repetition of doing a show. If people say something is wonderful on opening night I want to say, "Please come back in two months when I'm actually relaxed and truly know what I'm doing." To me the idea of trying to achieve perfection—which no one ever achieves—is very gratifying. You have this run of a play where you can see if you can reach the point where you're at 99 percent with the material. I'm someone who once I deliver a line it's like cutting a diamond. I think, *That's the perfect way to do it. I will do that line exactly the same way for twenty-five years.*

Martin Short

**BERNADETTE PETERS:** Annie Oakley is an iconic, fabulous role, and I was happy to have a chance to play her. When I did the revival of *Annie Get Your Gun*, it was important to me that it would not be a walk down memory lane. Even though the songs and the story were familiar to some of the audiences, we made it come alive in a way that was different from the original production in 1946.

Irving Berlin's music is wonderful. It was so much fun singing "Anything You Can Do I Can Do Better" with Tom Wopat. "Moonshine Lullaby" is such a pretty song, and "You Can't Get a Man with a Gun" is fantastic. It's such a fun show with great music.

# ACCEPTANCE SPEECHES THROUGH THE YEARS

**NIGEL HAWTHORNE (1991):** I'm very proud of this. *Shadowlands* was a very special play to me, and I was certainly very proud to be in it. They say pride is a sin, but perhaps I might be allowed a lapse on this particular occasion....I'd like particularly to say how grateful we all were to our producers for steering us through a very difficult time. We had after all, a long winter, a recession, the Gulf War, and Frank Rich. But we ran for five months, and for an emotional play like *Shadowlands*, that ain't half bad. I'm very proud.

**MERCEDES RUEHL (1991):** This is one of the great moments of my life. It's very hard to breathe. With all due respect to the great house of Chanel, the dress doesn't make it any easier.

> To be the first recipient of the Brooks Atkinson Award is an overwhelming experience that I shall not even attempt to describe in bumbling prose. **AL HIRSCHFELD (1984)**

Mercedes Ruehl and Nigel Hawthorne

**BARRY MILLER (1985):** Mostly I'd like to thank Mr. Neil Simon, because besides writing a very funny play, he also wrote a play of great feeling and beauty and compassion and dignity, and trusted me with a character that embodies those ideals, and for that I will always be grateful. He is a wonderful and a generous man, and I owe this to him.

**LEN CARIOU (1979):** This is a cutthroat business, they had no other choice....It's an incredible thrill to stand up here, but it is in a sense—at least to me—somewhat inevitable in this sense. I was with two geniuses in the theatre. One of them being Mr. Harold Prince, whose conceptual genius of *Sweeney Todd*—and his casting genius—are, well, they're without peer. The other one is Stephen Sondheim...I would like, though, to say a very special thank you to our conductor, Mr. Paul Gemignani, who is so incredibly sensitive to us up on that stage. It's like having another actor, and that is a joy.

**GREG CHAMPION (1981):** My father (Gower Champion) always said to me that he felt very fortunate in his life to have loved his work, the work that he did, and I know that he would have been very grateful to get this award for a show which was so important to him. It meant so much to him continuing his association with David Merrick, Mike Stewart. He would have been very proud, and we're very proud to have him as our father.

> Let me just say thank you to all the marvelous people who helped with the show and say that they could not have done it without me.
> **BOB FOSSE (1973)**

# I cannot tell you how this beats the alternative. ROBERT FALLS (1999)

**RICARDO KHAN (1999):** To the league, the Theatre Wing, and the American Theatre Critics Association, I am honored and so grateful on behalf of all of Crossroads for this moment to finally stand here and say to the dreamer that is inside of us all that regardless of your color, it is possible. And to say that for over twenty years we faced the odds, and folks said it couldn't be done. Don't ever let anybody try to convince you that it can't because of the color of your skin or anything else, because it can....I want to acknowledge the Negro Ensemble Company and the New Federal Theatre and the Robesons and the Hansberrys, who came before us to kick the doors open so that we could stand here today and do our work....Hold fast to dreams.

**PHYLICIA RASHAD (2004):** Often I've wondered what does it take for this to happen. And now I know it takes effort, and grace. Tremendous self-effort, and amazing grace. In my life that grace has taken numerous forms. The first is the family into which I was born. Parents who loved and wanted me, and a mother who fought fearlessly, courageously, consistently so that her children above all else could realize their full potential as human beings. Teachers who wanted to be teachers. Art all my life. A brilliant play. A magnificent role. A producer with a vision. A producer with a heart. And a director who dares to see me as an artist capable of many things. I thank God for everything, every single thing. For my mother, for my sister, for my brothers, for my children. And for this.

**ROBERT NEMIROFF (1974):** It has been fifteen years since Lorraine Hansberry wrote the play *A Raisin in the Sun*, which is the solid rock on which all of our achievements in *Raisin* have been based. It was Lorraine Hansberry who sat down to write a play to express the glory and the laughter and the joy and the heroism that came to her out of a Black experience in America, and who created words and a view of life which has illuminated our theater and illuminated our lives ever since.

**PHILIP J. SMITH (2011):** We may live in a world of smartphones and iPads, but nothing will ever replace the magic of Broadway.

Jonathan Larson

**JULIE LARSON (JONATHAN LARSON'S SISTER, 1996):** My brother, Jonathan, loved musical theatre, and he dreamed of creating a youthful, passionate piece that would be pertinent and...bring a new generation to the theatre so they too could enjoy the theatre as much as he did and get as much joy out of it as he did. That dream became *Rent*.

It took Johnny fifteen years of really hard work to become an overnight sensation. So we'd like to share this award with all those who are out there still working in restaurants, or driving taxis, or doing whatever they have to, to scrape by for their art. Stay true to yourselves and to dreams. I know they can come true. This is for you.

**BEN HARNEY (1982):** I'd like to share this award with Obba Babatundé, Cleavant Derricks, Tony Franklin, and Vondie Curtis-Hall. This one's for the Dreamboys.

**KEN HOWARD (1970):** There are a lot of people you feel you should thank at this time, but I feel I should especially thank the admissions officers of several law schools who inadvertently encouraged me to go into this business a few years ago.

**MIKE NICHOLS (2012):** There's not a person in this theater that doesn't know what it is to be a salesman. To be out there in the blue, riding on a smile and a shoeshine. As we know, a salesman has got to dream. It goes with the territory.

This is without a doubt the greatest thrill of my life .... Since this is the year of tap dancing, there is one element that I must acknowledge. Ladies and gentlemen, in my case, it's Father Time. He let me stay here long enough. **CHARLES HONI COLES (1983)**

**EDWARD HERRMANN (1976):** I often wondered what it would be like to receive one of these. It's like catching a home run in the bleachers hit by Al Kaline.

**JERRY HERMAN (2009):** It just doesn't get any better than this, does it? Did you know I was born on this street and that my mother thought there was something special about the fact that her hospital window had a great view of the Winter Garden marquee? Well, here I am, seventy-seven years later. Still on 50th Street. But enjoying the ultimate moment of my life. The journey from Mom's window to this iconic stage has been filled with so much joy and excitement and laughter and lifelong friendships that the only way I know how to say thanks to the hundreds of thousands of people who helped get me here is to say enormous heartfelt thank-you to every soul who has touched my life in the musical theatre. The thing I want you to know is that I will hold this moment fast because the best of times is now, is now, is definitely now.

Charles Honi Coles

I've stood on the sidelines for over half a century and watched other people receive the Tony Awards. And now as we face the millennium at last, I get my own Tony Award.

**ISABELLE STEVENSON (1999)**

# the '2000s

# WINNERS ◎ 2000

**PLAY:** *Copenhagen*, Michael Frayn

Produced by Michael Codron, Lee Dean, The Royal National Theatre, James M. Nederlander, Roger Berlind, Scott Rudin, Elizabeth I. McCann, Ray Larsen, Jon B. Platt, Byron Goldman, Scott Nederlander

**MUSICAL:** *Contact*

Produced by Lincoln Center Theater, André Bishop, Bernard Gersten

**BOOK OF A MUSICAL:** Richard Nelson, *James Joyce's The Dead*

**ORIGINAL SCORE (MUSIC AND/OR LYRICS) WRITTEN FOR THE THEATRE:**
Elton John (music), Tim Rice (lyrics), *Aida*

**REVIVAL OF A PLAY:** *The Real Thing*

Produced by Anita Waxman, Elizabeth Williams, Rob Kastner, Miramax Films, The Donmar Warehouse

**REVIVAL OF A MUSICAL:** *Kiss Me, Kate*

Produced by Roger Berlind, Roger Horchow

**ACTOR IN A LEADING ROLE IN A PLAY:**
Stephen Dillane, *The Real Thing*

**ACTRESS IN A LEADING ROLE IN A PLAY:**
Jennifer Ehle, *The Real Thing*

Michael Frayn

Martin Pakledinaz

**ACTOR IN A LEADING ROLE IN A MUSICAL:**
Brian Stokes Mitchell, *Kiss Me, Kate*

**ACTRESS IN A LEADING ROLE IN A MUSICAL:**
Heather Headley, *Aida*

**ACTOR IN A FEATURED ROLE IN A PLAY:**
Roy Dotrice, *A Moon for the Misbegotten*

**ACTRESS IN A FEATURED ROLE IN A PLAY:**
Blair Brown, *Copenhagen*

**ACTOR IN A FEATURED ROLE IN A MUSICAL:**
Boyd Gaines, *Contact*

**ACTRESS IN A FEATURED ROLE IN A MUSICAL:**
Karen Ziemba, *Contact*

**SCENIC DESIGN:** Bob Crowley, *Aida*

**COSTUME DESIGN:** Martin Pakledinaz, *Kiss Me, Kate*

**LIGHTING DESIGN:** Natasha Katz, *Aida*

**DIRECTION OF A PLAY:** Michael Blakemore, *Copenhagen*

**DIRECTION OF A MUSICAL:** Michael Blakemore, *Kiss Me, Kate*

**CHOREOGRAPHY:** Susan Stroman, *Contact*

**ORCHESTRATIONS:** Don Sebesky, *Kiss Me, Kate*

**SPECIAL TONY AWARD FOR LIFETIME ACHIEVEMENT IN THE THEATRE:**
T. Edward Hambleton

**REGIONAL THEATRE AWARD:** The Utah Shakespearean Festival

**SPECIAL TONY AWARD:** *Dame Edna: The Royal Tour*

**TONY HONOR:** Eileen Heckart; Sylvia Herscher; City Center Encores

Double winner Michael Blakemore, who won for Direction of a Play (*Copenhagen*) and Direction of a Musical (*Kiss Me, Kate*)

Karen Ziemba

2000 ∘ 149

**NATASHA KATZ:** Lighting has come far in the last fifteen to twenty years. When I started out, you'd hang lights on the pipe. If the director wanted something moved, we'd have to get out a ladder—four people had to be at the bottom of the ladder—and one electrician would go up and refocus the light. That took a lot of time, and it wasn't always right. You'd do it over and over again. Now they're robotic. Somebody sits behind a computer and just moves the light. It's a miracle.

Lighting is an amazing thing. It can change the whole feel of the moment in just a second. It is instant gratification. I did a show with Marvin Hamlisch called *Sweet Smell of Success*. He was the first person to say to me, "Lighting is exciting!" I love that expression. Lighting can make something very quiet into—without anyone even realizing it—a burst of energy. At the snap of the fingers, it can change what everything looks like.

Being a Tony winner means everything to me. I can't imagine anything better than being recognized by my peers. It's a validation. I'm thrilled to have seven Tony Awards.

**ROSEMARY HARRIS:** My daughter [Jennifer Ehle] and I were both nominated for Tonys the same year. Of course, I knew I wouldn't get it, and I was fairly sure that Jennifer wouldn't either. There was a lovely actress, Claudia Shear, who sat behind us that night, who starred as Mae West in *Dirty Blonde*. She'd written that play, so I felt sure that she was the favorite and both Jennifer and I would be disregarded. I don't know if Jennifer or I was more surprised when she won! I know that I was out of my mind with happiness.

**SUSAN STROMAN:** Most of the times you do a show, it comes from a novel or a screenplay or it's a revival. In the case of *Contact* it came from a vision. I happened to be in a dance club downtown on Hudson and Hubert at one o'clock in the morning. In this club was a sea of good New Yorkers wearing black, and this girl walked in wearing a yellow dress. She would step forward when she wanted to dance with someone. When she was done with them, she'd retreat back to the bar and wait. I got obsessed watching her. I thought she was going to change some man's life that night. About two weeks later André Bishop called me from Lincoln Center Theater and asked me to come up. He

had seen my work in *Steel Pier*, which was very poetic and filled with choreography. He said, "If you have an idea, we will help you develop it." I couldn't believe I was hearing that. A lot of artists don't get to hear that. I told him I had an idea and would come back to him in a week. I called my good friend John Weidman, who wrote *Assassins* and *Pacific Overtures*. We got together and created this story about a girl in a yellow dress in a club changing some man's life. John and I loved it so much. The dancers loved doing it. It was a very special experience, but it was so unique we didn't know how it was going to be embraced. In fact, it was really embraced and ran for a very long time up at Lincoln Center. It was a gift from André Bishop and Bernie Gersten to see an artist's work and think that maybe I had another idea. It was a very special show.

I cast Boyd Gaines because he's such a strong actor, and I also wanted someone who didn't really dance. Part of the idea was that these dancers represent obstacles that you have to get through to get to this girl in the yellow dress. If that character that Boyd played, Michael Wiley, if he didn't make contact with that girl, he would die. It was better for me to have a very strong actor that didn't move. Ultimately, he does dance at the end. It's more triumphant when he embraces the dance and makes contact with the girl, because he wasn't a dancer.

**BRIAN STOKES MITCHELL:** It's so stereotypical to say, but winning a Tony was a dream come true. I was raised on the stage. What is most gratifying is that it's conferred on you by your peers, and people who understand the subtleties and eccentricities and the artistry of the work. There's a title that comes with it. All of a sudden, I became Tony Award winner Brian Stokes Mitchell when I was introduced at events. But I still had to pay my rent. The title helps with that. It puts you in a different kind of strata.

I wanted to let people that had been part of my career and my receiving the award enjoy it. I started with my dad. I sent him the Tony with the idea that he would keep it for about a month and then pass it on to someone else. My dad held on to it for a couple of years! It went to my brother, my sister, my theatre parents—Don and Bonnie Ward—who started me in theatre when I was fourteen years old in San Diego, and some other teachers. It did this grand tour for about four years.

I loved working with Michael Blakemore on *Kiss Me, Kate*. He won two Tonys that year! If there was a scene that wasn't working for him, he would demonstrate with the perfect line reading. He would always follow it up by sincerely saying, "But don't say it like that. You'll find it." He was an actor as well. I learned to start with his line reading and then made it my own. I was happy to be his student. I eventually got to the place where I understood the rhythm and style of the comedy in the show, and I added my own touches to the show. I always knew I was within the structure of the show thanks to Michael.

At the very beginning of the process, Marin Mazzie and I decided we were going to have the most fun ever doing *Kiss Me, Kate*. We did a little pinky shake on it. We said "most fun ever" before every show. I still say that now before I start a show with anybody. Marin and I did have the most fun ever. She was such a brilliant singer and comic actress. She was like Lucille Ball. She was amazing, and I just loved her madly as a human being. My greatest disappointment when I won the Tony was that she did not win.

Lead acting winners (L to R) Brian Stokes Mitchell, Heather Headley, Jennifer Ehle, and Stephen Dillane

Dodger Theatricals: Brad
Bartell, Ed Strong, Joop van
den Ende, Michael David,
and Robin DeLevita

# WINNERS ◎ 2001

**PLAY:** *Proof*, David Auburn

Produced by Manhattan Theatre Club, Lynne Meadow, Barry
Grove, Roger Berlind, Carole Shorenstein Hays, Jujamcyn
Theaters, Ostar Enterprises, Daryl Roth, Stuart Thompson

**MUSICAL:** *The Producers, the New Mel Brooks Musical*

Produced by Rocco Landesman, SFX Theatrical Group, The Frankel-Baruch-Viertel-Routh Group, Bob and
Harvey Weinstein, Rick Steiner, Robert F.X. Sillerman, Mel Brooks, James D. Stern/Douglas Meyer

**BOOK OF A MUSICAL:** Mel Brooks and Thomas Meehan, *The Producers,
the New Mel Brooks Musical*

**ORIGINAL SCORE (MUSIC AND/OR LYRICS) WRITTEN FOR THE THEATRE:**
Mel Brooks, *The Producers, the New Mel Brooks Musical*

**REVIVAL OF A PLAY:** *One Flew over the Cuckoo's Nest*

Produced by Michael Leavitt, Fox Theatricals, Anita Waxman, Elizabeth Williams, John York Noble,
Randall L. Wreghitt, Dori Berinstein, The Steppenwolf Theatre Company

**REVIVAL OF A MUSICAL:** *42nd Street*
Produced by Dodger Theatricals,
Joop van den Ende, Stage Holding

**ACTOR IN A LEADING ROLE IN A PLAY:**
Richard Easton, *The Invention of Love*

**ACTRESS IN A LEADING ROLE IN A PLAY:**
Mary-Louise Parker, *Proof*

**ACTOR IN A LEADING ROLE IN A MUSICAL:**
Nathan Lane, *The Producers, the
New Mel Brooks Musical*

Mary-Louise Parker

August Wilson and
Viola Davis

Andrea Bowen and
Gary Beach

**ACTRESS IN A LEADING ROLE IN A MUSICAL:** Christine Ebersole, *42nd Street*

**ACTOR IN A FEATURED ROLE IN A PLAY:** Robert Sean Leonard, *The Invention of Love*

**ACTRESS IN A FEATURED ROLE IN A PLAY:** Viola Davis, *King Hedley II*

**ACTOR IN A FEATURED ROLE IN A MUSICAL:** Gary Beach, *The Producers, the New Mel Brooks Musical*

**ACTRESS IN A FEATURED ROLE IN A MUSICAL:** Cady Huffman, *The Producers, the New Mel Brooks Musical*

**SCENIC DESIGN:** Robin Wagner, *The Producers, the New Mel Brooks Musical*

**COSTUME DESIGN:** William Ivey Long, *The Producers, the New Mel Brooks Musical*

**LIGHTING DESIGN:** Peter Kaczorowski, *The Producers, the New Mel Brooks Musical*

**DIRECTION OF A PLAY:** Daniel Sullivan, *Proof*

**DIRECTION OF A MUSICAL:** Susan Stroman, *The Producers, the New Mel Brooks Musical*

**CHOREOGRAPHY:** Susan Stroman, *The Producers, the New Mel Brooks Musical*

**ORCHESTRATIONS:** Doug Besterman, *The Producers, the New Mel Brooks Musical*

**SPECIAL THEATRICAL EVENT:** *Blast!*

**SPECIAL TONY AWARD FOR LIFETIME ACHIEVEMENT IN THE THEATRE:** Paul Gemignani

**REGIONAL THEATRE AWARD:** Victory Gardens Theater, Chicago, Illinois

**TONY HONOR:** Betty Corwin and the Theatre on Film and Tape Archive of the New York Public Library for the Performing Arts; New Dramatists; Theatre World

Edie Falco and
Robert Sean Leonard

2001 153

**PETER KACZOROWSKI:** As a lighting designer, I get to decide an awful lot. I can focus where people should look, and in what way they should look. I love composing the stage and framing it in an emotional way that is perfect for the text and for the moment. When you feel the audience lean forward a little bit because you've made a cue that draws attention to something, that's very satisfying.

**NATHAN LANE:** I was in Paris staying at the Ritz hotel and had gone down to the pool. There were only two people in the pool, and to my surprise it was the great Mel Brooks and his lovely wife, the great Anne Bancroft. So, I got in and we started chatting. I had met them once when they came to see Neil Simon's *Laughter on the 23rd Floor*. They had been extremely gracious and kind after the performance. In the play there was a character based on Mel, and I remember him saying dramatically, "That character based on me, it was a tissue of lies!" Anyway, eventually Anne went upstairs and Mel stayed in the pool with me, which was surprising. And then he said, "I want to talk to you about a project. I'm writing a musical based on *The Producers*, and I think you and Marty Short are the only two people I can see doing this." I said, "Wow. That would be a tremendous honor. I'd be thrilled." A couple of years went by and we did a reading of it and people went crazy. Marty Short had just done *Little Me* in New York, and didn't want to leave his family again for that long. He lives in Los Angeles, so Evan Pappas played Leo that day. And then eventually someone had the brilliant idea to ask Matthew Broderick to do the show, who was perfection, and the rest is history. But that first reading was such a huge success, they offered Mel the St. James Theatre during the intermission. It doesn't hurt that it has one of the greatest comic plots ever written, but that was one of those times when all the right people came together and it was magical and the show just became a true phenomenon.

**MEL BROOKS:** David Geffen bothered me every day to make a musical out of my film *The Producers*. I would say, "Forget it. It's a perfectly good little movie. Let's leave it alone." He persisted until I said yes. When we were ready, David was forming a new company and couldn't produce it. But he was the catalyst that started it all.

Susan Stroman's direction was unerringly correct. I was going to throw out "Along Came Bialy." She said, "No! Leave it alone. I've got a great idea for it." What a brilliant woman! She was very gifted at moving the production. One scene would gracefully slide into another scene without anyone even realizing it. She was a genius at that. Stro was so valuable to that show. She would find things and then turn them into gold.

She lost her husband, Mike Ockrent, when we were in rehearsal. He was directing *The Producers*, and Stro was the choreographer. He had great ideas; he was funny. He was just the right person to direct. And then he died from leukemia. Everybody came up with ideas for another director. Tom and I had just seen her show *Contact*. We looked at each other and said, "That's our director." She was hesitant. I said, "Look, you can't cry all day. You wake up, you'll cry in the morning. You'll come to work, take your mind off it. You'll leave rehearsal and cry at night." She was heartbroken. I told her, "The only way out of grief is work. I know that." We were so lucky and pleased. She did a magnificent job of staging that show.

Tom Meehan was incredibly invaluable in how *The Producers* would go from a movie to a musical. We used to go to Madame Romaine De Lyon, a restaurant on the corner of 61st and Third. She only served omelets. We'd meet there every morning around ten thirty or eleven o'clock, and we'd have our omelet. It was always tomato and cheese. Afterwards we had coffee and wrote down ideas. Then we'd either go to down to the Village, where he lived, or uptown, where I live, and continue working. We'd work about four or five hours a day. We loved eating our omelets and getting to work on *The Producers*. It literally was a labor of love; it was never hard. It was a joyous collaboration. He was such a great writer and a great human being: good-natured, sweet, giving. We were equal partners. I miss him every day.

The Tony is a very special, sacred salute from the most talented people in the world. I started wanting to only be in theatre. When I originally wrote *The Producers* years ago, I sent it to my friend, the producer Kermit Bloomgarden. He said the standard was for a show to have one set, five characters. It was the most inexpensive way to produce a play. He said, "You've got twenty sets and thirty-five characters. This is not a play. I think it's a movie." And it became a movie.

When David Geffen was still involved, he felt I wasn't ready to write the music and lyrics and sent me to Jerry Herman. I met with Jerry, and he listened to the two songs I had already written for the show. He played "Prisoners of Love" and "Springtime for Hitler" and said, "You're a great writer. You're a natural songwriter. Write another eight songs, and you've got a big hit." Thanks to Jerry Herman, I got the job of writing the score.

**ROBERT SEAN LEONARD:** When I was a teenager, I did a horrible TV movie with Cleavant Derricks. I remember hearing someone say that he had a Tony Award, and that made him a bit of a conspicuous character! I didn't really know what it meant at the time.

I almost didn't do *The Invention of Love*. I read it and called the director, Jack O'Brien, to tell him I didn't see the theatricality. Jack had me come and meet with him and Richard Easton, who was playing the older version of A. E. Houseman. They both told me I had to do the play. Because I trusted them, I agreed, but going in I had no idea how I was going to play it and was very uncertain as to why anyone would want to see it. It turned out that I was a fool, because when Jack O'Brien is at the helm and you've got Bob Crowley painting the world around you, things tend to work out.

I played the younger version of Richard Easton's A.E. Houseman. Richard came in completely off book and ready to go. His scenes were done from the very first read-through; he knew what he wanted to do. He did all his work before the

Thomas Meehan and Mel Brooks

first rehearsal. I respected and applauded and enjoyed working with him. And because his Houseman was done and mine was very much uncooked, what he did informed how I played the character. I often had questions answered by observing Richard. Just little things like how to stand, to talk, how to inflect a particular line. I based a lot of what I did on just observing Richard. It was like playing tennis in slow motion and getting to see how McEnroe hits the ball right before you hit. It was an incredibly helpful rehearsal process. I have great memories of working with him. He made things much easier for me.

**SUSAN STROMAN:** Max Bialystock danced very differently from Leo Bloom. You don't really see them come together and dance until the very end as they come to be comrades and friends. Max dances with great abandon and big energy. Leo Bloom dances in a very lyrical way. Much smaller and more careful. When you're choreographing, you have to make sure that the way the actors move exemplifies their character and strengthens it.

To win for directing *The Producers* was very special. To be a woman in a male-dominated field and then to be a woman in something that became such a blockbuster was significant. I was thrilled to receive that Tony Award for all the women who were finally being seen as directors. Mel Brooks gave me complete respect and support. I learned a lot from Mel about comedy. I felt his support every second of the way. I knew it was a big deal that he was putting that script in my hands. I only ever felt love and support from him, and we're still wonderful friends to this day.

Mel wrote this song "Along Comes Bialy." It was about a little old lady. I had the idea to have twenty-five little old ladies with walkers come after Max Bialystock. I went into a studio and got a walker to see what I could do. I didn't know

if you could dance with a walker. In fact, you can not only tap with it; it holds you. You can lift it up and do acrobatic steps with it. That idea heightened the comedy even more.

People would ask me what it was like being a woman in charge. I kept thinking, *Why aren't women in charge?* I felt it at the time for all the young women who were trying to break through, who had a lot to say and a lot to offer. But even after that it still took a long time to have more women in charge. Richard Easton

# WINNERS ◎ 2002

PLAY: *Edward Albee's The Goat, or Who Is Sylvia?*, Edward Albee

Produced by Elizabeth Ireland McCann, Daryl Roth, Carole Shorenstein Hays, Terry Allen Kramer, Scott Rudin, Bob Boyett, Scott Nederlander, Sine/ZPI

MUSICAL: *Thoroughly Modern Millie*

Produced by Michael Leavitt, Fox Theatricals, Hal Luftig, Stewart F. Lane, James L. Nederlander, Independent Presenters Network, L. Mages/M. Glick, Berinstein/Manocherian/Dramatic Forces, John York Noble, Whoopi Goldberg

BOOK OF A MUSICAL: Greg Kotis, *Urinetown the Musical*

ORIGINAL SCORE (MUSIC AND/OR LYRICS) WRITTEN FOR THE THEATRE:

Mark Hollman (music), Mark Hollman and Greg Kotis (lyrics), *Urinetown the Musical*

REVIVAL OF A PLAY: *Private Lives*

Produced by Emanuel Azenberg, Ira Pittelman, Scott Nederlander, Frederick Zollo, Nicholas Paleologos, Broccoli/Sine, James Nederlander, Kevin McCollum, Jeffrey Seller, Duncan C. Weldon and Paul Elliott for Triumph Entertainment Partners Ltd.

REVIVAL OF A MUSICAL: *Into the Woods*

Produced by Dodger Theatricals, Stage Holding/Joop van den Ende, TheatreDreams

ACTOR IN A LEADING ROLE IN A PLAY: Alan Bates, *Fortune's Fool*

ACTRESS IN A LEADING ROLE IN A PLAY:
Lindsay Duncan, *Private Lives*

ACTOR IN A LEADING ROLE IN A MUSICAL:
John Lithgow, *Sweet Smell of Success*

ACTRESS IN A LEADING ROLE IN A MUSICAL:
Sutton Foster, *Thoroughly Modern Millie*

John Rando

Elaine Stritch accepting for *Elaine Stritch at Liberty*

**ACTOR IN A FEATURED ROLE IN A PLAY:** Frank Langella, *Fortune's Fool*

**ACTRESS IN A FEATURED ROLE IN A PLAY:** Katie Finneran, *Noises Off*

**ACTOR IN A FEATURED ROLE IN A MUSICAL:** Shuler Hensley, *Oklahoma!*

**ACTRESS IN A FEATURED ROLE IN A MUSICAL:**
Harriet Harris, *Thoroughly Modern Millie*

**SCENIC DESIGN:** Tim Hatley, *Private Lives*

**COSTUME DESIGN:** Martin Pakledinaz, *Thoroughly Modern Millie*

**LIGHTING DESIGN:** Brian MacDevitt, *Into the Woods*

**DIRECTION OF A PLAY:** Mary Zimmerman, *Metamorphoses*

**DIRECTION OF A MUSICAL:** John Rando, *Urinetown the Musical*

**CHOREOGRAPHY:** Rob Ashford, *Thoroughly Modern Millie*

**ORCHESTRATIONS:** Doug Besterman and Ralph Burns, *Thoroughly Modern Millie*

**SPECIAL TONY AWARD FOR LIFETIME ACHIEVEMENT IN THE THEATRE:**
Robert Whitehead; Julie Harris

**REGIONAL THEATRE AWARD:**
Williamstown Theatre Festival

**SPECIAL THEATRICAL EVENT:**
*Elaine Stritch at Liberty*

Mary Tyler Moore and Whoopi Goldberg.
Goldberg won a Tony for producing *Thoroughly
Modern Millie,* which cemented her EGOT status.

Lead acting winners (L to R) John Lithgow, Lindsay Duncan, Sutton Foster, and Alan Bates

**SUTTON FOSTER:** I grew up watching the Tonys from my living room outside of Detroit, Michigan. Never in a million years did I think I would ever be on them, let alone have won two! When I won for *Millie*, it was so surreal. When I was fifteen, I would dream of that moment and practice my Tony speech with my hairbrush.

What makes the Tonys so special is that it's not just your show; it's all the shows. You're cheering each other on. It's a celebration. You get to see your friends and feel the sense of community. Every time I've performed at the Tonys it's been an honor. Most people don't realize what Tony day is like. We're not just going to an award show. That morning we did a full dress rehearsal, then we did a matinee, then

got glammed up for the red carpet, then you get pulled from your seat to get into costume and perform. It's a thrill, but it's not just sitting in a chair all night. Many of us are still the entertainment!

**MICHAEL DAVID:** Unpredictable moments make the Tonys exciting. The year we produced *Urinetown* we went to the Tonys thinking we didn't have a prayer of winning Best Musical. Then we won for Best Book, then Best Music and Lyrics, then we won for Best Director. So, we were thinking that we were surprisingly now looking like the favorite. Until Best Musical went to *Thoroughly Modern Millie*. Or when *Wicked* saw the Tony go to *Avenue Q*.

**SHULER HENSLEY:** *Oklahoma!* is one of those shows you grow up with. I had seen the movie, so I was very familiar with the character of Jud Fry, but the character's song "Lonely Room" was missing from the film. Mary Rodgers told me that "Lonely Room" was one of her father's top five songs that he composed. It is such a tone poem with these chord clusters and dissonant harmonies. It beautifully helps create the sound of someone in pain, but also deeply troubled. The lyrics also reveal that Jud has a lot of the same hopes and fears in life that we all do. I felt like Jud was a role people might not have fully understood and that there was an opportunity to show a deeper side to his character. It was a great opportunity as an actor to challenge people's preconceived notions about who Jud is. If you can find characteristics that people can relate to on a personal level, like loneliness or wanting to be included, and you can express that, it puts people in a very uncomfortable state. They don't want to like someone like Jud, but they can relate to him on that level.

Shuler Hensley and Hugh Jackman

# WINNERS ◯ 2003

Sisters Vanessa and Lynn Redgrave

PLAY: *Take Me Out*, Richard Greenberg
Produced by Carole Shorenstein Hays, Frederick DeMann,
The Donmar Warehouse, The Public Theater

MUSICAL: *Hairspray*

Produced by Margo Lion, Adam Epstein, The Baruch-Viertel-Routh-Frankel Group,
James D. Stern/Douglas L. Meyer, Rick Steiner/Frederic H. Mayerson, SEL & GFO,
New Line Cinema, Clear Channel Entertainment, A. Gordon/E. McAllister,
D. Harris/M. Swinsky, J. & B. Osher

BOOK OF A MUSICAL: Mark O'Donnell and Thomas Meehan, *Hairspray*

ORIGINAL SCORE (MUSIC AND/OR LYRICS) WRITTEN FOR THE THEATRE:

Marc Shaiman (music), Scott Wittman and Marc Shaiman (lyrics), *Hairspray*

REVIVAL OF A PLAY: *Long Day's Journey into Night*

Produced by David Richenthal, Max Cooper, Eric Falkenstein, Anthony and Charlene Marshall,
Darren Bagert, Kara Medoff, Lisa Vioni, Gene Korf

REVIVAL OF A MUSICAL: *Nine the Musical*

Produced by Roundabout Theatre Company, Todd Haimes,
Ellen Richard, Julia C. Levy

ACTOR IN A LEADING ROLE IN A PLAY:
Brian Dennehy, *Long Day's Journey into Night*

ACTRESS IN A LEADING ROLE IN A PLAY:
Vanessa Redgrave, *Long Day's Journey into Night*

ACTOR IN A LEADING ROLE IN A MUSICAL:
Harvey Fierstein, *Hairspray*

ACTRESS IN A LEADING ROLE IN A MUSICAL:
Marissa Jaret Winokur, *Hairspray*

ACTOR IN A FEATURED ROLE IN A PLAY:
Denis O'Hare, *Take Me Out*

ACTRESS IN A FEATURED ROLE IN A PLAY:
Michele Pawk, *Hollywood Arms*

Denis O'Hare

Michele Pawk

*Movin' Out* co-orchestrators
Billy Joel and Stuart Malina

**ACTOR IN A FEATURED ROLE IN A MUSICAL:** Dick Latessa, *Hairspray*

**ACTRESS IN A FEATURED ROLE IN A MUSICAL:** Jane Krakowski, *Nine the Musical*

**SCENIC DESIGN:** Catherine Martin, *La Bohème*

**COSTUME DESIGN:** William Ivey Long, *Hairspray*

**LIGHTING DESIGN:** Nigel Levings, *La Bohème*

**DIRECTION OF A PLAY:** Joe Mantello, *Take Me Out*

**DIRECTION OF A MUSICAL:** Jack O'Brien, *Hairspray*

**CHOREOGRAPHY:** Twyla Tharp, *Movin' Out*

**ORCHESTRATIONS:** Billy Joel and Stuart Malina, *Movin' Out*

**SPECIAL THEATRICAL EVENT:** *Russell Simmons' Def Poetry Jam on Broadway*

**SPECIAL TONY AWARD FOR LIFETIME ACHIEVEMENT IN THE THEATRE:** Cy Feuer

**REGIONAL THEATRE AWARD:** The Children's Theatre Company, Minneapolis, Minnesota

**TONY HONOR:** The principal ensemble of *La Bohème*; Paul Huntley; Johnson-Liff Casting Associates; The Acting Company

A number from *Nine* (front row) Laura Benanti, Mary Stuart Masterson, Jane Krakowski; (middle row) Mary Beth Peil, Rona Figueroa, Nell Campbell, Antonio Banderas, Saundra Santiago, Stephanie Bast, Myra Lucretia Taylor; (back row) Kathy Voytko, Linda Mugleston, Sara Gettelfinger, Deidre Goodwin, Rachel deBenedet, Elena Shadow, Jessica Leigh Brown, Kristin Marks

*Hairspray*'s Thomas Meehan, Mark O'Donnell, Harvey Fierstein, and Dick Latessa

*Hairspray*'s Jack O'Brien and Jerry Mitchell

Jed Bernstein and Cy Feuer

**JACK O'BRIEN:** I will never forget; it was one of our first previews of *Hairspray* in Seattle. After the curtain call everybody left the stage, and the audience wouldn't go home. Finally, the stage manager had to go up to the dressing room and get Harvey, who was out of his drag, out of his wig, out of his makeup, out of his brassiere, to come down to the stage and wave to the people and say, "Go home." We realized then that this was not ordinary. One sort of watched with wonder as this little project teetered away from us and became kind of legendary.

There's part of you that doesn't believe it. There's part of you that thinks that tomorrow night it's not going to work. And yet it does. It's a mitzvah; it's a gift. I take it with great humility knowing that half a step away is a disaster, and there are no guarantees that you're going to do it again.

**JOE MANTELLO:** Not being an aficionado of professional baseball, my main way in to *Take Me Out* was through (playwright) Richard Greenberg. Rich came to baseball later in life, and when there was a Major League Baseball game on television, we would talk on the phone. He would explain things to me, but so much of what I gleaned was through listening to him describe what he was seeing and hearing his real-time reactions to the game as it was being

played. I realized what I was trying to capture: not a literal representation, but a romanticized version of the game as Rich and the character Mason Marzac experienced it. That became very liberating, because the play wasn't trying to be a documentary; it was trying to capture the romance of the sport.

**HARVEY FIERSTEIN:** When Marissa won her Tony for Best Actress in a Musical, I grabbed her and I whispered something in her ear. I said, "Your name has now been changed. You were Marissa Jaret Winokur, you are now Tony Award winner Marissa Jaret Winokur. No matter what else happens, they can never take that away from you."

I auditioned for *Hairspray* assuming they didn't want me. They had me sing everything I had with me, which was about ten songs. I left the audition and called my manager, Richie Jackson, on the pay phone. We didn't have cellphones in those days. I said, "They were so wonderful to me, please call them and thank them for being so nice. Tell them I will be there on opening night throwing flowers at them." He said, "Are you done? You got the role. They already called."

Playwright Richard Greenberg (center) accepting for *Take Me Out* with producers including Frederick DeMann, Pilar DeMann, Carol Shorenstein Hays, and Michael Grandage

# WINNERS ◎ 2004

Lead acting winners (L to R) Idina Menzel, Hugh Jackman, Phylicia Rashad, and Jefferson Mays

PLAY: *I Am My Own Wife*, Doug Wright
Produced by Delphi Productions, Playwrights Horizons

MUSICAL: *Avenue Q*
Produced by Kevin McCollum, Robyn Goodman, Jeffrey Seller,
Vineyard Theatre, The New Group

BOOK OF A MUSICAL: Jeff Whitty, *Avenue Q*

ORIGINAL SCORE (MUSIC AND/OR LYRICS) WRITTEN
FOR THE THEATRE: Robert Lopez and Jeff Marx, *Avenue Q*

REVIVAL OF A PLAY: *Henry IV*
Produced by Lincoln Center Theater, André Bishop, Bernard Gersten

REVIVAL OF A MUSICAL: *Assassins*
Produced by Roundabout Theatre Company, Todd Haimes, Ellen Richard, Julia C. Levy

ACTOR IN A LEADING ROLE IN A PLAY:
Jefferson Mays, *I Am My Own Wife*

ACTRESS IN A LEADING ROLE IN A PLAY:
Phylicia Rashad, *A Raisin in the Sun*

ACTOR IN A LEADING ROLE IN A MUSICAL:
Hugh Jackman, *The Boy from Oz*

ACTRESS IN A LEADING ROLE IN A MUSICAL:
Idina Menzel, *Wicked*

Anika Noni Rose

Todd Haimes

*Wicked* set designer Eugene Lee

**ACTOR IN A FEATURED ROLE IN A PLAY:**
Brian F. O'Byrne, *Frozen*

**ACTRESS IN A FEATURED ROLE IN A PLAY:**
Audra McDonald, *A Raisin in the Sun*

**ACTOR IN A FEATURED ROLE IN A MUSICAL:**
Michael Cerveris, *Assassins*

**ACTRESS IN A FEATURED ROLE IN A MUSICAL:**
Anika Noni Rose, *Caroline, or Change*

**SCENIC DESIGN:** Eugene Lee, *Wicked*

**COSTUME DESIGN:** Susan Hilferty, *Wicked*

**LIGHTING DESIGN:** Jules Fisher and Peggy Eisenhauer, *Assassins*

**DIRECTION OF A PLAY:** Jack O'Brien, *Henry IV*

**DIRECTION OF A MUSICAL:** Joe Mantello, *Assassins*

**CHOREOGRAPHY:** Kathleen Marshall, *Wonderful Town*

**ORCHESTRATIONS:** Michael Starobin, *Assassins*

**SPECIAL TONY AWARD FOR LIFETIME ACHIEVEMENT
IN THE THEATRE:** James M. Nederlander

**REGIONAL THEATRE AWARD:** Cincinnati Playhouse in the Park

**TONY HONOR:** The cast of the 2003 Broadway production
of *Big River*; Nancy Coyne; Frances and Harry Edelstein
and Vincent Sardi Jr.; Martha Swope

Susan Hilferty

can start to construct curves and arcs into the play of light. The more curved it is, the more organic and human it has the potential of feeling. A computer becomes more like a piano, or a violin.

**JULES FISHER:** When I started working with Peggy my work got better. She was my assistant for many years. There was a very early moment when I said, "I think all of my work will look better if we're partners." One of the thrills of working together is coming up with ideas. We've always agreed that there's no pride of authorship. If one of us comes up with an idea, it's now *our* idea.

**HUGH JACKMAN:** You have to remember, I am from the suburbs of Australia. My excitement of just coming to Broadway in the late nineties was off the charts. And at that point I had no idea I'd ever be on Broadway. But that was the dream.

Now, many years later, just to be part of this community means so much to me. Actually, being honored by this community with a Tony Award…well, that is truly and deeply moving to me. I have had some of the best times of my life at that ceremony. To host, to present, and as a nominee.

I will never forget when Nicole [Kidman] read out my name. I was standing side of stage. Time stopped; the world stopped. I just tried to take in that somehow, I was realizing my dream at that very moment.

**PEGGY EISENHAUER:** Being a Tony recipient means I belong to a collective of theatre artists and

*Assassins' co-lighting designers Jules Fisher and Peggy Eisenhauer*

businesspeople who consider my design as an expression of artistry.

The ephemeral and amorphous nature of light allows each story to be expressed uniquely. There is never a preconceived way to convey music and drama with light. Every time we begin with a director, we're seeking to interpret their vision of the play. The freedom, the blank canvas of that, is what's truly terrifying and exciting. The opportunity as an artist is to find some way to reveal with light, in a way that has never been expressed before.

Technology in lighting has changed drastically since my practice began, but the emotional impact retains the same power. Digital technology has given us an enormous amount of creative headroom in the control of light. We can shave down the attributes of lighting to such small fractions of time, intensity, color, and movement that we

**JOE MANTELLO:** When actors you've directed win the Tony, it's like having a child who really excels at something. Some of my proudest moments have been when those actors have stepped onto that stage and been acknowledged for their performances. The year Idina Menzel won for *Wicked* was as proud a moment as I've ever had, even though I got the Tony that year for *Assassins*. We had a long road together. We were always rolling up our sleeves. Sometimes it was working, and other times it wasn't. We knew we had a lot of work to do on that character. We put in the work—she definitely put in the work. There were moments along the way where we struggled and got frustrated with each other. We also held each other's hand. We would recommit if we had a bump in the road. I always go to the theater the performance

Hugh Jackman as Peter Allen calls Sarah Jessica Parker up from the audience for some fun

From right: Jeffrey Seller, Kevin McCollum, Robert Lopez, Robyn Goodman, Jeff Marx (with mother)

Doug Wright

after opening night to check in, no matter how the show is received. I remember Idina being incredibly sad because the *New York Times* had barely mentioned her. It was upsetting to her because she'd worked so hard. I remember saying to her, "This isn't the end of the story. Show up. Do your work. Keep getting better and see what happens." So to see her have that triumphant moment, for that win to be the culmination of our collaboration was just extraordinary.

**KRISTIN CHENOWETH:** It was like a relative of mine had won when Idina Menzel won the Tony. I know how hard she worked, and I was proud of her. We support each other in the theatre.

**KATHLEEN MARSHALL:** Growing up in the sixties and seventies, there were only a few chances to see Broadway. You could see it at the Tony Awards. You could see it on the Macy's Thanksgiving Day parade. Sometimes the Jerry Lewis Labor Day telethon would have a New York studio, and sometimes Broadway performers would be on. There weren't a lot of opportunities to see it if you weren't in a position to go to New York and see shows. The Tonys have always had that magical place for me because it gave me that little window into the world of Broadway.

Idina Menzel as Elphaba in *Wicked*

**PHYLICIA RASHAD:** Receiving a Tony signals new beginnings.

# WINNERS ◎ 2005

---

**PLAY:** *Doubt*, John Patrick Shanley

Produced by Carole Shorenstein Hays; MTC Productions, Inc.; Lynne Meadow;
Barry Grove; Roger Berlind; Scott Rudin

**MUSICAL:** *Monty Python's Spamalot*

Produced by Boyett Ostar Productions, The Shubert Organization, Arielle Tepper, Stephanie McClelland,
Lawrence Horowitz, Élan V. McAllister/Allan S. Gordon, Independent Presenters Network, Roy Furman,
GRS Associates, Jam Theatricals, TGA Entertainment, Clear Channel Entertainment

**BOOK OF A MUSICAL:** Rachel Sheinkin, *The 25th Annual Putnam County Spelling Bee*

**ORIGINAL SCORE (MUSIC AND/OR LYRICS) WRITTEN FOR THE THEATRE:**
Adam Guettel, *The Light in the Piazza*

**REVIVAL OF A PLAY:** *Glengarry Glen Ross*

Produced by Jeffrey Richards, Jerry Frankel, Jam Theatricals, Boyett Ostar Productions, Ronald Frankel,
Philip Lacerte, Stephanie P. McClelland/CJM Productions, Barry Weisbord, Zendog Productions, Herbert
Goldsmith Productions, Roundabout Theatre Company, Todd Haimes, Ellen Richard, Julia C. Levy

**REVIVAL OF A MUSICAL:** *La Cage aux Folles*

Produced by James L. Nederlander, Clear Channel Entertainment, Kenneth Greenblatt,
Terry Allen Kramer, Martin Richards

**ACTOR IN A LEADING ROLE IN A PLAY:** Bill Irwin, *Edward Albee's*
*Who's Afraid of Virginia Woolf?*

**ACTRESS IN A LEADING ROLE IN A PLAY:** Cherry Jones, *Doubt*

**ACTOR IN A LEADING ROLE IN A MUSICAL:** Norbert Leo Butz, *Dirty Rotten Scoundrels*

Alan Alda, Liev
Schreiber, and
Brian F. O'Byrne

**ACTRESS IN A LEADING ROLE IN A MUSICAL:**
Victoria Clark, *The Light in the Piazza*

**ACTOR IN A FEATURED ROLE IN A PLAY:**
Liev Schreiber, *Glengarry Glen Ross*

**ACTRESS IN A FEATURED ROLE IN A PLAY:**
Adriane Lenox, *Doubt*

**ACTOR IN A FEATURED ROLE IN A MUSICAL:**
Dan Fogler, *The 25th Annual Putnam County Spelling Bee*

**ACTRESS IN A FEATURED ROLE IN A MUSICAL:**
Sara Ramirez, *Monty Python's Spamalot*

**SCENIC DESIGN OF A PLAY:** Scott Pask, *The Pillowman*

**SCENIC DESIGN OF A MUSICAL:** Michael Yeargan,
*The Light in the Piazza*

**COSTUME DESIGN OF A PLAY:** Jess Goldstein, *The Rivals*

**COSTUME DESIGN OF A MUSICAL:** Catherine Zuber, *The Light in the Piazza*

**LIGHTING DESIGN OF A PLAY:** Brian MacDevitt, *The Pillowman*

**LIGHTING DESIGN OF A MUSICAL:** Christopher Akerlind, *The Light in the Piazza*

**DIRECTION OF A PLAY:** Doug Hughes, *Doubt*

**DIRECTION OF A MUSICAL:** Mike Nichols, *Monty Python's Spamalot*

**CHOREOGRAPHY:** Jerry Mitchell, *La Cage aux Folles*

**ORCHESTRATIONS:** Ted Sperling, Adam Guettel, and Bruce Coughlin,
*The Light in the Piazza*

**SPECIAL THEATRICAL EVENT:** *Billy Crystal 700 Sundays*

**SPECIAL TONY AWARD FOR LIFETIME ACHIEVEMENT IN THE THEATRE:**
Edward Albee

**REGIONAL THEATRE AWARD:** Theatre de la Jeune Lune, Minneapolis, Minnesota

**TONY HONOR:** Peter Neufeld; Theatre Communications Group

Bill Irwin

**CATHERINE ZUBER:** I never dreamed that I would get one Tony, let alone eight. They are at my studio on 38th Street. They are next to my high school basketball trophies, a trophy I won for winning Best Costume at Marc Jacobs's Christmas party in 2006, and two Olivier Awards. If I ever feel a bit unsure, they give me a boost of confidence to trust my instincts.

**BARTLETT SHER:** People underestimate what it means when you have a good collaborator. Cathy (Zuber) can do anything. She's very good at being deep in the period, but at the same time making something very original cohesive.

Adam Guettel's work on *Light in the Piazza* is an incredible piece of musical theatre writing that is very close to my heart. It's in the spirit of the great musicals of his grandfather Richard Rodgers and Oscar Hammerstein II, and I feel very lucky to have been a part of it.

**JOHN PATRICK SHANLEY:** When an actor wins a Tony, they get up, go onstage, get their award, and then go back to their seat. When they say Best Play, it seems like half the audience gets up! It's a package deal. Producers get up, the artistic director of the theater gets up; you have to fight your way to get to the front of the line! I see that as support. These are my people. They helped me get this damn thing up, and I'm so happy they're up here with me.

Playwright John Patrick Shanley (center) with *Doubt* producers Barry Grove and Lynne Meadow of Manhattan Theatre Club

I think that any play or film that breaks through to a larger audience is a fluke. You've stumbled into the zeitgeist of the moment. Whether you realize it or not, you're writing about the times that you live in. As it happens, during the period when I wrote *Doubt*, there were an awful lot of people who seemed very certain about things that I didn't feel certain about at all. I had doubts. It turns out, there was a lot of people that felt like me.

**JERRY MITCHELL:** I had sixteen of the greatest male dancers to work with on *La Cage aux Folles*. Director Jerry Zaks gave me his full support and complete freedom to do whatever I wanted with the choreography. I was a fan of drag, and a fan of the danger of drag to people who are enticed, but afraid. That's part of what *La Cage* is about. I went to town with that show. I was throwing dancers over the orchestra pit into the splits. I had acros in it who could really do stuff. I called my aerial people for the end of the birdcage; I had people on a swing. It was just great fun.

**SCOTT PASK:** Something magical happened in *The Pillowman*. Martin McDonagh's incredible play is centered in storytelling and its consequence—detailing the writing of gruesome stories and the acts they inspire within a deeply guarded police state. After approaching the initial design, while considering various audience seating configurations (we were within the malleable Dorfman space of the National Theatre in London), I alongside the director John Crowley conceived a traditional end stage to best facilitate the elaborate visual language that we developed to accompany the stories being told within the play. The action first takes place within an interrogation room during the questioning of our protagonist, a writer, and then later in an adjoining cell. We enter into the imagined world (or is it?) of his stories—which magically appear up above him, as he tells them, within the wall of the cell—and continue in that manner throughout the evening. This illusion of architecture dematerializing into ever shifting images became a very unexpected, and sometimes shocking piece of theatre. It was my first Tony nomination, and my twin brother Bruce and my mom and stepfather were with me that incredible night. When Idina Menzel announced my name I was so shocked, and it took my brother's shoulder nudge to get up and go while the TV camera was in the aisle aimed at me. I remember my feet hitting the steps of the stage, and getting that statuette from Idina, hugging her, and being completely floored. I don't know how I got through my speech—but the moment I turned away from the podium to walk offstage, I became a sobbing mess. I had a full breakdown of disbelief. Anita Shevett, the photographer backstage, so kindly pulled me into a stairwell and helped me gather myself together for the official photograph with the award in hand. I later found out that when I won, my stepfather jumped out of his seat yelling at the top of his lungs, "That's my son! That's my son!" My heart could not be more full of my love for him. His immense pride in my accomplishment, and my family members being there, made every detail of that night absolutely unforgettable.

Design winners (L to R): Christopher Akerlind, Jess Goldstein, Scott Pask, Michael Yeargan, Brian MacDevitt, and Catherine Zuber

**VICTORIA CLARK:** To me theatre is alchemy, the transformation of elements from the everyday to the transcendent. Theatre at its best can change your life, as it has mine, both as a theatre practitioner and as an audience member. Growing up in Texas, the yearly Tony Awards broadcast was my sole visceral connection to New York theatre. I watched the Tony performances and dreamed of being a part of them one day, having no idea how. Watching such iconic stars as Angela Lansbury, Carol Burnett, Bernadette Peters, Ben Vereen, Leslie Uggams, and Patti LuPone, and marveling at the dancing ensembles swirling around the camera shots, I was deeply engrossed in my element. Given that the medium itself is live performance, I was thrilled watching these live broadcasts, and amazed at the grace and poise of these diverse artists.

When I first read and heard *The Light in the Piazza*, I was dazzled by the incredible writing of Craig Lucas (book) and Adam Guettel (music and lyrics). It was a moving story based on the novella by Elizabeth Spencer, which explored all different sides of love: love between parent and child, romantic love, abiding friendship, flirtation, longing, waning love, waxing love. In the role of Margaret Johnson I found a kind of sacred space in which to disappear. I was no less dazzled by the work of our creative team

Victoria Clark and her son, T.L.

and my collaborators as I played this role during the run, for the mastery of their work became *The Light in the Piazza's* Adam Guettel, Ted Sperling, and Bruce Coughlin more and more evident to me with the passage of time.

Our director, Bartlett Sher, crafted the show with nuance; our choreographer, Jonathan Butterell, galvanized the style and subtlety of our movement; our musical director, my friend and longtime colleague Ted Sperling, shaped the score in miraculous detail. My castmates Kelli O'Hara, Matthew Morrison, Mark Harelik, Patti Cohenour, Michael Berresse, Sarah Uriarte Berry, and Beau Gravitte became my new family and taught me both how to lead and to enjoy a long run. Quite simply, it was a magical time.

Everything I wanted to say in my life at that time was somehow sewn into the fabric of *The Light in the Piazza*: grace is possible, forgiveness is possible. A new beginning is possible. My encounter with this fictional character Margaret became deeply personal—it was the meeting of role and soul.

**BILLY CRYSTAL:** Being a Tony winner means a great deal to Janice and myself. That was a project we ended up doing together that was based on my family's history, which ultimately became Janice's also. Working on Broadway to me is the epitome of an actor's talents and commitment. In movies or television, you usually get a chance to do something over again. When you come onstage it is as pure as it gets, and you have to bring it every night. With *700 Sundays* it was two and a half hours of playing different characters and telling the narrative of my family's history, both the joys and the sorrows of it. To be recognized for that meant a great deal.

I couldn't imagine doing the show without Janice. I knew she would be a fantastic producer, which she was, not only creatively with notes and suggestions, but she took the burden off of me for the business side of things. She worked with fellow producer Larry Magid and the Shuberts and the staff at both the Broadhurst and Imperial Theatres. Janice was the pit bull. The Broadhurst is right next to the Shubert Theatre. There's a common alleyway behind. Very often *Spamalot* would come down before we did. There was often noise, which filtered into our theater. Janice would time it and go outside and tell people like Mike Nichols to hold it down.

**JANICE CRYSTAL:** And not to slam the doors!

**BILLY CRYSTAL:** *700 Sundays* was an amazing experience from beginning to end. It was a show that was in preproduction since 1948. It was a show that just hit people. I don't know what their expectations were. Maybe they thought it would be a stand-up show. But it was so much more than that. It's a real play. It's a two-act journey from when I was a little kid up until present day. It was an incredible emotional experience. It was personal and it touched people. Seven hundred Sundays was the sad limit I had with my father over the fifteen years that I knew him. That is a universal message for people and something that bonds us. Loss is loss, and we dealt with it with humor and dignity and the right amount of sentimentality and pathos. It was an honest show, and it struck a chord with people. It didn't matter whether you were a Jewish family, an Italian family, a white family, an African American family… families are families. The dynamic of loving and losing and recovering is a universal theme.

**JANICE CRYSTAL:** A lot of the letters that we received were telling us how cathartic the show was and how it helped them. That was the most rewarding part.

There's nothing like live theatre. I would often watch from the back so I could see the audience's reactions. That was always thrilling, as was seeing the change from show to show. It was exciting when Billy came up with something

700 Sundays' Janice Crystal and Billy Crystal

new, an ad-lib or something, and I would wonder how he came up with it.

**BILLY CRYSTAL:** I just can't come out and be a mimeograph machine and do what I did the night before. I always have to find something new, and the audience leads you there. Their excitement has always made my brain go to a different place and keep it fresh.

Doing eight shows a week on Broadway is very wearing, very tiring, but it's the most innovating and exciting and stimulating thing that any actor can do. The magic of Broadway is amazing. You have these streets, 44th Street, 45th Street, etc., and they're jammed with people ten minutes before showtime, they're all clamoring, and then suddenly, the streets are bare. Everyone's in their theaters experiencing something different. To be part of that, that they're clamoring to see you, they're on line, you hear them from behind the curtain, has never changed for me. I remember being in my first play in third grade, and that experience has never changed. I remember the teachers putting makeup on me and the smell of the powder, and it's still the same. It's all the same. I was always destined for this. It's an amazing thing to experience, to go from the darkness of backstage into the lights and into the audience's consciousness. It's a great thing.

Matthew Broderick and Mike Nichols

Dan Fogler and Rachel Sheinkin from *The 25th Annual Putnam County Spelling Bee*

*Spamalot*'s Sara Ramirez, Eric Idle, and Tim Curry

# WINNERS ◎ 2006

**PLAY:** *The History Boys*, Alan Bennett

Produced by Boyett Ostar Productions, Roger Berlind, Debra Black, Eric Falkenstein,
Roy Furman, Jam Theatricals, Stephanie P. McClelland, Judith Resnick, Scott Rudin,
Jon Avnet/Ralph Guild, Dede Harris/Mort Swinsky, The National Theatre of Great Britain

**MUSICAL:** *Jersey Boys*

Produced by Dodger Theatricals, Joseph J. Grano, Pelican Group, Tamara and Kevin Kinsella,
Latitude Link, Rick Steiner/Osher/Staton/Bell/Mayerson Group

**BOOK OF A MUSICAL:** Bob Martin and Don McKellar, *The Drowsy Chaperone*

**ORIGINAL SCORE (MUSIC AND/OR LYRICS) WRITTEN FOR THE THEATRE:**
Lisa Lambert and Greg Morrison, *The Drowsy Chaperone*

**REVIVAL OF A PLAY:** *Awake and Sing!*

Produced by Lincoln Center Theater, André Bishop, Bernard Gersten

**REVIVAL OF A MUSICAL:** *The Pajama Game*

Produced by Roundabout Theatre Company, Todd Haimes, Harold Wolpert, Julia C. Levy,
Jeffrey Richards, James Fuld Jr., Scott Landis

**ACTOR IN A LEADING ROLE IN A PLAY:** Richard Griffiths, *The History Boys*

**ACTRESS IN A LEADING ROLE IN A PLAY:**
Cynthia Nixon, *Rabbit Hole*

Julia Roberts and Richard Griffiths

Hal Holbrook, Kristen Bell,
and Bernard Gersten

**ACTOR IN A LEADING ROLE IN A MUSICAL:**
John Lloyd Young, *Jersey Boys*

**ACTRESS IN A LEADING ROLE IN A MUSICAL:**
LaChanze, *The Color Purple*

**ACTOR IN A FEATURED ROLE IN A PLAY:**
Ian McDiarmid, *Faith Healer*

**ACTRESS IN A FEATURED ROLE IN A PLAY:** Frances de la Tour, *The History Boys*

**ACTOR IN A FEATURED ROLE IN A MUSICAL:** Christian Hoff, *Jersey Boys*

**ACTRESS IN A FEATURED ROLE IN A MUSICAL:** Beth Leavel, *The Drowsy Chaperone*

**SCENIC DESIGN OF A PLAY:** Bob Crowley, *The History Boys*

**SCENIC DESIGN OF A MUSICAL:** David Gallo, *The Drowsy Chaperone*

**COSTUME DESIGN OF A PLAY:** Catherine Zuber, *Awake and Sing!*

**COSTUME DESIGN OF A MUSICAL:** Gregg Barnes, *The Drowsy Chaperone*

**LIGHTING DESIGN OF A PLAY:** Mark Henderson, *The History Boys*

**LIGHTING DESIGN OF A MUSICAL:** Howell Binkley, *Jersey Boys*

**DIRECTION OF A PLAY:** Nicholas Hytner, *The History Boys*

**DIRECTION OF A MUSICAL:** John Doyle, *Sweeney Todd*

**CHOREOGRAPHY:** Kathleen Marshall, *The Pajama Game*

**ORCHESTRATIONS:** Sarah Travis, *Sweeney Todd*

**SPECIAL TONY AWARD FOR LIFETIME ACHIEVEMENT IN THE THEATRE:** Harold Prince

**REGIONAL THEATRE AWARD:** Intiman Theatre, San Francisco, California

**SPECIAL TONY AWARD:** Sarah Jones

**TONY HONOR:** BMI Lehman Engel Musical Theatre Workshop; *Forbidden Broadway* and Gerard Alessandrini; Samuel (Biff) Liff; Ellen Stewart

Howell Binkley

**BRADLEY KING:** I learned so much from Howell Binkley, specifically how to work fast. He taught me how to sketch it all in and clean it up later. I loved his use of color and his cueing. He had such an amazing musical sensibility about him that I really latched on to.

**DES McANUFF:** Howell was so gifted that he didn't require very much direction. We hit a point some years in where we had telepathic communication. He was very quiet. He assembled a wonderful team; I'm still working with his protégés. He was fiercely devoted to me, and I stuck with him through all kinds of times, thick or thin. I learned a lot from him. I used to call him the pharaoh of the photon. He painted with light and always understood that it was about performance and story. He was a joy to work with and a very dear friend. I miss him every day.

**BARTLETT SHER:** We strategically chose to do *Awake and Sing* at the Belasco Theatre, the same theater it was presented in in 1935. The theater was just about to be renovated—after we were done. Audiences literally were walking into an art installation that was the same one they would have seen it in seventy years earlier.

**KATHLEEN MARSHALL:** A challenge in directing and choreographing *Pajama Game* is "Steam Heat." *Pajama Game* was originally a Bob Fosse show, and "Steam Heat" is probably one of the most famous pieces of theatre choreography ever created. It was a challenge to pay homage but still make it my own. Richard Adler, who wrote the music with Jerry Ross, insisted it still be a trio with bowler hats. I had a different character, Mae, lead the number. It usually was Gladys, originally played by Carol Haney. It didn't make sense to me to have her character in that scene. In doing research of jazz choreography from the 1950s I learned that everybody was doing the same style. Fosse just crystallized it into something much more specific. I realized I could do some of that hunched over style with knock knees and dragging the feet and tucked-in elbows because it wasn't just Fosse. That was 1950s jazz.

**JAMES CORDEN:** The whole experience of doing *The History Boys* was life changing. I signed up to do a play at the National Theatre for six months, and three years later I was living in New York having traveled to Hong Kong and Australia and shot a film and a radio play and made best friends. It was an extraordinary bunch of people. Sometimes you can be in something which is good, but nobody really sees it. Sometimes you can be in something that isn't very good, but commercially it's very successful. And every now and then you can be in something which is critically acclaimed and commercially a smash. That is so rare. *The History Boys* was one of those things. The icing on the cake was from London right the way through New York watching Richard Griffiths win every single Best Actor award he was ever eligible for. It was an amazing time, and we all knew it. We knew this was unique. Often you only know those things retrospectively, but we knew every single day. We did one show in New York where sitting in the same row was David Bowie, James Taylor, and Steven Spielberg. It was extraordinary being in this thing that had become the thing to see. It was never, ever anything less than utterly thrilling.

**MICHAEL DAVID:** Early on, in 1992, we Dodgers produced *The Who's Tommy*. We were excited to bring elements to the show that hadn't been seen on Broadway before. We didn't think about what things cost, only to painfully and to vividly have demonstrated that the key to running is the math and the cost of running weekly. To stay alive. We all feel *Tommy* should still be running in terms of that production, but it couldn't afford itself. And that was sad. The life of *Jersey Boys* is a consequence of the lesson we learned with *Tommy*. It has good math. We saw to it from the start. It was on Broadway for over thirteen years and on the road for almost twenty. We got smarter!

It's thrilling and terrifying to produce a show from scratch. And a joy when the idea you had at the beginning turns out as good or better than you imagined. And of course we've experienced the reverse when we weren't so smart after all. The Dodgers have a history creating what turn out be "warm" hits—when a good show walks the perilous wire from week to week, fighting to keep it from falling off. Finding ways to keep it breathing and keeping audiences coming. We've been fortunate enough to keep a number of shows alive for two to three years. A more satisfying kind of success. Especially for each company's cast and crew—onstage and off—who are counting on you keeping their respective families breathing healthfully too.

LaChanze with Judy Kaye

Christian Hoff

*The History Boys* playwright Alan Bennett (center) with producers including Bil Haber, Roy Furman, and Bob Boyett

# WINNERS ◎ 2007

**PLAY:** *The Coast of Utopia*, Tom Stoppard

Produced by Lincoln Center Theater, André Bishop, Bernard Gersten, Bob Boyett

**MUSICAL:** *Spring Awakening*

Produced by Ira Pittelman, Tom Hulce, Jeffrey Richards, Jerry Frankel, Atlantic Theater Company, Jeffrey Sine, Freddy DeMann, Max Cooper, Mort Swinsky/Cindy and Jay Gutterman/Joe McGinnis/ Judith Ann Abrams, ZenDog Productions/CarJac Productions, Aron Bergson Productions/Jennifer Manocherian/Ted Snowdon, Harold Thau/Terry Schnuck/Cold Spring Productions, Amanda Dubois/ Elizabeth Eynon Wetherell, Jennifer Maloney/Tamara Tunie/Joe Cilibrasi/StyleFour Productions

**BOOK OF A MUSICAL:** Steven Sater, *Spring Awakening*

**ORIGINAL SCORE (MUSIC AND/OR LYRICS) WRITTEN FOR THE THEATRE:** Duncan Sheik (music), Steven Sater (lyrics), *Spring Awakening*

**REVIVAL OF A PLAY:** *Journey's End*

Produced by Boyett Ostar Productions, Stephanie P. McClelland, Bill Rollnick, James D'Orta, Philip Geier

**REVIVAL OF A MUSICAL:** *Company*

Produced by Marc Routh, Richard Frankel, Tom Viertel, Steven Baruch, Ambassador Theatre Group, Tulchin/Bartner Productions, Darren Bagert, Cincinnati Playhouse in the Park

**ACTOR IN A LEADING ROLE IN A PLAY:** Frank Langella, *Frost/Nixon*

Jay Johnson with producers including Robert Alan Gindi and Herbert Goldsmith

**ACTRESS IN A LEADING ROLE IN A PLAY:**
Julie White, *The Little Dog Laughed*

**ACTOR IN A LEADING ROLE IN A MUSICAL:**
David Hyde Pierce, *Curtains*

**ACTRESS IN A LEADING ROLE IN A MUSICAL:**
Christine Ebersole, *Grey Gardens*

**ACTOR IN A FEATURED ROLE IN A PLAY:** Billy Crudup, *The Coast of Utopia*

**ACTRESS IN A FEATURED ROLE IN A PLAY:** Jennifer Ehle, *The Coast of Utopia*

**ACTOR IN A FEATURED ROLE IN A MUSICAL:** John Gallagher Jr., *Spring Awakening*

**ACTRESS IN A FEATURED ROLE IN A MUSICAL:** Mary Louise Wilson, *Grey Gardens*

**SCENIC DESIGN OF A PLAY:** Bob Crowley and Scott Pask, *The Coast of Utopia*

**SCENIC DESIGN OF A MUSICAL:** Bob Crowley, *Mary Poppins*

**COSTUME DESIGN OF A PLAY:** Catherine Zuber, *The Coast of Utopia*

**COSTUME DESIGN OF A MUSICAL:** William Ivey Long, *Grey Gardens*

**LIGHTING DESIGN OF A PLAY:** Brian MacDevitt, Kenneth Posner, and Natasha Katz, *The Coast of Utopia*

**LIGHTING DESIGN OF A MUSICAL:** Kevin Adams, *Spring Awakening*

**DIRECTION OF A PLAY:** Jack O'Brien, *The Coast of Utopia*

**DIRECTION OF A MUSICAL:** Michael Mayer, *Spring Awakening*

**CHOREOGRAPHY:** Bill T. Jones, *Spring Awakening*

**ORCHESTRATIONS:** Duncan Sheik, *Spring Awakening*

**SPECIAL THEATRICAL EVENT:** *Jay Johnson: The Two and Only*

**REGIONAL THEATRE AWARD:** Alliance Theatre, Atlanta, Georgia

**TONY HONOR:** Gemze de Lappe; Alyce Gilbert; Neil Mazzella; Seymour "Red" Press

---

*Spring Awakening*'s Duncan Sheik and Steven Sater

**BILL T. JONES:** My work matters not only Bill T. Jones in the art world, but in the world of advocacy. Arnie Zane was a five-foot-four Jewish Italian man, and with the Bill T. Jones/Arnie Zane Company, he and I were the first same-sex duet couple ever in the world. I'm not just for hire on Broadway. I choose shows that I think are going to inspire discussion in the culture.

There is something about bodies in motion that has a meaning and a mystery that eludes text.

I hope there are questions that we can take on after seventy-five years of Tony Awards. I think there's still work to do to include more people of color on Broadway. I think tickets should be priced in a way that more people can afford to go. The creatives and the producers ultimately shape the tastes of the public.

**JACK O'BRIEN:** It isn't the winning that makes the difference; it's the company you keep. It's the fact that whatever you're doing somehow is registered in the public consciousness to the degree that it's considered to be exceptional. That's enough for anybody.

The thing that I'm proudest of is that my Tony Awards are for all entirely different categories. A show, in an odd way, can only be as good as the season was good. To have survived, to have been accorded a success, and then to be singled out and awarded for it is like the frosting on the cake. For those of us who are in the business of making frosting, we don't expect awards.

**MICHAEL MAYER:** *Spring Awakening* Michael Mayer would not have had anything near the life that it had without those key Tony nominations and those wins. When we started at the O'Neill, ticket sales were terrible. When the show got rave reviews ticket sales went up, but it was not at all what we needed to survive. It wasn't until the Tony nominations came out and we got eleven nominations that the box office took a giant leap. Suddenly we were a contender. I wasn't so concerned with whether or not I was going to win. I understood that the Tony for Best Musical is a guaranteed box office bump. That win gave me the push to keep working on Broadway, trying to make the most risky, provocative, and super creative work I could make.

**ANDRÉ BISHOP:** It was very audacious for us at Lincoln Center Theater to attempt *three plays in repertory* devoted to semi-well-known nineteenth-century Russian intellectuals! *The Coast of Utopia* was so beautiful, and it was so beautifully done and so beautifully designed that it turned into one of our biggest box office hits.

**BILLY CRUDUP:** The part of Belinsky in *Coast of Utopia* is so well written by Tom Stoppard. He's got a monologue in the first play series, and if you don't screw it up, you should win something. It is the kind of speech that brings an audience into the play in such a visceral way. He's the guy who's thumbing his nose at ancestry and heritage and asking articulately and passionately for a better future for the community, the country, the world. I don't think there's any mistaking that there was a correlation between that part and some accolades.

The experience of being in something that people want to see on Broadway while living in New York is as exhilarating and great a feeling as I'm sure anyone in the world can have. *The Coast of Utopia* was a one-of-a-kind, once-in-a-lifetime experience.

**SCOTT PASK:** When I watched the Tonys growing up, I could see the models of the set design and costume design sketches and the lighting designers' work. There was usually some footage where they would go to the studios, and show backstage views of the work in progress. I was fascinated with it all. I don't think I would have had the wherewithal to choose this profession if I had not seen that, because back then I thought it was a bunch of talented people with a very elaborate hobby! The broadcast was so important to me as a child, because it gave me that insight into how these productions happened and seeing the people who were responsible for creating that magical work.

Billy Crudup

Tom Stoppard

John Gallagher Jr.

Mary Louise Wilson

Lead acting winners (L to R) Frank Langella, Christine Ebersole, Julie White, and David Hyde Pierce

Stew

# WINNERS ◎ 2008

**PLAY:** *August: Osage County*, Tracy Letts

Produced by Jeffrey Richards, Jean Doumanian, Steve Traxler, Jerry Frankel,
Ostar Productions, Jennifer Manocherian, The Weinstein Company,
Debra Black/Daryl Roth, Ronald & Marc Frankel/Barbara Freitag,
Rick Steiner/Staton Bell Group, The Steppenwolf Theatre Company

**MUSICAL:** *In the Heights*

Produced by Kevin McCollum, Jeffrey Seller, Jill Furman, Sander Jacobs,
Goodman/Grossman, Peter Fine, Everett/Skipper

**BOOK OF A MUSICAL:** Stew, *Passing Strange*

**ORIGINAL SCORE (MUSIC AND/OR LYRICS) WRITTEN FOR THE THEATRE:**

Lin-Manuel Miranda, *In the Heights*

**REVIVAL OF A PLAY:** *Boeing-Boeing*

Produced by Sonia Friedman Productions, Bob Boyett, Act Productions, Matthew Byam Shaw,
Robert G. Bartner, The Weinstein Company, Susan Gallin/Mary Lu Roffe, Broadway Across America,
Tulchin/Jenkins/DSM, The Araca Group

**REVIVAL OF A MUSICAL:** *Rodgers & Hammerstein's South Pacific*

Produced by Lincoln Center Theater, André Bishop, Bernard Gersten, Bob Boyett

**ACTOR IN A LEADING ROLE IN A PLAY:** Mark Rylance, *Boeing-Boeing*

**ACTRESS IN A LEADING ROLE IN A PLAY:** Deanna Dunagan, *August: Osage County*

**ACTOR IN A LEADING ROLE IN A MUSICAL:**

Paulo Szot, *Rodgers & Hammerstein's South Pacific*

**ACTRESS IN A LEADING ROLE IN A MUSICAL:**

Patti LuPone, *Gypsy*

**ACTOR IN A FEATURED ROLE IN A PLAY:**

Jim Norton, *The Seafarer*

**ACTRESS IN A FEATURED ROLE IN A PLAY:**

Rondi Reed, *August: Osage County*

**ACTOR IN A FEATURED ROLE IN A MUSICAL:**

Boyd Gaines, *Gypsy*

*Gypsy*'s Laura Benanti and Boyd Gaines

ACTRESS IN A FEATURED ROLE IN A MUSICAL:

Laura Benanti, *Gypsy*

SCENIC DESIGN OF A PLAY: Todd Rosenthal, *August: Osage County*

SCENIC DESIGN OF A MUSICAL: Michael Yeargan,
*Rodgers & Hammerstein's South Pacific*

COSTUME DESIGN OF A PLAY: Katrina Lindsay, *Les Liaisons Dangereuses*

COSTUME DESIGN OF A MUSICAL: Catherine Zuber,
*Rodgers & Hammerstein's South Pacific*

LIGHTING DESIGN OF A PLAY: Kevin Adams, *The 39 Steps*

LIGHTING DESIGN OF A MUSICAL: Donald Holder,
*Rodgers & Hammerstein's South Pacific*

SOUND DESIGN OF A PLAY: Mic Pool, *The 39 Steps*

SOUND DESIGN OF A MUSICAL: Scott Lehrer, *Rodgers & Hammerstein's South Pacific*

DIRECTION OF A PLAY: Anna D. Shapiro, *August: Osage County*

DIRECTION OF A MUSICAL: Bartlett Sher, *Rodgers & Hammerstein's South Pacific*

CHOREOGRAPHY: Andy Blankenbuehler, *In the Heights*

ORCHESTRATIONS: Alex Lacamoire and
Bill Sherman, *In the Heights*

SPECIAL TONY AWARD FOR LIFETIME
ACHIEVEMENT IN THE THEATRE:
Stephen Sondheim

REGIONAL THEATRE AWARD: Chicago Shakespeare Theater

SPECIAL TONY AWARD:
Robert Russell Bennett

Jim Norton

Rondi Reed

**TRACY LETTS:** *August: Osage County* started at Steppenwolf Theatre, which is my company in Chicago. I went to our artistic director Martha Lavey and told her I had a play that was three acts with a lot of characters in it. She was very encouraging from the beginning. She was never daunted by the size or the scope of the piece. She had to find some extra money to put it on because it was an expensive production. We could tell from early in previews that we were onto something. I'd never seen audiences so responsive to a piece before. My agent came from New York to Chicago and saw the show. He said, "That's a Broadway play." That had never occurred to me. I was just writing a play for my company. I'd never had a play on Broadway, so I didn't necessarily know what constituted a Broadway play.

My dad was in the original production of *August*. He was an English teacher and became an actor, and I put him in my play on Broadway. It was a wonderful experience. He died during the course of the production, a couple of months before the Tony Awards. The ceremony turned out be on Father's Day, of all things. Bittersweet doesn't even capture it. It was a tough night in a lot of ways. I'm very proud of *August: Osage County* and that production. It felt like such a group effort on the part of Steppenwolf, my theatre company. It was not just my play. It was also a statement about what our theatre company does and what Chicago theatre is and what ensemble theatre is all about. I embraced it very much in that sense.

**JILL FURMAN:** At the end of 2002 an actor I had worked with called me to say I needed to go see this show that was being workshopped in the basement of the Drama Bookshop. He compared it to *Rent*. At that point everything was being compared to *Rent*. I went, and saw a reading of a very, very early version of *In the Heights*. Lin came out onstage, and I was completely blown away by him. I needed to be in his life! He was so young, but so talented. I'd never heard rap onstage like that. I knew he was special.

At that point in the show's development, he had written everything—the book, the music and lyrics. He was green back then, so my partners Kevin McCollum, Jeffrey Seller, and I found a book writer to work with him (Quiara Alegría Hudes). Lin's a genius (I don't use that word lightly), but it was his first time out and so young. We felt that writing the book, lyrics, and music all by himself and starring in it might be biting off more than he could chew.

It was incredible when *In the Heights* won four Tonys, including Best Musical. I got to accept it, which was insane and heady and thrilling! It was one of the most special moments of my life. I believed in Lin's talent early, and I stuck with it. I feel like we changed a lot of people's lives, both onstage and behind the scenes, as well as the audience members who saw themselves up on that stage and realized they can do that too. That's what happened for Lin when he saw *Rent* (which Jeffrey and Kevin produced). *In the Heights* felt like a family from the very beginning.

**BARTLETT SHER:** I directed *South Pacific* in 2008. The show had not been on Broadway for sixty years. The last time it was on Broadway was following World War II. That had an impact on that particular universe. I had to go deep into the text and look at what they were exploring. It wasn't about guys in hula skirts. It was really about race. The more research I did, the more I found that Hammerstein was becoming obsessed with this. That happened in the first year that had a platform on race at the Democratic National Convention. I did other research on what the actual conditions were like in the Navy at the time, especially when it came to segregation of soldiers, etc. It was alarming and shocking to me how intense that was. That helped me develop how deep I wanted the approach to be.

**PATTI LuPONE:** The part of Rose requires a lot of energy. In the first twenty minutes you're shot out of a cannon. I didn't know how I was going to make it. Gillian Lynne recommended a nutritionist, Oz Garcia, who got me through it with vitamins. Rose is brutal physically. I can sing it and I can definitely understand it from an acting standpoint. But the whole show you're gearing up for "Rose's Turn," so you have to be fortified by that point.

Our *Gypsy* started at City Center. On our first day Arthur Laurents (who wrote the book and was directing) brought in his prompt book with the stage management from the production he directed in 1989. He considered that was the last successful production of *Gypsy*, and he wanted to replicate his success. During the first couple of days of rehearsals he would say, "No! This is how you do it." You could see the cast sort of imploding because we were being stifled. We were not being able to discover these parts for ourselves. But Laura Benanti, Boyd Gaines, and I continued to ask him questions about his script, and at some point, it flipped, the director took the hat off and the playwright put the hat on. He was rediscovering his play with the actors he chose. From then on, he had every cast member, down to the absolute smallest part, own their roles. It was joyful, committed, passionate. We did it for the love of Arthur, who did it for the love of his partner, Tom. We had an incredible experience with Arthur Laurents.

**SCOTT LEHRER:** I won the first Tony Award for Sound Design of a Musical in 2008. There had not been a sound design Tony Award prior to that. I think for about fifteen years before then sound designers felt that it was a mature design area, and it was time to be recognized in the same way as the other designers. There really weren't any credited sound designers until the late 1960s when people started to pay more attention to sound, as shows like *Hair* and the early Andrew Lloyd Webber musicals required more sophisticated attention.

Musicals and plays are two different types of design work. Doing sound for a play is much more focused on creating effects and soundscapes. You also often work with a composer or are the music supervisor, finding music that works appropriately for the show for moments like underscores, transitions, and music that plays in scenes as part of the storytelling. In musicals your job is primarily concerned with sonically reinforcing the show, putting microphones on the musical instruments and the actors, and figuring out how to clearly deliver the performance to the audience with a dynamic and sonic quality that's appropriate to the style of the production.

Jean Doumanian, Steve Traxler, David Hawkanson, and Tracy Letts accepting the award for *August: Osage County*

*South Pacific*'s Scott Lehrer and Michael Yeargan

Lead Actors in a Musical winners Paulo Szot and Patti LuPone

Deanna Dunagan

Bartlett Sher

The Sound Design category has been controversial. After several years of giving out the awards, the decision was made to eliminate the category. That was incredibly frustrating and painful for many of us. It took a lot of work, but the award was reinstated four years later. It was important for us to have those sound awards and receive the respect from our community that other design areas had gotten for many years.

It was mind-boggling to win that first Tony. On the one hand, I wondered how this was possible. I had fallen into this career and developed my own system of working. On the other hand, I felt like my work on *South Pacific* was the best I'd ever done for a musical. I cracked the code on doing a musical at the Beaumont with the house sound person Marc Salzberg. People have had a hard time doing sound at the Beaumont. It's hard to get the entire theater properly covered sonically so that all the audience is hearing the show in a similar way at consistent levels and not feeling like it's disassociated from the actors onstage. Marc and I finally figured that out for *South Pacific*. There was also a theatrical coup of Michael Yeargan's and Bart Sher's to have the orchestra revealed as the stage pulled away during the overture. It was a sound designer's dream. Marc and I found a way to support that reveal without it feeling like an obvious sonic effect. We did something sonically there that made the audience feel the orchestra differently as the stage opened up and revealed the musicians without them thinking we just made it louder, creating an enveloping sphere of sound around the audience. Audiences were excited and moved. In response to our vocal reinforcement people would say, "For the first time at the Beaumont I felt like I was actually hearing people singing onstage as if there were no speakers." I felt like I had worked towards that Tony Award for a good part of my career. Everyone's work on *South Pacific* was outstanding. Michael Yeargan's set design and Don Holder's lighting were amazing. As always, Cathy Zuber's costumes were incredible. Bart Sher made *South Pacific* feel like a new show. It's unusual for a revival to sweep the Tonys, and that we were all rewarded for it felt right. *South Pacific* was such an extraordinary experience, and it has meant so much to me and my career. I would never have had a chance to work with Mike Nichols at the end of his life if I hadn't done that show. When he did *Death of a Salesman* he said, "I want the guy who did *South Pacific*."

**KELLI O'HARA:** When the soldiers march off to war at the end of *South Pacific* it's understood by "Honeybun," which is a bright up-tempo song. For our production Bart Sher couldn't change the song, but he could change the tempo. So, these young soldiers and nurses were marching slowly, and possibly going to their deaths. Simply by changing the tempo, that moment had so much more meaning.

**LIN-MANUEL MIRANDA:** For most people, including me, the Tony Awards are your only chance to glimpse Broadway shows. I remember watching and seeing *Rent*, *Bring in 'da Noise, Bring in 'da Funk*. I remember when *Avenue Q* pulled off their stunning upset. That was the first time I ever knew someone on TV winning an award because I went to the same school as Bobby Lopez. At that point I was working on *In the Heights* in the basement of the Drama Bookshop. It was exciting and aspirational to see people not too much older than us accepting their awards. It meant the world to me every time I was nominated. There's something magic about the theatre community coming together at the Tonys every year, and every year it feels like the greatest crossover episode of all time to see all those casts side by side running around backstage. I've now worked for the Tonys in every capacity. I've been a nominee, I've been a presenter, I've been a writer. I was lucky enough to write Neil Patrick Harris's opening number this year. It was the closest I ever got to *The Muppet Show* for real. Our subject matter was every show that season. It was such a joy. Neil Patrick Harris was of course encouraging us to go as big as possible, so Tom Kitt and I went to town, and it actually worked. We had a half hour with each cast, and we didn't rehearse the whole thing with all the casts until the Sunday morning of the event. It really felt like we put together this impossible domino rally, and we had two tries to see if it would work! I don't think I've ever felt the way Tom and I felt when it actually worked and all of the dominos knocked each other down, and the magic trick worked. Neil paused for applause at the Tom Hooper joke so he could catch his breath for the rap section. So many things had to go right in that Rube Goldberg of a number. If he had not made the Hula-Hoop jump in *Pippin*, it could have been over.

Kevin McCollum, Lin-Manuel Miranda, and Jeffrey Seller

Jill Furman was one of the first folks to see *In the Heights* in the basement. She said, "I think what you guys are doing is magical, and more people need to see it." She helped us connect with Ars Nova. That was our first New York production. She was the first person in the theatre world to take a chance on us.

If you're a theatre kid and your school has just cut your art program and you're selling candy so you can get microphones for your school musical—I've been in that position—the Tonys are like oxygen. To get that glimpse of musicals at the highest level. There's going to be someone whose life has changed because they saw some number on that show. Or they saw some acceptance speech on that show that made them feel less alone wherever they were out in the world. I wrote in that opening number for Neil: "'Cause I promise you all of us up here tonight, we were that kid and now we're bigger." That was the way of making "Bigger" mean more than just a big musical number. What we do here can be a rocket that can reverberate and reach someone that we don't even know about yet.

The core creative team writing *In the Heights* were all having their first time at the dance. It was Tommy Kail's first Broadway show, Quiara Alegría Hudes's first Broadway show, Alex Lacamoire's first Broadway show as the main music director, Bill Sherman, Andy Blankenbuehler. The grown-ups were on our design team: Anna Louizos, Nevin Steinberg, Paul Tazewell, and Howell Binkley. Howell was so brilliant at carving with light. He was singular in the way he would create. Our relationship began on *In the Heights*, which is a single set of a neighborhood. I remember asking how we were going to do the interiors, and Tommy said, "Howell is going to make us interiors with light." It was such an education for me about theatre and imagination. I remember also asking in total ignorance as a first-time writer, "I wrote the lyric 'Look at the fireworks,' how are we going to do that? Are we going to do video projections of fireworks?" Tommy said Howell was going to make us fireworks. What was so incredible is what you saw was not literal fireworks. You saw the way the light of the fireworks spilled off of the actors' faces as they looked out into the house. It was so much more evocative and beautiful than the literal answer. We took that to the *n*th degree on *Hamilton* with seventy different scenes over a hundred years and it was a single set. Howell and Tommy really carved those together. Howell was the kindest, most patient soul. He had candy at his tech table. I would always go over. He noticed that I would always take the Reese's Peanut Butter Cups. The next day it was all Reese's Peanut Butter Cups. That's like something your grandparents would do when they find out you love something. That's who Howell was.

I just love our people. Honestly, who gives better speeches than theatre kids? We should never be played off. I love how honest-to-God happy we are to be at the Tonys and what a joy it is.

**ALEX LACAMOIRE:** I was working at *Wicked* when we started *In the Heights*, so I had seen what it takes to put up a new musical on Broadway. I knew what it took to finish something quickly, what it took to not rest until something was perfect, what it took to be responsible and accountable and meet the deadlines, and work around the clock. When it came time for me to be in the driver's seat with *In the Heights* I knew what it was going to be like, and I felt like I could do it. It didn't feel outside of my reach.

It's always a different experience working with different composers, but what doesn't change is the act of me being a conduit for them. The composers I've been fortunate enough to work with, I feel like I can read their minds enough, and I feel like I hear their music and instinctively have a point of view about it. There are moments of self-doubt and uncertainty, but at the core I had enough of a true understanding of what the writers were going for, such that when it came time to put pen to paper, or put mouse to screen, I knew what to do. I had enough of a knowledge about how a band works to be able to put those songs to life. Whether that was the vocal arrangement or the band makeup, it's just chemistry. It just clicks. With Lin-Manuel and Pasek and Paul, I just knew.

My voice as a writer is really present in *In the Heights* because Lin was gracious enough to leave that space for me to put my imprint on it. That's a rare thing. Lin welcomes that kind of collaboration and highlights it. Not all composers are willing to share that kind of glory and attention. I'm very lucky that Lin and also Justin and Benj on *Dear Evan Hansen* were able to give me some shine in that way.

# WINNERS ◎ 2009

**PLAY:** *God of Carnage*, Yasmina Reza

Produced by Robert Fox, David Pugh & Dafydd Rogers, Stuart Thompson, Scott Rudin, Jon B. Platt, The Weinstein Company, The Shubert Organization

**MUSICAL:** *Billy Elliot, the Musical*

Produced by Universal Pictures Stage Productions, Working Title Films, Old Vic Productions, Weinstein Live Entertainment

**BOOK OF A MUSICAL:** Lee Hall, *Billy Elliot, the Musical*

**ORIGINAL SCORE (MUSIC AND/OR LYRICS) WRITTEN FOR THE THEATRE:** Tom Kitt (music), Brian Yorkey (lyrics), *Next to Normal*

**REVIVAL OF A PLAY:** *The Norman Conquests*

Produced by Sonia Friedman Productions, Steven Baruch, Marc Routh, Richard Frankel, Tom Viertel, Dede Harris, Tulchin/Bartner/Lauren Doll, Jamie deRoy, Eric Falkenstein, Harriet Newman Leve, Probo Productions, Douglas G. Smith, Michael Filerman/Jennifer Manocherian, Richard Winkler, Dan Frishwasser, Pam Laudenslager/Remmel T. Dickinson, Jane Dubin/True Love Productions, Barbara Manocherian/Jennifer Isaacson, The Old Vic Theatre Company

**REVIVAL OF A MUSICAL:** *Hair*

Produced by The Public Theater; Oskar Eustis; Andrew D. Hamingson; Jeffrey Richards; Jerry Frankel; Gary Goddard Entertainment; Kathleen K. Johnson; Nederlander Productions, Inc.; Fran Kirmser Productions/ Jed Bernstein; Marc Frankel; Broadway Across America; Barbara Manocherian/Wencarlar Productions; JK Productions/Terry Schnuck; Andy Sandberg; Jam Theatricals; The Weinstein Company/Norton Herrick; Jujamcyn Theaters; Joey Parnes; Elizabeth Ireland McCann

*Billy Elliot*'s Lee Hall, Elton John, and Peter Darling

**ACTOR IN A LEADING ROLE IN A PLAY:** Geoffrey Rush, *Exit the King*

**ACTRESS IN A LEADING ROLE IN A PLAY:** Marcia Gay Harden, *God of Carnage*

**ACTOR IN A LEADING ROLE IN A MUSICAL:** David Alvarez, Trent Kowalik, and Kiril Kulish, *Billy Elliot, the Musical*

**ACTRESS IN A LEADING ROLE IN A MUSICAL:** Alice Ripley, *Next to Normal*

**ACTOR IN A FEATURED ROLE IN A PLAY:** Roger Robinson, *Joe Turner's Come and Gone*

**ACTRESS IN A FEATURED ROLE IN A PLAY:** Angela Lansbury, *Blithe Spirit*

**ACTOR IN A FEATURED ROLE IN A MUSICAL:** Gregory Jbara, *Billy Elliot, the Musical*

**ACTRESS IN A FEATURED ROLE IN A MUSICAL:** Karen Olivo, *West Side Story*

**SCENIC DESIGN OF A PLAY:** Derek McLane, *33 Variations*

**SCENIC DESIGN OF A MUSICAL:** Ian MacNeil, *Billy Elliot, the Musical*

**COSTUME DESIGN OF A PLAY:** Anthony Ward, *Mary Stuart*

**COSTUME DESIGN OF A MUSICAL:** Tim Hatley, *Shrek the Musical*

**LIGHTING DESIGN OF A PLAY:** Brian MacDevitt, *Joe Turner's Come and Gone*

**LIGHTING DESIGN OF A MUSICAL:** Rick Fisher, *Billy Elliot, the Musical*

**SOUND DESIGN OF A PLAY:** Gregory Clarke, *Equus*

**SOUND DESIGN OF A MUSICAL:** Paul Arditti, *Billy Elliot, the Musical*

**DIRECTION OF A PLAY:** Matthew Warchus, *God of Carnage*

**DIRECTION OF A MUSICAL:** Stephen Daldry, *Billy Elliot, the Musical*

**CHOREOGRAPHY:** Peter Darling, *Billy Elliot, the Musical*

**ORCHESTRATIONS:** Martin Koch, *Billy Elliot, the Musical*; Michael Starobin and Tom Kitt, *Next to Normal*

**SPECIAL THEATRICAL EVENT:** *Liza's at the Palace*

**SPECIAL TONY AWARD FOR LIFETIME ACHIEVEMENT IN THE THEATRE:** Jerry Herman

**ISABELLE STEVENSON AWARD:** Phyllis Newman

**REGIONAL THEATRE AWARD:** Signature Theatre, Arlington, Virginia

**TONY HONOR:** Shirley Herz

Roger Robinson

David Alvarez, Kiril Kulish, and Trent Kowalik winning for alternating in the role of *Billy Elliot*

Derek McLane and Brian
MacDevitt

**DEREK McLANE:** Winning the Tony is so meaningful because it means the people in my work community recognized my design. It's a very different thing from the appreciation of the general public or a critic. These are people that I love, but also people with whom I have sometimes complicated, competitive relationships. Getting that recognition from that group of people feels very special. It is a profound feeling of belonging.

*33 Variations* made me appreciate the value of experimenting. Moisés Kaufman wrote and directed the show, and when I started designing, it didn't have a fully formed plot yet, which is often how Moisés works. It was a series of scenes that eventually turned into a story. I designed the set that served as a kind of kit of parts. One of the main features of the set was about three thousand gray cardboard boxes. Another was hundreds of pages of hanging sheet music. The challenge became how to make these extremely plain things look beautiful. It was an interesting box to design myself into and then find my way out of.

**OSKAR EUSTIS:** I had been thinking about a revival of

*Hair* even before I came to the Public, but it just seemed to need a powerful raison d'être. I arrived at the Public two years before the show's fortieth anniversary. That was a great reason to revive *Hair*. I wanted to do a concert version. I had always felt that there was a *Hair* inside *Hair* that had never entirely come out. We did *Hamlet* and *Hair* in the park in the summer of 2008. The publicity department asked me for blurbs. I sent them one, and they thanked me for sending one for *Hamlet*, but they also needed one for *Hair*. I said, "It is a synopsis of *Hair* too. Same story." That idea of a young man who is completely disillusioned with his elders and the way the country is being run, who knows that something terrible is going on but doesn't really know the right way to oppose it, ultimately tries to, but fails and dies. That's *Hamlet*. And that's *Hair*. I thought if we viewed *Hair* through the lens of *Hamlet*, if we viewed it as a tragedy all the way through, not a pure celebration of the hippie lifestyle but simultaneously a celebration and elegy for what these kids of this generation couldn't do, we could come up with something beautiful. Fortunately, Jim Rado and Galt MacDermot were happy to keep working on it.

Oskar Eustis and the cast of *Hair*

Geoffrey Rush

Lead Actress winners Alice Ripley and Marcia Gay Harden

# ACCEPTANCE SPEECHES THROUGH THE YEARS

*Thank God for letting me live this long to be here.* **BILL McCUTCHEON (1988)**

**ANN REINKING (1997):** This is such a curious thing to do, to decide you want to be a dancer for the rest of your life. And then realize you can't be a dancer for the rest of your life. It's a curious thing that dancers must do. It's sort of an unwritten law, and we're supposed to pass on what we know and give back. I can't thank you enough for this opportunity....I thank the opportunity to give back. I thank my teachers. I thank the one man who stood up for me so many times. This one's for you, Bobby.

**MAURICE CHEVALIER (ON THE EVE OF HIS EIGHTIETH BIRTHDAY, 1968):** I want to thank the American public and the American show people and the American critics for having helped me feel that life and the theatre can still be more marvelous at eighty years of age than before.

**L. SCOTT CALDWELL (1988):** I'm accepting this award for the entire *Joe Turner* company and family and also for all of the actors everywhere who are dreaming and hoping. This is for all of us.

**B.D. WONG (1988):** I also thank the most important teacher and friend and a beautiful man into whose eyes I look every night at the Eugene O'Neill Theatre and see two kinds of love. The love of a poor deluded white devil for his butterfly, and the love of a seasoned professional brilliant actor for his young protégé.

**DOUG BESTERMAN (2002):** The passing of Ralph Burns last November was a tremendous loss to the musical theatre community, but it was particularly felt by the creative team of *Thoroughly Modern Millie*, for whom he was a cherished collaborator. Ralph's career spanned six decades, and he was probably most well known for his work with Woody Herman and then his collaborations with the director Bob Fosse, which included musicals such as *Sweet Charity, Chicago, Dancin'*, and the film *All That Jazz*. I first met Ralph working on the Broadway show *Fosse*, and three years ago had the privilege of sharing this stage with him. I'm sad to be here without him this evening. But the opportunity to continue the work on *Thoroughly Modern Millie* that he began will surely remain one of the highlights of my career.

Linda Lavin, John Randolph, and Kathleen Turner

**JOHN RANDOLPH (1987):** I'm just honored and excited to get this award. You know, I didn't go into acting to win any awards. I just couldn't do anything else. And being honored by your colleagues and peers with a Tony is worth forty-seven years of struggling as an actor. I must thank Neil Simon for the seventy-seven-year-old colorful rebel I play, who is so beautifully written with humor. And representing those of us who have passed seventy on this earth as still being filled with life and fighting spirit no matter what shape the body looks like on the outside.... I'm glad I'm back in the theatre world again, our first love that sustained us through rough times. Peace, love, and brown rice to all of you.

> To Jon—Jonathan Larson—whom I often dreamed of moments like this, with him. I know you're here tonight, so this is for you.
>
> **ROGER BART (1999)**

Bernadette Peters and Jackie Mason

Roger Bart and William Hurt

**TONY KUSHNER (1994):** Twenty-five years ago, on June 27, the night Judy Garland was laid to rest, was the Stonewall uprising, which marked the official beginning of the gay and lesbian liberation movement. I'd like to dedicate this award tonight to my gay and lesbian brothers the world over who are fighting for both a cure and for citizenship.

**JACKIE MASON (1987):** I don't know who to thank for this. Nobody believed in this whole show. I'd like to thank my cast, but I got no cast. I'd like to thank the director, I'd like to thank the writer, but I'm the director and I'm the writer. I don't think it looks nice for me to thank myself. I'll tell you the truth if not for me there would be no show here at all….I feel like Ronald Reagan right now. Because Ronald Reagan, let's be honest about it, he was an actor all his life, knew nothing about politics and became the president of the United States. Here I am, an ex-rabbi who knew nothing about acting, and I'm holding a Tony Award in my hand. It proves an amazing thing: that if you don't know what to do and you don't know what you're doing at all, you can become the biggest man in your field.

Tony Kushner and Stephen Spinella

# the '20 10s

*Fela!*'s Robert Kaplowitz and Lillias White

Sean Hayes and Levi Kreis at the piano

# WINNERS ◎ 2010

**PLAY:** *Red*, John Logan

Produced by Arielle Tepper Madover, Stephanie P. McClelland, Matthew Byam Shaw, Neal Street, Fox Theatricals, Ruth Hendel/Barbara Whitman, Philip Hagemann/Murray Rosenthal, The Donmar Warehouse

**MUSICAL:** *Memphis*

Produced by Junkyard Dog Productions; Barbara and Buddy Freitag; Marleen and Kenny Alhadeff; Latitude Link; Jim and Susan Blair; Demos Bizar Entertainment; Land Line Productions; Apples and Oranges Productions; Dave Copley; Dancap Productions, Inc.; Alex and Katya Lukianov; Tony Ponturo; 2 Guys Productions; Richard Winkler; Lauren Doll; Eric and Marsi Gardiner; Linda and Bill Potter; Broadway Across America; Jocko Productions; Patty Baker; Dan Frishwasser; Bob Bartner/Scott and Kaylin Union; Loraine Boyle/Chase Mishkin; Remmel T. Dickinson/Memphis Orpheum Group; ShadowCatcher Entertainment/Vijay and Sita Vashee

**BOOK OF A MUSICAL:** Joe DiPietro, *Memphis*

**ORIGINAL SCORE (MUSIC AND/OR LYRICS) WRITTEN FOR THE THEATRE:**
David Bryan (music), Joe DiPietro and David Bryan (lyrics), *Memphis*

**REVIVAL OF A PLAY:** *Fences*

Produced by Carole Shorenstein Hays, Scott Rudin

**REVIVAL OF A MUSICAL:** *La Cage aux Folles*

Produced by Sonia Friedman Productions; David Babani; Barry and Fran Weissler and Edwin W. Schloss; Bob Bartner/Norman Tulchin; Broadway Across America; Matthew Mitchell; Raise The Roof 4 Richard Winkler/Bensinger Taylor/Laudenslager Bergère; Arelene Scanlan/John O'Boyle; Independent Presenters Network; OlympusTheatricals; Allen Spivak; Jerry Frankel/Bat-Barry Productions; NederlanderPresentations, Inc./Harvey Weinstein; Menier Chocolate Factory

**ACTOR IN A LEADING ROLE IN A PLAY:** Denzel Washington, *Fences*

**ACTRESS IN A LEADING ROLE IN A PLAY:** Viola Davis, *Fences*

**ACTOR IN A LEADING ROLE IN A MUSICAL:** Douglas Hodge, *La Cage aux Folles*

**ACTRESS IN A LEADING ROLE IN A MUSICAL:**
Catherine Zeta-Jones, *A Little Night Music*

**ACTOR IN A FEATURED ROLE IN A PLAY:** Eddie Redmayne, *Red*

ACTRESS IN A FEATURED ROLE IN A PLAY:
Scarlett Johansson, *A View from the Bridge*

ACTOR IN A FEATURED ROLE IN A MUSICAL:
Levi Kreis, *Million Dollar Quartet*

ACTRESS IN A FEATURED ROLE IN A MUSICAL:
Katie Finneran, *Promises, Promises*

SCENIC DESIGN OF A PLAY: Christopher Oram, *Red*

SCENIC DESIGN OF A MUSICAL: Christine Jones, *American Idiot*

COSTUME DESIGN OF A PLAY: Catherine Zuber, *The Royal Family*

COSTUME DESIGN OF A MUSICAL: Marina Draghici, *Fela!*

LIGHTING DESIGN OF A PLAY: Neil Austin, *Red*

LIGHTING DESIGN OF A MUSICAL: Kevin Adams, *American Idiot*

SOUND DESIGN OF A PLAY: Adam Cork, *Red*

SOUND DESIGN OF A MUSICAL: Robert Kaplowitz, *Fela!*

DIRECTION OF A PLAY: Michael Grandage, *Red*

DIRECTION OF A MUSICAL: Terry Johnson, *La Cage aux Folles*

CHOREOGRAPHY: Bill T. Jones, *Fela!*

ORCHESTRATIONS: Daryl Waters and
David Bryan, *Memphis*

SPECIAL TONY AWARD FOR LIFETIME
ACHIEVEMENT IN THE THEATRE:
Alan Ayckbourn; Marian Seldes

ISABELLE STEVENSON AWARD: David Hyde Pierce

REGIONAL THEATRE AWARD:
The Eugene O'Neill Theater
Center, Waterford, Connecticut

TONY HONOR: Alliance of Resident Theatres/
New York; B.H. Barry; Midtown North &
South New York City Police
Precincts; Tom Viola

David Hyde Pierce and
Kelsey Grammer

Michael Douglas and Catherine Zeta-Jones

2010 · 203

Sean Hayes, Katie Finneran, and Kristin Chenoweth

Ellen Barkin and Don Cheadle

*Fences*'s Viola Davis and Denzel Washington

Lifetime Achievement winners Marian Seldes and Alan Ayckbourn

Adam Cork, Christopher Oram, Michael Grandage, John Logan, and Arielle Tepper Madover of *Red*

**BILL T. JONES:** When we decided that *Fela!* would be centered in Fela's historic, legendary shrine, I wanted someone to help me think through what the shrine was physically and as a state of mind. We were also looking for ways that the dramaturgy could be on the walls of the theater. We wanted it to be immersive; we wanted the show to begin when people walked in. Marina (Draghici) and her team of Romanian street artists graffitied the set. She did a brilliant job with the costumes as well. The Nigerian women in the play looked the way they did because Marina was up in Harlem at the location that African women themselves might go to find gele cloth. She studied how it was done, and we brought it to Broadway. Working with Marina was very exciting. It almost felt like an art project.

**JOHN LOGAN:** Winning a Tony was like all the childhood dreams come true. I was one of those theatre kids. I spent my junior high and high school years in Milburn, New Jersey, and I always went to see Broadway and Off-Broadway shows on the weekends. I'd go to the TKTS booth, and the great things about that was the fact that you didn't know what you'd be seeing until you got to the front of that line. They had placards there with the names of the available shows on them. It was a wonderful surprise grab bag of theatre. Sometimes it was *Sweeney Todd*, and sometimes it was *Key Exchange* at Circle in the Square. It was great.

I was the kid who watched the Tonys every year. It was so exciting. It seemed to me the quintessence of glamour. I still remember to this day Angela Lansbury and Bea Arthur doing a number together. You would see all the big shows performed, but then you'd also see a number from a show like *Big Deal* (the Bob Fosse show that only ran for two months). It's preserved there forever. Now we can see it on YouTube. I remember and cherish those moments, so to actually be invited to the Tonys was amazing.

Winning an award myself was a lovely thing. But seeing the people I worked with win awards was equally gratifying. When you work in theatre, you're in the trenches together. There are no privates or generals. The fact that other people have been inspired by my work and I've been able to give them the opportunity to do something magnificent on their own is the best thing in the world. We all made the show together.

Anytime your peers value and appreciate your work it's valuable. I grew up as a theatre rat, so everything in the theatre is more meaningful to me than it is in movies or TV. That's my DNA. I still wake up as a playwright every day who gets the nice opportunity to work on movies.

A play can exist entirely on dialogue and metaphor and character. The temporal reality of the theatre is very different than the temporal reality of cinema. A movie can have quick cuts and flash pans, while in the theatre you're watching a story evolve in real time.

I was in London working on the movie of *Sweeney Todd*, and I would go to the Tate frequently. I found Rothko's Seagram murals so moving and powerful. I read the description on the gallery wall of how Rothko painted them. I instantly knew it was a two-hander play. I spent a year researching. It wasn't only the biographical research about Rothko; it was also learning everything about painting—which I knew nothing about. Rothko was a very scholarly painter and deeply aware of the painters that came before him. To understand Rothko you have to understand Manet, Monet, El Greco. You have to understand the artists that influenced him.

**MICHAEL GRANDAGE:** The theatre year is more formally structured in New York than it is anywhere else in the world. The Tony Awards are designed to be at the end of a season, so there is a palpable sense of something coming to a conclusion. A big, glamorous prize-giving ceremony in June allows the industry to take a breather over the summer months before starting again in the fall. It feels entirely different to how we work in the UK, where the Olivier Awards are part of the more general awards season honoring the previous year and where there is no real sense of a cutoff point. Both have their merits, and both seem to represent the needs of the theatregoing public in each country.

The moment I read John Logan's script, I knew I wanted to direct *Red* at the Donmar, where I was artistic director at the time. It spoke to the nature of creative energy in a very profound way, but it also had something important to say about mentorship. I have always believed good mentorship should never be about an older person just giving information to a younger person. It should work

both ways, and at the end of the relationship, the more senior figure should have learned just as much as the younger person. The play articulates this beautifully—Rothko is too much of an egotist to consider he is being mentored or is even receiving information, but by the end, he has learned as much as his pupil.

We cast Eddie Redmayne, who at the time was on the rise here in the UK, and as Rothko, I asked Alfred Molina. There was never anyone else even to consider, to be honest. It was fascinating that one of our American producers—Stephanie McClelland—said, "You're sitting on something here that is much bigger than you know. This will resonate in America more than it's resonating here." In England, we like the underdog story, so we were backing the Eddie Redmayne character a lot more. But another of our American producers, Arielle Tepper, said, "We want to know about Rothko. He's a New Yorker. In America we will take both those characters and bring them to ourselves. Here in England, you are enjoying it, but this would be much bigger in America." They were both right. The reviews were infinitely more celebratory in New York.

Arielle Tepper flew in all of the seven nominees to attend the Tony Awards. She didn't need to, but she did. It was one of the most special evening of our lives. *Red* was a piece of work that we were all incredibly proud of. On the night, it was the biggest Tony winner. That production with only two actors won more Tony Awards than Best Musical. It felt like

a thank-you for bringing the show to America. I think that moment of appreciation meant more than anything we'd ever had. It was only in America, through the Tonys, that we understood how big that show was to so many people. *Red* is a truly glorious journey from start to finish.

**CHRISTOPHER ORAM:** The Golden Theatre is one of the more intimate Broadway houses, which worked well for *Red*. It made it easy to blend the world of the play into the auditorium without having to cross the proscenium. The play would have gotten lost in a bigger theater.

An artists' studio is a beautiful, creative space. Rothko's studio though was as much a functional factory for making his work rather than an aesthetic space. It was an industrial space. The studio that we recreated was on the Bowery. The building is still there. It used to be the YMCA, the old gymnasium, so it was a room he repurposed. That was the attitude that we took with the design.

**JOE DiPIETRO:** The day after I won a Tony Award I wasn't a better writer, but everyone else thought I was.

# WINNERS ◎ 2011

Lily and David Rabe

**PLAY:** *War Horse*, Nick Stafford

Produced by Lincoln Center Theater, André Bishop, Bernard Gersten, National Theatre of Great Britain, Nicholas Hytner, Nick Starr, Bob Boyett, War Horse LP

**MUSICAL:** *The Book of Mormon*

Produced by Anne Garefino, Scott Rudin, Roger Berlind, Scott M. Delman, Jean Doumanian, Roy Furman, Important Musicals LLC, Stephanie P. McClelland, Kevin Morris, Jon B. Platt, Sonia Friedman Productions, Stuart Thompson

**BOOK OF A MUSICAL:** Trey Parker, Robert Lopez, and Matt Stone, *The Book of Mormon*

**ORIGINAL SCORE (MUSIC AND/OR LYRICS) WRITTEN FOR THE THEATRE:**
Trey Parker, Robert Lopez, and Matt Stone, *The Book of Mormon*

**REVIVAL OF A PLAY:** *The Normal Heart*

Produced by Daryl Roth, Paul Boskind, Martian Entertainment, Gregory Rae, Jayne Baron Sherman/Alexander Fraser

George C. Wolfe, Larry Kramer, William David Webster, and Joe Mantello

**REVIVAL OF A MUSICAL:** *Anything Goes*

Produced by Roundabout Theatre Company, Todd Haimes, Harold Wolpert, Julia C. Levy

**ACTOR IN A LEADING ROLE IN A PLAY:** Mark Rylance, *Jerusalem*

**ACTRESS IN A LEADING ROLE IN A PLAY:** Frances McDormand, *Good People*

**ACTOR IN A LEADING ROLE IN A MUSICAL:** Norbert Leo Butz, *Catch Me If You Can*

**ACTRESS IN A LEADING ROLE IN A MUSICAL:**
Sutton Foster, *Anything Goes*

**ACTOR IN A FEATURED ROLE IN A PLAY:**
John Benjamin Hickey, *The Normal Heart*

**ACTRESS IN A FEATURED ROLE IN A PLAY:**
Ellen Barkin, *The Normal Heart*

**ACTOR IN A FEATURED ROLE IN A MUSICAL:**
John Larroquette, *How to Succeed in Business without Really Trying*

*Anything Goes*'s Adam Godley, Kathleen Marshall, and Derek McLane

Rae Smith

**ACTRESS IN A FEATURED ROLE IN A MUSICAL:** Nikki M. James, *The Book of Mormon*

**SCENIC DESIGN OF A PLAY:** Rae Smith, *War Horse*

**SCENIC DESIGN OF A MUSICAL:** Scott Pask, *The Book of Mormon*

**COSTUME DESIGN OF A PLAY:** Desmond Heeley, *The Importance of Being Earnest*

**COSTUME DESIGN OF A MUSICAL:** Tim Chappel and Lizzy Gardiner, *Priscilla Queen of the Desert*

**LIGHTING DESIGN OF A PLAY:** Paule Constable, *War Horse*

**LIGHTING DESIGN OF A MUSICAL:** Brian MacDevitt, *The Book of Mormon*

**SOUND DESIGN OF A PLAY:** Christopher Shutt, *War Horse*

**SOUND DESIGN OF A MUSICAL:** Brian Ronan, *The Book of Mormon*

**DIRECTION OF A PLAY:** Marianne Elliott and Tom Morris, *War Horse*

**DIRECTION OF A MUSICAL:** Casey Nicholaw and Trey Parker, *The Book of Mormon*

**CHOREOGRAPHY:** Kathleen Marshall, *Anything Goes*

**ORCHESTRATIONS:** Larry Hochman and Stephen Oremus, *The Book of Mormon*

**SPECIAL TONY AWARD FOR LIFETIME ACHIEVEMENT IN THE THEATRE:** Athol Fugard; Philip J. Smith

**ISABELLE STEVENSON AWARD:** Eve Ensler

**REGIONAL THEATRE AWARD:** Lookingglass Theatre Company, Chicago, Illinois

**SPECIAL TONY AWARD:** Handspring Puppet Company

**TONY HONOR:** William Berloni; The Drama Book Shop; Sharon Jensen and Alliance for Inclusion in the Arts

___

Tim Chappel and Lizzy Gardiner with costumes they designed for *Priscilla Queen of the Desert*

**CASEY NICHOLAW:** Trey Parker and Matt Stone do satire so well, and their writing is always smart. For me as a director it's so much easier to stage something that's smart and makes sense and is funny. I came to *Book of Mormon* somewhat late in the process. Matt and Trey and Bobby Lopez had been working on the show a long time, so I was able to be fresh eyes for them. They were wonderful partners. It was a fantastic time and a very creative collaboration. I was so happy when the show won so many Tonys. We're all part of each other's success with the show. It was a very emotional night for me—winning a Tony was a childhood dream come true. But I never dreamed it would be for directing an original musical! I got to thank my parents on national TV. They were the ones that gave me the love of theatre. They weren't in theatre, but had four show albums that I wore out when I was growing up, and that was the start of the obsession for me!

**SCOTT PASK:** I grew up with such modest beginnings, and wasn't exposed to much theatre—and could never have imagined that winning a Tony Award was even a realistic dream to have. I considered it beyond the realm of reality to even be working in the business, so to be a Tony winner stretches beyond my wildest dreams.

**NIKKI M. JAMES:** Six months before I won the Tony Award, I had a side gig as a shopgirl selling lipstick because I wanted extra money to buy Christmas gifts for my family. The thought of that makes me emotional because it illustrates the true story of both an overnight success and years and years of hard work. By the time I won the Tony I had been working on Broadway for ten years.

When I was growing up in New Jersey, my best friend Shannon and I would have our private Tony Award party every year. We'd have Smarties candies, Diet Coke, and Baked Lay's. We would record the show on VHS and then play it back so we could memorize the speeches and the performances. We were so obsessed with the Tonys and the theatre community. To a twelve-year-old me, winning a Tony shows that dreams come true, and to the adult me, that win is a testament to everyone's work on the show.

That was a very special collection of people. I remain close with them. I did not feel like it was my award; I felt like it was an award for every single person who had worked on that show. It was a real family. I stayed at a hotel that night, and the next morning there was a knock on my door. It was a messenger who was there to pick up the dress and the shoes and the jewelry and the bag because it was all borrowed. That was a stark reminder of the fleeting nature of the win. But on the other hand, winning that award was like being knighted. Your name changes for the rest of your life. I'm now Tony Award winner Nikki M. James.

I felt and continue to feel a huge sense of responsibility to go out there every night and deliver a performance that was worthy of this title. Those first couple of months after was the first time in my life I ever had stage fright. I feel like I'm part of a legacy. I won in 2011, and more women have been added to that list of names. I'm counted among these incredible artists who get to share this unique honor. I wrote a song with my friend Amy Wolk called "The Ladies Who Tony," where I make a rhyme with every woman who's won Best Featured Actress in a Musical. There's Lotte Lenya, Melba Moore, Lena Hall. It's a long song. When you hear the names of these women, it's inspiring.

**TREY PARKER:** Our first experience with a musical with *South Park* was the Mr. Hanky Christmas show. It was a twenty-minute musical, and we thought we should do a bigger version of that, which was the *South Park* movie. Like everything we do, we thought it would be the last thing we did in Hollywood, so we figured we'd do exactly what we wanted. Musicals were not popular when we made the *South Park* movie.

**MATT STONE:** With the *South Park* movie we were making fun of the Disney formula. Ours was a demented or bizarro version of that. It was important to us that it actually be a good musical.

**TREY PARKER:** If you look at all the marketing material it almost never said it was a musical. They thought if people knew they wouldn't want to see it.

**MATT STONE:** They definitely didn't want us to say it was a musical, but then Trey got nominated for an Academy Award for Best Music! The conventional wisdom was that

Brian Bedford and Mark Rylance

Anne Garefino and Casey Nicholaw with their Tonys for *The Book of Mormon*

Nikki M. James

*The Book of Mormon*'s Trey Parker and Matt Stone

the typical fans of *South Park*, sixteen-to-twenty-year-old boys, were not going to want to see a musical. But they were wrong.

**TREY PARKER:** We knew we wanted to do a musical about Mormons. At first, we were thinking in terms of a movie, because that's what we knew. We met Bobby Lopez and discussed musicals in general, and he said that he had always wanted to do a musical about *Mormons!* We wrote the songs first because we wanted the songs to matter so much that if you took one out, the show would no longer make sense. Bobby was the one that taught us how a musical is put together. We'd never heard of doing a workshop, but we followed Bobby's lead. There was a moment when we just decided to put it onstage, that it was meant for the theatre.

Since the music was critical, we decided to make an album. Matt and Bobby and I would get together and talk about each song. We'd discuss the jokes and how the songs would move the story forward. We'd workshop each song until we had eight songs. I played them for my dad, who had no idea what the show was about. And he understood what the show was, just by listening to those eight songs.

**MATT STONE:** We had story meetings where we discussed ideas. An early idea was to do a Joseph Smith musical, but that ultimately didn't feel right. Somehow missionaries came up. That clean-cut Mormon aesthetic is so cheesy. If you go to their churches, it's like being in the 1950s. We thought the idea of sending these two missionaries somewhere challenging would work. We could flash back and learn about Mormons, but the world of the play would be today's world.

The characters being missionaries provided a lot of reasons for them to address the audience and sing to them that seemed natural.

**TREY PARKER:** That's what missionaries do; they approach people and try to talk to them. Casey Nicholaw was a huge help. We knew we were in good hands when he came on. We learned a lot from him as well as from Bobby Lopez.

**MATT STONE:** We usually don't ever watch our stuff in the presence of other people. We do it and it goes on TV.

When *South Park* shows on Wednesday nights, we're doing something else. When we started doing the first workshops of *Book of Mormon*, there were thirty of our friends there. It was like doing a high-wire act worrying about whether something would go wrong. I remember how emotionally intense it was when we went into previews. It was going great, but I was still worried and then relieved when they made it through another show!

**TREY PARKER:** There was this sense of nervousness from the company about how Mormons would react to the show. Would they try to burn the theater down? We knew better. We told them, "Mormons kill you with niceness; they don't burn down buildings."

Tony night was very special. What made it so fun was everyone feeling that reward and getting that accolade. When we started out, people would say, "What are you guys doing? You have a successful TV show. You could go make a movie. Why are you wasting your time on Broadway? That community isn't going to like this." We were warned that there would be a lot of old people in the audience. We were around forty at the time, so not spring chickens! I remember watching the kind of people they described in the theater turning to each other and laughing. That was when I knew we were going to be fine.

**MATT STONE:** It was amazing that we had the opportunity to do a Broadway show. It's tough to pull off. It took us seven years to write.

**TREY PARKER:** Everyone we worked on *Book of Mormon* with are just dear friends now. We felt the love from the company and could see how much fun everyone was having. It was an amazing group of people and a fantastic experience.

**SUTTON FOSTER:** I was intimidated by Reno Sweeney; she was probably my scariest role. I struggled to find her and own her, or even own that piece of myself. For a while I felt like I was just wearing my mom's clothes and playing dress-up. I was very different from the actresses who came before me in the role—Patti LuPone and Ethel Merman. I ended up working with an acting coach, Larry Moss, who

helped me find her humanity and her sexuality and to own my talent and my power. I tend to apologize for everything and deflect with humor. Reno is not like that at all, so it was a turning point for me as a performer and as a person to step into her and own her fully.

Act 1 ends with the song "Anything Goes," which in our production included an eight-minute tap number that was so incredibly choreographed by Kathleen Marshall. She just knocked it out of the park. She delivered masterful storytelling through song and dance. She gave me such a gift. I remember my third grade self in tap class and singing, and all of those dreams came true.

I feel proud to be a part of Tony history, and that I have established a name for myself in this community that I love so much. I'm most proud to be recognized and be part of a list of such extraordinary performances and people who I admire so much. I recognize the responsibility that I may represent something to a fifteen-year-old out there who might be watching me waiting for the torch to be passed.

Philip J. Smith

Christopher Shutt

John Larroquette

*War Horse*'s Nick Stafford, Nicholas Hytner, André Bishop, Bernand Gersten, Bob Boyett, and Nick Starr

*Newsies*'s Alan Menken
and Jack Feldman

# WINNERS ◎ 2012

**PLAY:** *Clybourne Park*, Bruce Norris

Produced by Jujamcyn Theaters, Jane Bergère, Roger Berlind/
Quintet Productions, Eric Falkenstein/Dan Frishwasser, Ruth Hendel/
Harris Karma Productions, JTG Theatricals, Daryl Roth, Jon B. Platt,
Center Theatre Group, Lincoln Center Theater, Playwrights Horizons

**MUSICAL:** *Once*

Produced by Barbara Broccoli, John N. Hart Jr., Patrick Milling Smith,
Frederick Zollo, Brian Carmody, Michael G. Wilson, Orin Wolf,
The Shubert Organization, Robert Cole, New York Theatre Workshop

**BOOK OF A MUSICAL:** Enda Walsh, *Once*

**ORIGINAL SCORE (MUSIC AND/OR LYRICS) WRITTEN FOR THE THEATRE:**
Alan Menken (music), Jack Feldman (lyrics), *Newsies*

**REVIVAL OF A PLAY:** *Arthur Miller's Death of a Salesman*

Produced by Scott Rudin, Stuart Thompson, Jon B. Platt, Columbia Pictures, Jean Doumanian,
Merritt Forrest Baer, Roger Berlind, Scott M. Delman, Sonia Friedman Productions, Ruth Hendel,
Carl Moellenberg, Scott & Brian Zeilinger, Eli Bush

**REVIVAL OF A MUSICAL:** *The Gershwins' Porgy and Bess*

Produced by Jeffrey Richards, Jerry Frankel, Rebecca Gold, Howard Kagan, Cheryl Wiesenfeld/Brunish
Trinchero/Lucio Simons TBC, Joseph & Matthew Deitch, Mark S. Golub & David S. Golub, Terry Schnuck,
Freitag Productions/Koenigsberg Filerman, The Leonore S. Gershwin 1987 Trust, Universal Pictures Stage
Productions, Ken Mahoney, Judith Resnick, Tulchin/Bartner/ATG, Paper Boy Productions, Christopher
Hart, Alden Badway, Broadway Across America, Irene Gandy, Will Trice, American Repertory Theater

**ACTOR IN A LEADING ROLE IN A PLAY:** James Corden, *One Man, Two Guvnors*

**ACTRESS IN A LEADING ROLE IN A PLAY:** Nina Arianda, *Venus in Fur*

**ACTOR IN A LEADING ROLE IN A MUSICAL:** Steve Kazee, *Once*

**ACTRESS IN A LEADING ROLE IN A MUSICAL:** Audra McDonald,
*The Gershwins' Porgy and Bess*

**ACTOR IN A FEATURED ROLE IN A PLAY:** Christian Borle, *Peter and the Starcatcher*

**ACTRESS IN A FEATURED ROLE IN A PLAY:** Judith Light, *Other Desert Cities*

**ACTOR IN A FEATURED ROLE IN A MUSICAL:** Michael McGrath,
*Nice Work If You Can Get It*

**ACTRESS IN A FEATURED ROLE IN A MUSICAL:**
Judy Kaye, *Nice Work If You Can Get It*

**SCENIC DESIGN OF A PLAY:** Donyale Werle, *Peter and the Starcatcher*

**SCENIC DESIGN OF A MUSICAL:** Bob Crowley, *Once*

**COSTUME DESIGN OF A PLAY:** Paloma Young, *Peter and the Starcatcher*

**COSTUME DESIGN OF A MUSICAL:** Gregg Barnes, *Follies*

**LIGHTING DESIGN OF A PLAY:** Jeff Croiter, *Peter and the Starcatcher*

**LIGHTING DESIGN OF A MUSICAL:** Natasha Katz, *Once*

**SOUND DESIGN OF A PLAY:** Darron L. West,
*Peter and the Starcatcher*

**SOUND DESIGN OF A MUSICAL:**
Clive Goodwin, *Once*

**DIRECTION OF A PLAY:** Mike Nichols,
*Arthur Miller's Death of a Salesman*

**DIRECTION OF A MUSICAL:** John Tiffany, *Once*

**CHOREOGRAPHY:** Christopher Gattelli, *Newsies*

**ORCHESTRATIONS:** Martin Lowe, *Once*

**SPECIAL TONY AWARD FOR LIFETIME ACHIEVEMENT IN THE THEATRE:**
Emanuel Azenberg

**ISABELLE STEVENSON AWARD:** Bernadette Peters

**REGIONAL THEATRE AWARD:**
Shakespeare Theatre Company, Washington, DC

**SPECIAL TONY AWARD:** Actors' Equity Association / Hugh Jackman

**TONY HONOR:** Freddie Gershon, Artie Siccardi, TDF Open Doors

---

Michael McGrath

**JEFF CROITER:** They drill into you ahead of time that you have ninety seconds to finish your speech from the moment your name is called. At the luncheon they advised us that it would be more interesting to use that speech time to say something heartfelt, rather than recite a list of names. I wrote a speech ahead of time, just in case, and I didn't take that advice. There were people I needed to thank.

I barely remember anything from when they called my name! I do remember walking down the aisle and grabbing Roger Rees, who (with Alex Timbers) directed *Peter and the Starcatcher*, and Rick Elice, who wrote it. My friend Andrew Kato was a producer of the Tonys, and he told me afterwards, "Next time you win, try to look up from your speech. We wanted to put you on camera longer, but you didn't give us a chance!"

*Peter and the Starcatcher* was the first time that all four designers ever won for the same show. The design and the actors and script were all intertwined in a way that is rare for a play.

Ken Posner and Brian MacDevitt were people I met as a very young designer. It was Ken who actually suggested I go to college to study with Brian MacDevitt. I assisted them both eventually; they were my biggest mentors. I watched as their careers shot off into the stratosphere and they became Broadway juggernauts. That set the bar very high for me. Coincidentally, when I won, Ken Posner and Brian MacDevitt were also nominated in my category, along with Peter Kaczorowski, who I also assisted. All of the other nominees contributed to who I was as a designer, and to be nominated with them was special.

As a lighting designer I get to wear two hats. There's a technical side to lighting as well as the artistry of it. I get to put complicated puzzles together and also create art. That's one of the reasons that I do this. I also do it because I enjoy creating the lighting that can help tell the story to the audience. Lighting is another storytelling tool, and I love to take words on a page or music and a director's vision and present something to an audience that moves them in some way. It can teach them, it can make them cry, it can make them laugh, or it can make them do all of those things at the same time. It's all about what the people in the seats are receiving.

**JUDITH LIGHT:** Everybody in the theatre community knows what it means to do eight shows a week. Everybody knows that you don't have a life. Your whole day is geared for the performance. That is the familial understanding and ties us to each other in profound ways.

When I received the Tony for *Other Desert Cities*, I was so shocked I forgot to mention Joe Mantello, the director, and Jon Robin Baitz, the playwright. I felt terrible because they had to be acknowledged. I received this honor in large part because of them. However, both of them were totally understanding and kind, gracious, and generous. They were truly lovely.

It doesn't get any better than having the honor to originate a role and then be awarded with a Tony for it. When I was very young and first starting out, every summer I would pick a playwright to read. I would always open up the Samuel French play and look to see who had originated the role. It's a huge honor and acknowledgment. And it's also an honor to take over for somebody in a Broadway production. It's the creativity and the electricity of the community and the joy of connecting with the audience that makes the experience so special. This powerful connection, the interweaving and intimacy of creating with such

Jeff Croiter

talented people who have been in that production prior to your coming on board, all of that is part of the honor and the privilege and the warmth of being welcomed with open arms by your fellow performers.

**SCOTT LEHRER:** Mike Nichols directed a lot of *Death of a Salesman* by telling stories. He knew that these stories would motivate somebody in the room. If someone needed help, the stories would be an indirect way of enlightening and clarifying without telling anyone what to do in a scene or how to approach a role.

**JAMES CORDEN:** When I won my Tony in 2012, I said, "I think it's important on nights like this to remember there's no such thing as best." If you get to be in the room at the Tony Awards, you're doing all right.

There is an extraordinary compact and tight nature of Broadway, where all the shows happen so close together. You are literally on top of each other; you're sharing alleyways behind the theaters. It creates a company spirit within twenty companies. It's such an encouraging environment, and the pinnacle of that is the Tony Awards. It's a group of people so rarely celebrated publicly who actually are, pound for pound, the most talented people on Earth. Everybody wants everyone else to do well. It's such a supportive, warm, beautiful group. I love it. The feeling in the room is like no other award show on Earth. This isn't a room full of millionaires and billionaires. This is a room full of people who predominantly are pretty much hand to mouth. There's such a sense of celebration in the air.

I hosted the Tonys for the first time in 2016, the year of *Hamilton*. We had a brilliant writer on our show called David Javerbaum. He agreed to help me with the opening. I wanted to open with the question of how a boy like me ends up hosting the Tonys, and I told him I thought we could do that with *Hamilton*. It took him twenty-five minutes to come up with exactly what was done on the show. I also wanted to include something for every kid who lives for tonight. I wanted to make an opening that said that could be me up

James Corden with presenter Candice Bergen

there. Rob Ashford directed the opening. He had the incredible idea to get a group of kids that looked like all the acting nominees. They would be on the stage, and then the lights would come up and the actual grown-up nominees would be there. That was all Rob Ashford, and it was beautiful.

**BERNADETTE PETERS:** It was quite an honor to receive the Isabelle Stevenson Award for my work with Broadway Cares and Broadway Barks. To receive any Tony Award is special because it means you're part of a community and work in a world that is different from other worlds. The creative process is beautiful. You collaborate with others in the community to try to create lightning in a bottle. When that happens it's so fulfilling. Creativity is otherworldly, and it's beautiful that we get to share it.

Leon Rothenberg, Jennifer Anne Slattery, and Ted Chapin

Andrea Martin and Martin Short

# WINNERS ◎ 2013

**PLAY:** *Vanya and Sonia and Masha and Spike*, Christopher Durang

Produced by Joey Parnes, Larry Hirschhorn, Joan Raffe & Jhett Tolentino, Martin Platt & David Elliott, Pat Flicker Addiss, Catherine Adler, John O'Boyle, Joshua Goodman, Jamie deRoy/ Richard Winkler, Cricket Hooper Jiranek/Michael Palitz, Mark S. Golub & David S. Golub, Radio Mouse Entertainment, ShadowCatcher Entertainment, Mary Cossette/Barbara Manocherian, Megan Savage/Meredith Lynsey Schade, Hugh Hysell/Richard Jordan, Cheryl Wiesenfeld/ Ron Simons, S.D. Wagner, John Johnson, McCarter Theatre Center, Lincoln Center Theater

**MUSICAL:** *Kinky Boots*

Produced by Daryl Roth, Hal Luftig, James L. Nederlander, Terry Allen Kramer, Independent Presenters Network, CJ E&M, Jayne Baron Sherman, Just for Laughs Theatricals Judith Ann Abrams, Yasuhiro Kawana, Jane Bergère, Allan S. Gordon & Adam S. Gordon, Ken Davenport, Hunter Arnold, Lucy & Phil Suarez, Bryan Bantry, Ron Fierstein & Dorsey Regal, Jim Kierstead/Gregory Rae, BB Group/Christina Papagjika, Michael DeSantis/Patrick Baugh, Brian Smith/Tom & Connie Walsh, Warren Trepp, Jujamcyn Theaters

**BOOK OF A MUSICAL:** Dennis Kelly, *Matilda the Musical*

**ORIGINAL SCORE (MUSIC AND/OR LYRICS) WRITTEN FOR THE THEATRE:**

Cyndi Lauper, *Kinky Boots*

**REVIVAL OF A PLAY:** *Who's Afraid of Virginia Woolf?*

Produced by Jeffrey Richards, Jerry Frankel, Susan Quint Gallin, Mary Lu Roffe, Kit Seidel, Amy Danis & Mark Johannes, Patty Baker, Mark S. Golub & David S. Golub, Richard Gross, Jam Theatricals, Cheryl Lachowicz, Michael Palitz, Dramatic Forces/Angelina Fiordellisi, Luigi & Rose Caiola, Ken Greiner, Kathleen K. Johnson, Kirmser Ponturo Fund, Will Trice, GFour Productions, Steppenwolf Theatre Company

**REVIVAL OF A MUSICAL:** *Pippin*

Produced by Barry and Fran Weissler, Howard and Janet Kagan, Lisa Matlin, Kyodo Tokyo, A&A Gordon/ Brunish Trinchero, Tom Smedes/Peter Stern, Broadway Across America, Independent Presenters Network, Norton Herrick, Allen Spivak, Rebecca Gold, Joshua Goodman, Stephen E. McManus, David Robbins/ Bryan S. Weingarten, Philip Hagemann/Murray Rosenthal, Jim Kierstead/Carlos Arana/Myla Lerner, Hugh Hayes/Jamie Cesa/Jonathan Reinis, Sharon A. Carr/Patricia R. Klausner, Ben Feldman, Square 1 Theatrics, Wendy Federman/Carl Moellenberg, Bruce Robert Harris/Jack W. Batman, Infinity Theatre Company/ Michael Rubenstein, Michael A. Alden/Dale Badway/Ken Mahoney, American Repertory Theater

**ACTOR IN A LEADING ROLE IN A PLAY:** Tracy Letts, *Who's Afraid of Virginia Woolf?*

**ACTRESS IN A LEADING ROLE IN A PLAY:** Cicely Tyson, *The Trip to Bountiful*

**ACTOR IN A LEADING ROLE IN A MUSICAL:** Billy Porter, *Kinky Boots*

**ACTRESS IN A LEADING ROLE IN A MUSICAL:** Patina Miller, *Pippin*

Ann Roth

**ACTOR IN A FEATURED ROLE IN A PLAY:** Courtney B. Vance, *Lucky Guy*

**ACTRESS IN A FEATURED ROLE IN A PLAY:** Judith Light, *The Assembled Parties*

**ACTOR IN A FEATURED ROLE IN A MUSICAL:**
Gabriel Ebert, *Matilda the Musical*

**ACTRESS IN A FEATURED ROLE IN A MUSICAL:** Andrea Martin, *Pippin*

**SCENIC DESIGN OF A PLAY:** John Lee Beatty, *The Nance*

**SCENIC DESIGN OF A MUSICAL:** Rob Howell, *Matilda the Musical*

**COSTUME DESIGN OF A PLAY:** Ann Roth, *The Nance*

**COSTUME DESIGN OF A MUSICAL:** William Ivey Long,
*Rodgers + Hammerstein's Cinderella*

**LIGHTING DESIGN OF A PLAY:** Jules Fisher and
Peggy Eisenhauer, *Lucky Guy*

**LIGHTING DESIGN OF A MUSICAL:** Hugh Vanstone,
*Matilda the Musical*

**SOUND DESIGN OF A PLAY:** Leon Rothenberg, *The Nance*

**SOUND DESIGN OF A MUSICAL:** John Shivers, *Kinky Boots*

**DIRECTION OF A PLAY:** Pam MacKinnon, *Who's Afraid of Virginia Woolf?*

**DIRECTION OF A MUSICAL:** Diane Paulus, *Pippin*

**CHOREOGRAPHY:** Jerry Mitchell, *Kinky Boots*

**ORCHESTRATIONS:** Stephen Oremus, *Kinky Boots*

**SPECIAL TONY AWARD FOR LIFETIME ACHIEVEMENT IN THE THEATRE:**
Bernard Gersten; Paul Libin; Ming Cho Lee

**ISABELLE STEVENSON AWARD:** Larry Kramer

**REGIONAL THEATRE AWARD:** Huntington Theatre Company

**TONY HONOR:** Michael R. Bloomberg; Career Transition for Dancers;
William Craver; Peter Lawrence; *The Lost Colony*; Sophia Gennusa,
Oona Laurence, Bailey Ryon, and Milly Shapiro

Gabriel Ebert

Lifetime Achievement
winners Paul Libin, Ming Cho
Lee, and Bernard Gersten

Courtney B. Vance

**JOHN LEE BEATTY:** I felt my win for *The Nance* was also a recognition of my previous work, mostly plays. I'd done *The Heiress* and *A Delicate Balance*, and many other sets for plays that had been nominated before they split the design awards. I could have possibly had more Tonys, as I was often the only "play" designer nominated. That's not why I do the work, but it was really nice to receive this late Tony.

My partner, Freddy, is not in the business at all. We've been together for a long time. The first time he went to the Tonys was in 1992. I think he had gone with me for eleven or twelve times by the time I won for *The Nance*. It had become our spring ritual to get dressed up and go to the Tonys. This time I won, and I gave my speech, went backstage for the press. Freddy was so used to me not winning that I think he fell asleep and was surprised to find out that I had really won!

John Lee Beatty

**JUDITH LIGHT:** I was not expecting to be nominated for *The Assembled Parties*. Being nominated is another distinct honor. There are five of you, and every one of those people who are nominated could easily win. Every time I've been nominated, it's never felt like a competition. There was always this warmth and a sense of family.

I believe it was Laura Linney who came up with the idea for the Tony luncheon. She said something like this (and I am paraphrasing), "We're going to all go to the Tonys. We're not really going to get time with each other, so we need a time just for us to be together."

That luncheon is one of the most glorious parts of being nominated for a Tony. You're with your folk. It's like the family picnic. At one Tony luncheon Marian Seldes started to speak from a piece of paper on which she had written a speech. She was stumbling a bit and couldn't continue. Her

Tom Hanks and Judith Light

dear friend, the extraordinary actor Brian Murray, took the paper out of her hand and said, "This is what Marian wanted to say." There are so many wonderful moments like that at the Tony luncheon. There is a sense of camaraderie, not competition.

**TRACY LETTS:** George in *Who's Afraid of Virginia Woolf?* is an amazing role. He's such an unlikely hero. He's a pretty damaged person. He has this enormous intellect and a monstrous sense of humor, and a somewhat cruel sensibility. It's not the way we normally think of our heroes. He's brilliantly written.

What we found from doing hundreds of performances of the play was that the kernel of *Virginia Woolf* is the love story. The fact that George is fighting for something and someone that he loves is what makes him heroic. It's a wildly entertaining role. Martha is the more outsized personality. George has a stealthier way into things. It makes for such a great night in the theatre.

We opened *Who's Afraid of Virginia Woolf?* fifty years to the night after the original Broadway premiere. For us to take our curtain call and bring Mr. Albee out onto the stage fifty years later was certainly something I will never forget in my theatre career.

Winning the Tony was a surprise. The other actors nominated were Nathan Lane, Tom Hanks, David Hyde Pierce, and Tom Sturridge. It didn't seem like something that was going to happen, especially since our show had closed months earlier. It was a wonderful surprise.

I have such respect for the craft of acting. There's something about the craft of a stage actor that is so noble and quixotic. I take pride in being a stage actor.

**HARVEY FIERSTEIN:** *Kinky Boots* took five years to write because Cyndi Lauper was on the road. I had to catch her whenever she was in town. I would have to get on her to give me a song, which is why she calls me Mommie Dearest!

**BILLY PORTER:** I was introduced to theatre in the sixth grade in my middle school's after-school program, and that was it. They were doing *Babes in Arms*, and they said every part was going to be double cast. When the cast list went up, I got the role of Gus Fielding. It was the only role not double cast. For the first time in my life,

Billy Porter

I was being picked first instead of last. I was always picked last for sports in school. Once I started Hal Luftig, Cyndi Lauper, Daryl Roth, and Billy Porter of *Kinky Boots* doing theatre, the bullying stopped. That summer I stumbled across the Tony Awards. I just happened to be washing dishes in the kitchen when it came on. It was the year of *Dreamgirls*. Jennifer Holliday sang "And I Am Telling You I'm Not Going," and for me there was no turning back. I saw something that was close to who I was. I sang like that, and she's doing that on television. There was something about it being on television, even though it was theatre, that flipped the switch for me to understand that it was a career that I could go after. It became the original dream that I made when I was eleven years old. As I started working and experienced racism and homophobia, I learned to deepen my artistic vocabulary. I didn't have any work, so I investigated other ways of being creative—writing, directing, creating. As a result, my creative brain expanded, and I allowed my dreams to expand and mature. I moved on. Before *Kinky Boots* there was a decade where I didn't work as an actor very much. I was fulfilled behind the scenes, creating. I figured if it wasn't something as good as *Angels in America*, I didn't need to be doing it. And sure enough, *Angels in America* came around, and I got it. And then *Kinky Boots* came around and I got it. I had to jump through hoops of fire to get the part. It was not just offered to me. Jerry Mitchell always knew that he wanted me to play Lola. He and I have been friends since the late eighties. We have a trust with each other. We paid our dues and came up together. And he reached back and got me for *Kinky Boots* at a time when everybody else had basically given up on me.

There had never been a Lola before. There had never been a black, queer, out leading character who was the heart of the piece. I'm the first to do that. The change has happened. Because of my authenticity, every single person in my life, haters and allies alike, told me that my queerness would be my liability. And it was for decades, until that change. And now it's my superpower. It was a gift to play Lola, and to be able to tell a story of unconditional love and forgiveness, and to put that kind of energy and joy into the world every day.

**JERRY MITCHELL:** I knew Billy could bring what Lola required, so I started the dance to convince the producers and the writers and everyone else. At that time Billy had been gone a long time, and people were questioning whether vocally he could sustain eight shows a week. I said, "I can't worry about that. I can only worry about opening night, because that's the only night that's going to matter. I need the person I believe is Lola, and Billy Porter to me is Lola."

The message of *Kinky Boots* is accept yourself so you can accept others too. That message permeated the Al Hirschfeld Theatre the minute we walked in. I saw stagehands change their lives and their life choices because of the message of the show. I've worked on fifty musicals worldwide. I have never seen a musical change not just the audience but change everyone working on the piece.

**LEON ROTHENBERG:** The Tony Awards are an incredibly special thing to be a part of and to receive. It's a celebration.

Part of winning in sound is having something special that really stands out and that people take notice of and can relate to. A lot of the work we do is very subtle. It will be appreciated by our colleagues, but not necessarily by the larger theatre world. Winning a Tony for sound is always extraordinary, especially in a play, where things tend to be a little more subtle. *The Nance* is a play that feels like a musical. Nobody was wearing mics. The sound moved around as the set moved around. There was a lot there for people to notice, and we were able to make magic.

There was a fun scene change wipe that we did with lights and sound. It was a high squealing sound. I recorded that sound in the subway, and the effect was like wiping the stage as we turned, and we went to the next scene.

What makes theatre sound design different than other kinds of sound design is that it's as much about the space that it exists in as what it is. The space is the theater, but it's also other things that are in that space and how they interact. I don't feel a separation between the cues that I built for *The Nance* and the way that the voices sounded and the way that we amplified and delivered the music. That's both how loud it is and how present it is and what part it plays in the play as a whole, but also where it's coming from and where it exists in space. Some of the scenes took place in a cabaret. In those scenes with cabaret performance, we delivered the sound from where the pit would be, so it felt very much like the band was in the pit. As the set turned and the performance continued, the set turned to the backstage, and we did a scene backstage. The whole band sound turned with the set and then happened stage right. You could hear it moving. I didn't create that content per se, but delivering it in space is as much creating content as having written the music. As the set turned someone told a joke, and you can hear the audience laughing, but its sounds like its coming from backstage. That shift of perspective was a fun sound trick. You could hear it and tell. Nathan Lane had this long monologue, and he was getting heckled from the audience. I had those lines coming from within the audience. It was nasty heckling, and it was sort of terrifying. When you hear somebody yell out "Get off the stage," it would grab you. That's not because I recorded somebody saying "Get off the stage" really well. It's because it's playing a part of the space and using the space for telling the story.

I love the collaborative process of theatre. A director may say to me, "I want it to sound blue," and I have to turn that into volume. I can turn things up and down in very complex and subtle and sophisticated ways, but when it all comes down to it, it's turning things up and down. That's a vast oversimplification. There are many tools to do that in many different ways, from the sound system to the equipment that you use to the way it's mixed, etc.

**JOHN SHIVERS:** I wanted to bring the most important person in my world to the Tonys, my then eight-year-old daughter, Ruby. She was enormously excited, as you can imagine. Ruby knew most of people working on *Kinky Boots* as she had spent a lot of time in the theater while we were in technical rehearsals. Everyone always made a fuss over her when she visited. For the Tonys, Ruby chose a red dress and red high-heeled shoes in honor of the show. While she looked great, I actually had to carry her down the red carpet because she was struggling to walk in her heels. My only hesitation in bringing her was if by chance I won, she would be left sitting alone in a six-thousand-seat theater with nobody she knew seated near her. So, before the show started, we made sure to introduce ourselves to some of the nearby seat fillers who would possibly be taking my seat. I just wanted to make sure Ruby was going to be okay should I have to disappear for a

John Shivers and daughter, Ruby

half hour or so. As it was getting close to the time for my category to be announced, Ruby announced she had to go to the bathroom. "Can you wait, honey?" *"Absolutely not…"* We rushed to the bathroom, where I nervously waited… and waited…and waited…Finally Ruby reappeared. As we hurried back into the theater somebody was actually running up the aisle yelling for me to go sit down because the sound design award was about to be announced. Happily, Ruby made a seat filler friend.

I love the challenge of sound design for musical theatre. When I started my career working in the Village at Electric Lady studios, and then touring with Gregory Hines and Dionne Warwick, sound for musical theatre was considerably different. With concerts and studio work, sound was always the primary focus. Sound design for musical theatre, however, is just one small part of many creative disciplines that go into producing a show. As such, there are always negotiations and a great deal of collaboration necessary to achieve a successful design. I really enjoy the challenge of solving whatever complexities are presented to make every show sound the best it can. It's truly satisfying, magical even, in the moments when everything aligns.

I feel like I had quite a bit to offer to *Kinky Boots* because of my solid background in studio work and concert touring and because of my longtime fascination with sound for film. In film, the use of scoring, sound effects, and surround sound can be vastly effective in impacting and enhancing the overall experience. This has had a big influence on my philosophy and creative process for theatrical sound design. Beyond my basic design concepts, *Kinky Boots* gave me the opportunity to do some interesting things with rhythmically moving elements of the music around the theater. I judiciously chose specific moments for this in order to achieve the desired effect.

On the surface, sound design may not be particularly well understood. However, like a film score, a good design can be extremely powerful in helping to evoke emotions and support the story both viscerally and subliminally. If the sound design for a production calls attention to itself when not intending to do so, it can become distracting. My objective is to support and advance the narrative of the story being told through the book, music, and lyrics. With every design I endeavor to provide sonic clarity and energy, and enhance the live theatre experience.

**DIANE PAULUS:** *Pippin* is a musical that has touched people's lives over the years in a way that goes beyond its life as a Broadway show. People know the music because it is the soundtrack to their lives. It had been almost forty years since the original production premiered on Broadway in 1972. I knew in my bones I wanted to revive it.

Our revival came together when I partnered with circus creator Gypsy Snider, from the company Les 7 Doigts de la Main, and with choreographer Chet Walker, who had worked with Bob Fosse and performed in the original production. It was important to me to pay homage to Bob Fosse's work. He had made an indelible mark on *Pippin* for me and for so many others, and I knew that Fosse's choreography would be a key element in audiences' expectation of a revival. Chet told me early on in the process that Fosse never wanted to repeat himself, and that he was fascinated by both Fellini and the circus. If you look back at the original production of *Pippin*, elements of the circus were already there. The ensemble was a troupe—not a circus troupe exactly, but there was imagery of people juggling. So, it was Chet who encouraged me to pursue the idea of the circus setting. I had been a fan of Les 7 Doigts (which means "The Seven Fingers") for a long time, and I always thought it would be thrilling to experience their virtuosic acrobatics on Broadway. Gypsy told me the theme of being "extraordinary" in *Pippin* was so powerful for her, because that is the life of a circus artist—to literally defy the limits of the human body. As an acrobat, you pursue the quest to defy those limits in extraordinary physical ways. It felt like bringing *Pippin* into the world of the circus resonated with the core theme of the show, and was a natural extension of the way Fosse had worked on the original.

The script is structured like a medieval morality play; you have to move through the different stages of life: home, glory, the flesh, politics, ordinary life, to name a few. Our production concept embraced this series of life trials imagined as circus acts, culminating in the finale act when Pippin is asked to jump into fire. When Pippin doesn't jump, the Leading Player literally stops the show. She calls for the tent to be pulled down, and the whole world of the circus deconstructs. Pippin walks away with Catherine, his lover, taking their son, Theo, with them.

He doesn't want to be part of the circus anymore. For as long as we ran the production, this final moment was always met with different reactions from the audience. On certain nights people would applaud as Pippin departed, but on other nights, they were silent and applauded when the Leading Player reappeared, seducing Theo back to the world of the circus. I was never interested in there being a morality to the ending—there was no "right way" to respond. It was a moment for people to look at their own life and ask, what have I chosen to do in my life that is extraordinary? Is choosing love and family extraordinary? Did I ever want to run away with the circus? In the end, after trying to do so many things and please so many different people, Pippin listens to his own voice and makes a choice for himself. And Theo's re-entrance is a beautiful life lesson: this boy will have to go through the same journey of life trials and face the same tests confronted by his father.

I worked very closely with Stephen Schwartz and Roger O. Hirson on the production. They were both so supportive of our concept and the production we first created at the American Repertory Theater at Harvard University. We tailored the script and moved things around to support this version. Early on, I remember asking Stephen who the Leading Player is, because there's no description in the script. He told me that the most important thing about the Leading Player is that it's someone who is different from Pippin. I also knew this performer would have to be a quadruple threat—someone who could sing, dance, act, and do something in the circus. When Patina Miller walked through the door, I thought, this could be it. Her ability to handle the Fosse choreography on top of her incredible vocals made it clear that she was the right choice, not to mention her acting and the discovery throughout rehearsal that she was fearless on the trapeze. When I spoke with Andrea Martin about being in the cast, she told me that she would love to play Berthe, Pippin's grandmother, but only if she could be a part of the circus troupe. She did not want to sing her song sitting in a wicker chair like a granny. So Gypsy came up with the idea of Andrea doing a duo partner act on the trapeze. The day I pitched to Andrea the idea of singing the end of her song while hanging upside down from the trapeze, her eyes lit up. She trained rigorously for this, and it

Patina Miller

paid off. Her number literally stopped the show, getting a standing ovation in the middle of Act 1.

Winning a Tony Award was such a gift, because it gave me the opportunity to say thank you on a public platform to all the people who made it possible. I was also excited to be recognized as a female director. There haven't been that many of us—I was only the second woman to win the Tony for Best Direction of a Musical, after Julie Taymor for *The Lion King*. 2013 was also the first year that two women, at the same time, won a Tony for directing (myself for Pippin and Pam MacKinnon for *Who's Afraid of Virginia Woolf?*). I grew up watching the Tony awards. As both a woman and an Asian American artist, it meant so much to be able to give inspiration to aspiring directors out there watching.

Sophie Okonedo

Scenic Design winners Beowulf
Boritt and Christopher Barreca

# WINNERS ◎ 2014

**PLAY:** *All the Way*, Robert Schenkkan

Produced by Jeffrey Richards, Louise Gund, Jerry Frankel, Stephanie P. McClelland, Double Gemini Productions, Rebecca Gold, Scott M. Delman, Barbara H. Freitag, Harvey Weinstein, Gene Korf, William Berlind, Caiola Productions, Gutterman Chernoff, Jam Theatricals, Gabrielle Palitz, Cheryl Wiesenfeld, Will Trice, The Oregon Shakespeare Festival, American Repertory Theater

**MUSICAL:** *A Gentleman's Guide to Love and Murder*

Produced by Joey Parnes, S.D. Wagner, John Johnson, 50 Church Street Productions, Joan Raffe & Jhett Tolentino, Jay Alix & Una Jackman, Catherine & Fred Adler, Rhoda Herrick, Kathleen K. Johnson, Megan Savage, ShadowCatcher Entertainment, Ron Simons, True Love Productions, Jamie deRoy, Four Ladies & One Gent, John Arthur Pinckard, Greg Nobile, Stewart Lane & Bonnie Comley, Exeter Capital/Ted Snowdon, Ryan Hugh Mackey, Cricket-CTM Media/Mano-Horn Productions, Dennis Grimaldi/Margot Astrachan, Hello Entertainment/Jamie Bendell, Michael T. Cohen/Joe Sirola, Joseph & Carson Gleberman/ William Megevick, Green State Productions, The Hartford Stage, The Old Globe

**BOOK OF A MUSICAL:** Robert L. Freedman, *A Gentleman's Guide to Love and Murder*

**ORIGINAL SCORE (MUSIC AND/OR LYRICS) WRITTEN FOR THE THEATRE:**
Jason Robert Brown, *The Bridges of Madison County*

**REVIVAL OF A PLAY:** *A Raisin in the Sun*

Produced by Scott Rudin, Roger Berlind, Eli Bush, Jon B. Platt, Scott M. Delman, Roy Furman, Stephanie P. McClelland, Ruth Hendel, Sonia Friedman/Tulchin Bartner, The Araca Group, Heni Koenigsberg, Daryl Roth, Joan Raffe & Jhett Tolentino, Joey Parnes, S.D. Wagner, John Johnson

**REVIVAL OF A MUSICAL:** *Hedwig and the Angry Inch*

Produced by David Binder, Jayne Baron Sherman, Barbara Whitman, Latitude Link, Patrick Catullo, Raise the Roof, Paula Marie Black, Colin Callender, Ruth Hendel, Sharon Karmazin, Martian Entertainment, Stacey Mindich, Eric Schnall, The Shubert Organization

**ACTOR IN A LEADING ROLE IN A PLAY:** Bryan Cranston, *All the Way*

**ACTRESS IN A LEADING ROLE IN A PLAY:** Audra McDonald,
*Lady Day at Emerson's Bar & Grill*

**ACTOR IN A LEADING ROLE IN A MUSICAL:** Neil Patrick Harris,
*Hedwig and the Angry Inch*

**ACTRESS IN A LEADING ROLE IN A MUSICAL:** Jessie Mueller,
*Beautiful—The Carole King Musical*

**ACTOR IN A FEATURED ROLE IN A PLAY:** Mark Rylance, *Twelfth Night*

**ACTRESS IN A FEATURED ROLE IN A PLAY:**
Sophie Okonedo, *A Raisin in the Sun*

**ACTOR IN A FEATURED ROLE IN A MUSICAL:**
James Monroe Iglehart, *Aladdin*

**ACTRESS IN A FEATURED ROLE IN A MUSICAL:**
Lena Hall, *Hedwig and the Angry Inch*

**SCENIC DESIGN OF A PLAY:** Beowulf Boritt, *Act One*

**SCENIC DESIGN OF A MUSICAL:**
Christopher Barreca, *Rocky*

**COSTUME DESIGN OF A PLAY:** Jenny Tiramani,
*Twelfth Night*

**COSTUME DESIGN OF A MUSICAL:** Linda Cho, *A Gentleman's Guide to Love and Murder*

**LIGHTING DESIGN OF A PLAY:** Natasha Katz, *The Glass Menagerie*

**LIGHTING DESIGN OF A MUSICAL:** Kevin Adams, *Hedwig and the Angry Inch*

**SOUND DESIGN OF A PLAY:** Steve Canyon Kennedy, *Lady Day at Emerson's Bar & Grill*

**SOUND DESIGN OF A MUSICAL:** Brian Ronan, *Beautiful—The Carole King Musical*

**DIRECTION OF A PLAY:** Kenny Leon, *A Raisin in the Sun*

**DIRECTION OF A MUSICAL:** Darko Tresnjak, *A Gentleman's Guide to Love and Murder*

**CHOREOGRAPHY:** Warren Carlyle, *After Midnight*

**ORCHESTRATIONS:** Jason Robert Brown, *The Bridges of Madison County*

**SPECIAL TONY AWARD FOR LIFETIME ACHIEVEMENT IN THE THEATRE:**
Jane Greenwood

**ISABELLE STEVENSON AWARD:** Rosie O'Donnell

**REGIONAL THEATRE AWARD:** Signature Theatre, New York, New York

**TONY HONOR:** Joseph N. Benincasa; Joan Marcus; Charlotte Wilcox

*All the Way*'s Cindy Gutterman, Louise Gund, Diane Paulus, Gene Korf, Bill Rauch, Robert Schenkkan, Jay Gutterman, Jeffrey Richards, and Rebecca Gold

Mark Berger, David Binder, Stephen Trask, John Cameron Mitchell, and Neil Patrick Harris

2014 ○ 227

**LINDA CHO:** I did not expect to win the Tony! I was up against some
Alexander Dodge and Linda Cho
stiff competition. I saw all of the other nominees' work, and they were all amazing. I thought it would just be fun to go to the party. I actually wore my wedding gown to the Tonys because I didn't think I would win, so I didn't feel it was necessary to buy something new! When they called my name, I was shocked and amazed. I was so proud of the show and thought that it was something special.

My work as a costume designer is about uplifting the story. Its character based. Costumes can communicate what the character wants to portray to the world, what their socioeconomic background is, how they feel about themselves, and how they want other people to feel about them. I have a degree in psychology, which comes in very handy, because my work is a psychological study. Sometimes I'll give an actor something small like a necklace that most people in the audience will never see. But the actor knows the relevance it has to their character. I always loop in actors in the fitting and give them a say in the final decision. Nobody knows the characters better than they do.

**ROSIE O'DONNELL:** My mom was a big
Rosie O'Donnell
Broadway fan, and she handed that to me. It was the greatest gift she ever gave me. I remember growing up going to see a play and waiting at the stage door to see the actors come out. I remember thinking, *If you want to perform, this is the place to go.* I didn't know where Hollywood was. All I knew was there was a street in New York City where you could wait by an old dented gray door and see the people who just performed the magic for you onstage. That meant everything, because then I knew there was a destination for what I wanted to do.

There's nothing like going to see a Broadway show. You have that waxy Playbill in your hand, and the orchestra is tuning up. Then the lights go down and you know that what happens that night is just for you and the other people in the theater. Broadway has always been the life raft that comes in and saves me.

I knew Isabelle Stevenson. She was there and in charge when I hosted the Tony Awards. She had a gravitas to her, and everyone noticed when she came into a room. She cared so much and was such a part of the theatre community for

Audra McDonald and Will Swenson

Warren Carlyle and Jason Robert Brown

Kenny Leon

so many years. To win the award that bears her name for my philanthropic work is very touching for me. It is a huge honor. I have always felt so much love from the Broadway community. When I had my talk show, I always promoted a Broadway show by putting them on. I felt like the mayor of Broadway!

**KENNY LEON:** I always do a revival as if it were a new play. I look at it from the point of view of the people sitting in the seats. They're alive; they're now. How does this relate to them? When I did *A Raisin in the Sun* in 2014, I never even thought about the version I directed in 2004. The 2014 version came about because after we did *Fences* together, Denzel and I made a promise that we would try to do a show together every three or four years. We explored a lot of different American plays. One day he called me to say, "I don't want you to say anything, but just think about this. It's been ten years since you did *A Raisin in the Sun*. That production was huge and introduced a whole generation of theatregoers. Why can't we consider that?" I slept on it and called him the next day to say it was a great idea. There was some concern about Denzel's age for the character. But not once in the play do they mention his age. The play is about the pursuit of dreams, and what happens to those dreams if they're not realized. With an older Walter Lee, he's desperate to get that dream. He's got one shot.

Winning the Tony is confirmation that I belong as an artist in this country. I can play on the highest stage. I'm very proud of that. It makes me feel like I belong to Lloyd Richards and George C. Wolfe and Dan Sullivan, Audra McDonald, Natasha Katz, Phylicia Rashad, and Ruben Santiago-Hudson. We're all connected.

**JAMES MONROE IGLEHART:** To this day I am still mystified, surprised, and honored to have won a Tony Award. I started watching the Tonys religiously when I was about sixteen, and to actually have one is incredible.

I knew the character of the Genie in *Aladdin* inside out because I'm such a big Robin Williams fan, and such a big Disney nerd. When I thought about how I was going to approach the character, Jonathan Freeman (who played Jafar in the 1992 movie) changed my whole perspective. He told me Howard Ashman and Alan Menken originally saw the Genie as a Fats Waller, Cab Calloway type. He was originally supposed to be an African American man. If you listen to the music, it's big band music. Genie's music is so different from every other piece of music in the show and film. Once I knew that I found my way in. I'm very silly and I started coming up with my own jokes. I realized that the Genie is just someone who wants freedom, who wants a friend and just wants someone to love him. There's a part of him that uses his talent and showmanship to cover up his pain. Every performer understands that. Once I got that, I went out on a limb. I started to make up my own jokes. Every day I would come up with something different. The director, Casey Nicholaw, would say yes or no. Disney would say yes or definitely not! It was a moment of stepping out on faith. If the audience loved it, great. If they didn't, well, I gave it my best shot.

I have had so many twentysomethings come up to me and tell me that the first show they saw was *Aladdin*. I have had a lot of brown, round kids—girls, boys, other—walk up to me and say how much the show changed their lives. They wanted to do musical theatre but didn't think they could because they didn't see anybody that looked like them size wise, color wise. A lot of Rubenesque-type ladies tell me they didn't think they could be a character like that, until I said women could play the Genie too. I'm so thankful for that. It's such a blessing to be able to be a part of someone's life in a way that you didn't even know. You can touch someone's spirit without even meeting them. A performer's superpower is taking people away from the craziness of the world for a good two to three hours. To entertain someone, to make them smile or cry, to make them not think about what's going on outside those four walls for just a little bit is an amazing type of magic.

The day of the Tonys was a whirlwind. I walked the red carpet with my wife, I sat down in the theater, and they whisked me away to put makeup on and do the number with *Aladdin*. I thought I was going to go sit with my wife, but they called my name. I walked up to accept without a speech. I didn't write anything because I didn't think I was going to win. I was freestyling. I thanked my wife and Thomas Schumacher. There was a moment where I remembered when I was in church as a kid someone said,

AWARDS®

James Monroe Iglehart

"You feel the blessing so much that you don't have any words. You either sing or you dance." And so I danced, because I could not believe that they had just given me a Tony. The last thing I expected was for the audience to jump up in praise with me. I looked around and I saw the people. I went backstage and there was my friend Zachary Levi, and Bradley Cooper was there. It was the craziest moment because it went by so fast. It was a moment of dreams can come true, and then I had to go back to work on Tuesday.

After that night I felt like I had to give 110 percent when doing the show, because I wanted folks to know that my win wasn't a fluke. Every night for the next three years it was at that caliber.

Whenever I think about the fact that my name is up there with my heroes—Ted Ross and Chuck Cooper—in the same category, it's absolutely magical. The fantasy of being a Tony winner was never as sweet as the actual reality of being a part of this legacy. This is the elite; this is the cream of the crop of theatre.

BRYAN CRANSTON: When *Breaking Bad* ended I knew I wanted to do something different. I gave myself an arbitrary three-year hiatus from doing any television. I wanted to do theatre anyway. I asked my agent, Mark Subias at UTA, to find a play. It didn't have to be a starring role, but it had to be really good. He brought me *All the Way*. I read it and thought it was astonishingly well written. It scared the hell out of me to play a figure as iconic as LBJ, a president of the United States. He was controversial and bombastic and aggressive—he was bigger than life.

Playwright Robert Schenkkan and Bill Rauch, who was the artistic director of the Oregon Shakespeare Festival at the time (which is where the show originated), came to my house. I had been starting to play with the accent of Lyndon Johnson to see how it felt in my mouth as I was trying to embody it in some preliminary form. My agent told me ahead of time that this was not an audition and that I wouldn't be reading anything. But anytime you meet with anyone it's an audition. You're feeling each other out.

You're sensing if their comportment could match yours. I really liked them, so I said, "Do you want to read some of this?" Robert Schenkkan told me later that when I volunteered to read something it assuaged any fears they might have had. *All the Way* was a great gift.

I think most actors who do both Broadway and films looking for a creative experience, is best felt onstage. I've had more moments onstage of acting fulfillment than I've had on film. You get one shot at it: you're in real time going through it.

**NEIL PATRICK HARRIS:** I've been both a Tony host and a nominee, and it's a very different experience. When you're nominated, there are multiple outcomes that you can't predict. One involves a litany of names to say in a small amount of time and a lot of dopamine dripping into your brain. The other is a realization and then a process of how to continue. As a host you have a lot to do, but you've gotten a dress rehearsal. The responsibility of the host at the Tonys is to establish tone that is on par with the inspiring performances on the stage. The theatre community is a small, tight-knit group of people that have all worked together a lot and recognize how hard everyone works all week. Broadway performers are a step away from the Olympics to me. They are athletes. For one night to allow not two thousand, but two million people see them do it is a rare, exciting thing that no one in that theater that night takes lightly. It's a different vibe than anything I've ever experienced. There's a sense of appreciation for the show, for the community, for the producers. It's a celebration unlike anything I've ever seen. That's the tone that must be honored.

The first time I hosted involved a giant musical number with all the musicals of the season. I just came out at the end of it. A performer stayed onstage a bit longer than he was told to and got hit by a piece of scenery coming down. It was very jarring to watch from the wings. I was immediately wildly concerned that he was okay because from my vantage point it looked like something really terrible could have just happened; someone may have been beheaded live onstage in the first nine minutes of a three-hour show. I was very intent on finding out very quickly if things were okay because I might have to come out and tell people we'll be right back and cut to commercial and change the game very quickly. Thankfully, he was all right. That was definitely a case of being shot out of a cannon. In that same first show I wanted to try a magic trick of structure. With almost every award show once they announce the name of the winner of the last award, everyone changes the channel. Usually, fifty-five people climb up onstage and one producer, whom most people at home don't know, thanks a billion people. The host has to come out and say, "Thankseveryonethat'stheshowgoodnight!" as one word. I thought it would be fun to do an eleven o'clock number after the final award and recap the show, singing about everything that had happened to keep people tuned in, and also hopefully make everyone wonder how in the world we pulled that off because we were rhyming things that were about winners, information we didn't have before it happened live. That was very exciting. We got Marc Shaiman and Scott Wittman to write alternate versions of lyrics that once we got to the end we would plug in the teleprompter. It worked out well, and I got to do the same thing the following year as a long rap—a white boy rap, but thankfully written by Lin-Manuel Miranda. That was terrifying, because that was a lot of words they were writing on the fly. I left my hosting responsibilities for about twenty minutes near the end of the show to go downstairs into the bowels of the theater and practice and practice and practice this rap as fast as I could. It was, as you would expect, syncopated internal rhyme scansion done by Lin and Tommy Kail. We had to put that into the teleprompter, but we did all caps on the downbeat syllables of all the words. Once you started you were talking so fast, and everything was happening so quickly that you really couldn't get off or else you were really off. Thankfully it went as planned and I said good night and got to run off and give Lin a giant hug and exhale because we made it through. Those experiences pale in comparison to "Bigger," that big number we did when the Tonys went back to Radio City Music Hall. I think that was the most overtly triumphant experience that I've ever had as a host.

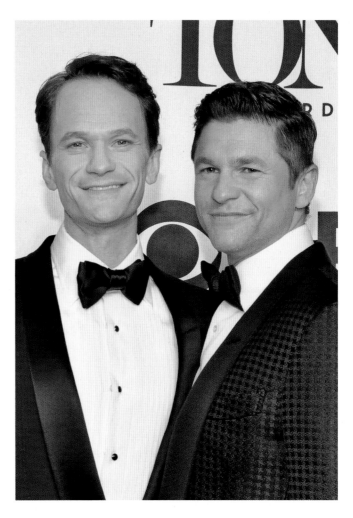

I feel so honored to be a Tony winner and to be considered part of a community that works so hard and is seen by so few. To be singled out amongst that group of people whose work I deeply admire and respect was surprising. It affirmed in me that I was one of them, and not on the outside fawning over others.

**JEFFREY RICHARDS:** As a producer, the Tony Award confirms for me, my partners, and investors—and for the entire company of artists—the merits of the production as the finest in its genre in that season. On a personal level, it's f-ing thrilling to hear the name of your play or musical announced.

Neil Patrick Harris and David Burtka

Alex Sharp

# WINNERS ○ 2015

**PLAY:** *The Curious Incident of the Dog in the Night-Time*, Simon Stephens

Produced by Stuart Thompson, Tim Levy for NT America, Warner Bros. Theatre Ventures, Nick Starr & Chris Harper for NT Productions, Bob Boyett, Roger Berlind, Scott M. Delman, Roy Furman, Glass Half Full Productions, Ruth Hendel, Jon B. Platt, Prime Number Group, Scott Rudin, Triple Play Broadway, The Shubert Organization, The National Theatre

**MUSICAL:** *Fun Home*

Produced by Fox Theatricals, Barbara Whitman, Carole Shorenstein Hays, Tom Casserly, Paula Marie Black, Latitude Link, Terry Schnuck/Jack Lane, The Forstalls, Nathan Vernon, Mint Theatrical, Elizabeth Armstrong, Jam Theatricals, Delman-Whitney, Kristin Caskey & Mike Isaacson, The Public Theater, Oskar Eustis, Patrick Willingham

**BOOK OF A MUSICAL:** Lisa Kron, *Fun Home*

**ORIGINAL SCORE (MUSIC AND/OR LYRICS) WRITTEN FOR THE THEATRE:**
Jeanine Tesori (music), Lisa Kron (lyrics), *Fun Home*

**REVIVAL OF A PLAY:** *Skylight*

Produced by Robert Fox, Scott Rudin, Eli Bush, Roger Berlind, William Berlind, Roy Furman, Jon B. Platt, The Shubert Organization, Stephanie P. McClelland, Catherine Adler, Jay Alix & Una Jackman, Scott M. Delman, Heni Koenigsberg, Spring Sirkin, Stuart Thompson, True Love Productions, The Araca Group, Carlos Arana, David Mirvish, Joey Parnes, Sue Wagner, John Johnson

**REVIVAL OF A MUSICAL:** *The King and I*

Produced by Lincoln Center Theater, André Bishop, Adam Siegel, Hattie K. Jutagir, Ambassador Theatre Group

**ACTOR IN A LEADING ROLE IN A PLAY:** Alex Sharp, *The Curious Incident of the Dog in the Night-Time*

**ACTRESS IN A LEADING ROLE IN A PLAY:** Helen Mirren, *The Audience*

**ACTOR IN A LEADING ROLE IN A MUSICAL:** Michael Cerveris, *Fun Home*

**ACTRESS IN A LEADING ROLE IN A MUSICAL:** Kelli O'Hara, *The King and I*

**ACTOR IN A FEATURED ROLE IN A PLAY:** Richard McCabe, *The Audience*

**ACTRESS IN A FEATURED ROLE IN A PLAY:** Annaleigh Ashford, *You Can't Take It with You*

**ACTOR IN A FEATURED ROLE IN A MUSICAL:** Christian Borle, *Something Rotten!*

**ACTRESS IN A FEATURED ROLE IN A MUSICAL:** Ruthie Ann Miles, *The King and I*

**SCENIC DESIGN OF A PLAY:** Bunny Christie and Finn Ross, *The Curious Incident of the Dog in the Night-Time*

**SCENIC DESIGN OF A MUSICAL:** Bob Crowley and 59 Productions, *An American in Paris*

**COSTUME DESIGN OF A PLAY:** Christopher Oram, *Wolf Hall Parts One & Two*

**COSTUME DESIGN OF A MUSICAL:** Catherine Zuber, *The King and I*

**LIGHTING DESIGN OF A PLAY:** Paule Constable, *The Curious Incident of the Dog in the Night-Time*

**LIGHTING DESIGN OF A MUSICAL:** Natasha Katz, *An American in Paris*

**SOUND DESIGN OF A PLAY:** Darron L. West, *Peter and the Starcatcher*

**SOUND DESIGN OF A MUSICAL:** Clive Goodwin, *Once*

**DIRECTION OF A PLAY:** Marianne Elliott, *The Curious Incident of the Dog in the Night-Time*

**DIRECTION OF A MUSICAL:** Sam Gold, *Fun Home*

**CHOREOGRAPHY:** Christopher Wheeldon, *An American in Paris*

**ORCHESTRATIONS:** Christopher Austin, Don Sebesky, and Bill Elliott, *An American in Paris*

**SPECIAL TONY AWARD FOR LIFETIME ACHIEVEMENT IN THE THEATRE:** Tommy Tune

**ISABELLE STEVENSON AWARD:** Stephen Schwartz

**REGIONAL THEATRE AWARD:** Cleveland Play House

**SPECIAL TONY AWARD:** John Cameron Mitchell

**TONY HONOR:** Arnold Abramson; Adrian Bryan-Brown; Gene O'Donovan

Helen Mirren and presenter Bradley Cooper

**BUNNY CHRISTIE:** The year we did *The Curious Incident of the Dog in the Night-Time*, the Tonys gave out the creative awards in the ad breaks of the filming. So as soon as they stopped filming everybody got up and went to the loo or said hello to someone across the aisle, but the show was still going on. When they announced my name, I had to excuse myself through all the people milling about. It was hilarious, but since not many people were paying attention, it really took the pressure off! The whole creative team winning together for *Curious* was wonderful. It was a very special show.

Designers work with such a huge team of people. We are part of every single bit of the production in a very unique way. We start with just the director, working for weeks together before the rest of the creative team join. Slowly layers of collaboration are added with the choreographer, musical director, sound, and crucially the lighting designer.

Scenic Design winners Finn Ross and Bunny Christie of *The Curious Incident of the Dog in the Night-Time*

Then we are sharing that with the builders, the painters, the prop people, the shoppers, buyers, and marketing in a way that nobody else really is. We move from the rehearsal room to production office. I do costume design as well as set, so I know the actors intimately. I see them in rehearsals and work with them to create their characters. I know how the set moves and what's going on in the wings as well as what's going on onstage.

Designers are at the center of this spinning team of hundreds of people who are making a show. All of that collaboration is what's gone into me picking up a Tony Award. I'm just one person and thus the filter for it. So, it's nice to have the opportunity when you win to say thank you. People have put time, energy, heart, and love into making shows and trying to get them right. The team is a massive team, and when you have a good team, it makes the work so much more fun.

**OSKAR EUSTIS:** *Fun Home* presented an interesting problem in adapting the book, the graphic novel by Alison Bechdel. What is the central story? There's an older Alison who's trying to write about her father, and a younger Alison discovering strange feelings, and a middle Alison who we see from the year before college until she goes to college and her dad dies. It only follows that middle Alison for about fifteen months. When the show originally came to the Public, it was heavily focused on the older and child Alisons. I felt that the protagonist was the middle Alison, who's finding out that she's gay and her finding out that her father's gay. Over the two years we worked on it, it changed quite a bit.

We had no idea that *Fun Home* would be so popular, but we knew it was something special. Samantha Power, who was the ambassador to the United Nations, brought the entire security council to see *Fun Home*. She didn't tell them what it was about. Most of the security council were from countries where being gay was illegal. They watched *Fun Home*. The next Monday the Orlando shooting took place. For the first and only time in the security council's history it issued a statement condemning violence against LGBTQ people. Samantha said it was because they saw *Fun Home* that she got everybody to sign off on the statement.

Fun Home's Alison Bechdel, Judy Kuhn, Emily Skeggs, Sydney Lucas, Sam Gold, Beth Malone, and Michael Cerveris

**CHRISTOPHER ORAM:** *Wolf Hall* was pretty much off the Richter scale in terms of how big of an enterprise it was. It was only really possible because it was an RSC production. They have this fantastic costume-making department the like of which no other building does in the UK. It's similar to the Met in New York. There were over twenty cast members, and they were all doubling and tripling. Some characters had costume journeys, while others had stock looks. A few characters had as many as ten outfits. If you get your job right, it feels like a smooth, seamless journey to the end result. *Wolf Hall* is set throughout Tudor England, from palaces and towers to boats on the river. I knew we were never going to physically represent all of that, so all the storytelling would have to be done through costumes. The set I created was a very cool, brutalist space that gave a sense to the religiosity. It was deliberately designed to show off the costumes and allow them to do the heavy lifting of the storytelling. All that feeds into it being a world you want to play in. It's a fantastic period for a costume designer, full of muscular bejeweled coats, beautiful ornate dresses, and every conceivable style of headwear.

**KELLI O'HARA:** When I signed on to do *The King and I*, and not knowing the show as well as other Rodgers and Hammerstein shows, I was expecting it to be a sweet revival. It turned out to be much more challenging and rewarding than I realized. Rodgers and Hammerstein's messages were so timely. They dug into these deep political and emotional themes but often dropped them inside fun musical comedy sounds. That experience was much more valuable to me than I ever imagined.

When you start out playing ingenue roles, you have a choice to make. You can try to hang on to the ingenue for the rest of your life, which can be devastating. I didn't

Richard McCabe, Marianne Elliott, and Bob Crowley

Christopher Austin and Bill Elliott of *An American in Paris*

Kelli O'Hara

was no way they were going to pass on those women and cast me. I was so green; I had never been on Broadway before. I was young and perhaps not formidable enough for this role. I thought she was the pivotal character in *The King and I*. When I auditioned for Bart Sher, I thought I was doing exactly what was expected of me. He threw his papers and asked what I was doing. I thought I was being Lady Thiang. I had an accent. I was a subservient woman, who was very respectful and perhaps cowing to Anna, the white woman in the room. Bart said, "Lady Thiang is Hillary Clinton. Lady Thiang is Imelda Marcos. She's just not allowed to say any of the things she's thinking." That absolutely blew my mind. He sent me home and told me to come back another day. I learned from that my accent didn't matter, my voice didn't matter, my look didn't matter. Everything had to do with my feelings that I could not say. That direction was absolutely world busting, changing, crack it open, life changing for me.　　Ruthie Ann Miles

want to do that. I was ready to move beyond the ingenue early in my career. The business doesn't necessarily want you to do that, and it's hard to make that change if you want to keep working. But you have to try. It's funny, I played younger than I was for a while, but the minute I went after roles that were stronger, I started playing older than myself, like *Bridges of Madison County* and *The King and I*. So when it came around to me doing something like *My Fair Lady*, I was told I was too old. So you make choices, and my choices led to me playing roles that were more meaningful to me with more gusto, heart, and intelligence. I don't regret that.

Winning the Tony was an amazing gift. Being part of this community means so much to me. I came up with people like Sutton Foster and Laura Benanti. We're all so different, yet we're all still finding places to make art. Sometimes we even get to do it together.

**RUTHIE ANN MILES:** I had a lot of auditions for *The King and I*. I was screened several times and then got in front of the team several times. I was very cognizant that the other women auditioning for the role were these beautiful performers who were ten to twenty years older than me. Lady Thiang is usually played by someone with a lot of gravitas and older than I was at the time. I thought there

Jim Parsons and Christian Borle

Annaleigh Ashford

Hosts Alan Cumming and Kristin Chenoweth with Lifetime Achievement winner Tommy Tune

# WINNERS ◎ 2016

Scenic Design winners David
Rockwell and David Zinn

**PLAY:** *The Humans*, Steven Karam

Produced by Scott Rudin, Barry Diller, Roundabout Theatre Company,
Fox Theatricals, James L. Nederlander, Terry Allen Kramer, Roy Furman, Daryl Roth,
Jon B. Platt, Eli Bush, Broadway Across America, Jack Lane, Barbara Whitman,
Jay Alix & Una Jackman, Scott M. Delman, Sonia Friedman, Amanda Lipitz,
Peter May, Stephanie P. McClelland, Lauren Stein, The Shubert Organization,
Joey Parnes, Sue Wagner, John Johnson, Roundabout Theatre Company,
ToddHaimes, Harold Wolpert, Julia C. Levy, Sydney Beers

**MUSICAL:** *Hamilton*

Produced by Jeffrey Seller, Sander Jacobs, Jill Furman, The Public Theater

**BOOK OF A MUSICAL:** Lin-Manuel Miranda, *Hamilton*

**ORIGINAL SCORE (MUSIC AND/OR LYRICS) WRITTEN FOR THE THEATRE:**
Lin-Manuel Miranda, *Hamilton*

**REVIVAL OF A PLAY:** *Arthur Miller's A View from the Bridge*

Produced by Scott Rudin, Lincoln Center Theater, Eli Bush, Robert G. Bartner, Roger Berlind, William
Berlind, Roy Furman, Peter May, Amanda Lipitz, Stephanie P. McClelland, Jay Alix & Una Jackman,
Scott M. Delman, Sonia Friedman, John Gore, Ruth Hendel, JFL Theatricals, Heni Koenigsberg, Jon B. Platt,
Daryl Roth, Spring Sirkin, Joey Parnes, Sue Wagner, John Johnson, The Young Vic

Paul Tazewell

**REVIVAL OF A MUSICAL:** *The Color Purple*

Produced by Scott Sanders Productions, Roy Furman, Oprah Winfrey, David Babani, Tom Siracusa,
Caiola Productions, James Fantaci, Ted Liebowitz, Stephanie P. McClelland, James L. Nederlander,
Darren Bagert, Candy Spelling, Adam Zotovich, Eric Falkenstein/Morris Berchard, Just for Laughs
Theatricals/Tanya Link Productions, Adam S. Gordon, Jam Theatricals, Kelsey Grammer,
Independent Presenters Network, Carol Fineman, Sandy Block, Quincy Jones,
Menier Chocolate Factory Productions

**ACTOR IN A LEADING ROLE IN A PLAY:** Frank Langella, *The Father*

**ACTRESS IN A LEADING ROLE IN A PLAY:** Jessica Lange,
*Long Day's Journey into Night*

**ACTOR IN A LEADING ROLE IN A MUSICAL:**
Leslie Odom Jr., *Hamilton*

**ACTRESS IN A LEADING ROLE IN A MUSICAL:**
Cynthia Erivo, *The Color Purple*

Jan Versweyveld and Ivo van Hove

Actors in a Musical winners
Daveed Diggs, Cynthia Erivo,
Leslie Odom Jr., and Renée
Elise Goldsberry

**ACTOR IN A FEATURED ROLE IN A PLAY:**
Reed Birney, *The Humans*

**ACTRESS IN A FEATURED ROLE IN A PLAY:**
Jayne Houdyshell, *The Humans*

**ACTOR IN A FEATURED ROLE IN A MUSICAL:**
Daveed Diggs, *Hamilton*

**ACTRESS IN A FEATURED ROLE IN A MUSICAL:**
Renée Elise Goldsberry, *Hamilton*

**SCENIC DESIGN OF A PLAY:** David Zinn, *The Humans*

**SCENIC DESIGN OF A MUSICAL:** David Rockwell, *She Loves Me*

**COSTUME DESIGN OF A PLAY:** Clint Ramos, *Eclipsed*

**COSTUME DESIGN OF A MUSICAL:** Paul Tazewell, *Hamilton*

**LIGHTING DESIGN OF A PLAY:** Natasha Katz, *Long Day's Journey into Night*

**LIGHTING DESIGN OF A MUSICAL:** Howell Binkley, *Hamilton*

**DIRECTION OF A PLAY:** Ivo Van Hove, *Arthur Miller's A View from the Bridge*

**DIRECTION OF A MUSICAL:** Thomas Kail, *Hamilton*

**CHOREOGRAPHY:** Andy Blankenbuehler, *Hamilton*

**ORCHESTRATIONS:** Alex Lacamoire, *Hamilton*

**SPECIAL TONY AWARD FOR LIFETIME ACHIEVEMENT
IN THE THEATRE:** Sheldon Harnick; Marshall W. Mason

**ISABELLE STEVENSON AWARD:** Brian Stokes Mitchell

**REGIONAL THEATRE AWARD:** Paper Mill
Playhouse, Milburn, New Jersey

**SPECIAL TONY AWARD:** National Endowment
for the Arts; Miles Wilkin

**TONY HONOR:** Seth Gelblum; Joan Lader; Sally Ann Parsons

*Hamilton*'s Thomas Kail, Oskar
Eustis, Andy Blankenbuehler,
and Alex Lacamoire

Sheldon Harnick

**CLINT RAMOS:** I grew up in the Philippines, Clint Ramos and when Lea Salonga won the Tony for *Miss Saigon*, it was a national event. At that point winning a Tony seemed so unattainable. When I won, I was so stunned. It was my first nomination. When I looked out into the crowd, the first face I saw was Oprah's! It was paralyzing, so I looked next to her and there was Whoopi Goldberg and Jessica Lange! All I could think about was my parents. I come from a long line of lawyers, and I think they had concerns. Looking back, I can't even remember what I said.

My award was the first one they presented that night. My mom was with me, and we brought a little bag of snacks. Since this was my first time, everyone told me I had to bring snacks. My mom started to feel a little dizzy, so I was digging through the bag looking for a granola bar when they called the category, and then I heard my name!

The characters in *Eclipsed* are African women. They were victims of a very prolonged war and were sex slaves. Audiences might not immediately relate to them. I used the costumes to bridge that gap. In my research I learned that Africa had become a repository of America's discards.

It was amazing to see the juxtaposition of women wearing traditional cloth with American T-shirts.

One of the most profound things to me was when I went backstage and a reporter told me I was the first person of color to win is this category [Best Costume Design for a Play]. This was 2016, which showed how behind we were. That gave my win more meaning and more weight. Maybe this could mean something to somebody out there watching. I was very happy when Montana Blanco won and this was continuing to occur.

**DAVID ZINN:** What's great about awards is feeling the pride of the folks who had invested in your career and your passion early in your life. It's impossible to thank those people enough, but that Tony moment is an opportunity to look back and say, "I see you and I celebrate you as the foundation of my work that's honored here, and I'm enjoying this experience for us." There are these magic people that see something in you when you're twelve, or thirteen, or fourteen—your parents, your sister, a drama teacher, a friend. Their belief in you is the fuel you need, desperately. Having the ability to say, in a big room, that their faith in you bore fruit, that we're here together because of—that's an honor just in itself, to get to say thank you.

When I won for *The Humans*, I got my award, and then was sent backstage for photos and interviews. From the press room you get fed backstage and at that moment there was a huge group rushing to the stage for a musical number. A bunch of people were scooting past me, and as I stepped back I looked up to see Bebe Neuwirth on the other side of this crowded stairway—I was holding my Tony Award, and she said, "Congratulations." I thanked her. And as I looked around at this whole scene, all lit by blue backstage light, I added, "It's really nice back here." It's true—it felt like home. And she smiled and said, "This is the best part." One of the pleasures of winning is that you get three experiences. You get the watching, then you get the super surreal experience where time stops and you're talking in front of a big group of people, and then you leave that into that beautiful, weird backstage zone. I remember that so deeply as a bounty of beautiful experiences. Walking home that night after the party, on a Sunday night after midnight with the streets empty, I just thought about all of the roads that got me to this beautiful place.

**DAVID ROCKWELL:** For me the Tonys lived in this mythic world that was so powerful because, even though theatre was my first love, I made my name in a completely different realm—in architecture. When I first started in theatre, I was so enamored with the community that there was an automatic concern that I'd be perceived as a dabbler or an interloper. The Tony was a lifelong dream for me, and when I won that ultimate symbol of belonging and validation it was a powerful embrace from a community of which I'm proud and gratified to count myself as a member.

**TODD HAIMES:** The Roundabout used to just have a 440-seat theater called the Laura Pels Theater. That's where we did new plays. I noticed over time that the critics were very harsh on our young playwrights. They reviewed their new plays as if they were on Broadway. I had this theory that they were looking at it incorrectly for emerging playwrights. Nine months passed since I had that thought, and we did a fantastic reading of a play that we really liked by this unknown person who had never written any public play, named Stephen Karam. It was called *Speech and Debate*. I wasn't comfortable putting the play in our big theater. We built a sixty-two-seat theater in our basement to do that play. We developed a program called The Underground for shows in that space. The mission was to give young American playwrights their first New York production and to commission their second play before the first play opened. I don't know if there's any Tony Award that made me happier then when Stephen Karam won for *The Humans*. We launched that career from The Underground and nurtured all of his plays. We really built that space because of his play.

**JILL FURMAN:** *Hamilton* entered the cultural conversation and was different from anything I'd ever seen before. People as varied as Michelle Obama and Busta Rhymes came to see it in the early days of The Public Theater production. David Brooks wrote an op-ed piece in the *New York Times* before we opened. I had never seen that before. It felt meaningful in a way that showed us it wasn't just a show. I'm so proud of it. I'm proud of my relationship with Lin. I think it's helping more theatre artists take risks. It shows that if you're very talented, you can write a musical about anything.

Jessica Lange

**JESSICA LANGE:** There's something unique about the Tonys. *Long Day's Journey into Night* was my third production on Broadway. I had done *Streetcar* back in the nineties, and then *Glass Menagerie*. I hadn't been nominated for either of those performances. I never felt a part of the theatrical community. I always felt like an outsider there, so I was thrilled to be nominated and know that the work was recognized. When I won it was one of the most special nights I can remember. I had my daughter and granddaughter there with me. It was a very magical evening.

Mary Tyrone is the most thrilling part I've ever played. *Long Day's Journey into Night* is one of the greatest plays of all time. You don't come across writing like that very often. Eugene O'Neill was writing from such a place of truth. He was exploring memories that were so profound and personal. It's an extraordinary gift for an actor to be given the opportunity to play something so truthful. The journey Mary Tyrone is on in the course of that one day is so complete. There's always more to explore as an actor, which is exhilarating when you're onstage eight times a week, week after week after week.

**BRIAN STOKES MITCHELL:** I immediately took my Isabelle Stevenson Award to the Actors Fund office. I said to the president, Joe Benincasa, "This is for everybody at the Actors Fund. We've all earned this together. Let people take this home if they want. It's for all of us." As long as I'm the chairman there, that award will be at the Actors Fund. The award was symbolically given to me, but Joe Benincasa and the entire staff are really doing the hard work. The award really belongs to the entire community.

I knew Isabelle Stevenson. She was a great supporter and a friend. I loved her spirit. To receive the award that was named after her, and what that award represents, was better than the acting award, as wonderful as that is. The Isabelle Stevenson Award is about the community, not only me. It's a representation of what happens when we try to do good in the world, and we do things for others. To have that validated is important. It shows the world that it's important to do things for others. We can accomplish so much when we have a common goal in mind. It's miraculous what human beings can do when we work together, which at its core is what a Broadway show does. We work together to create something that changes people, moves people, makes them happy, opens their hearts

Brian Stokes Mitchell and Marshall W. Mason

and minds. The Isabelle Stevenson Award acknowledges us all together doing something for the good of others. It's about the collective.

**LIN-MANUEL MIRANDA:** *Hamilton* is a bad elevator pitch: a musical about the Founding Fathers. It really does sound like some *Schoolhouse Rock* shit. But at the same time, I think that that book by Ron Chernow was unbelievably compelling. I couldn't believe no one else had made it into a musical. That's the only directive or impulse that means anything at all—what doesn't exist but should. I got to the end of the second chapter, and I went on Google to see if someone had written a *Hamilton* musical. When I realized no one had, I got to work. There had been a play that had been turned into a movie in the 1920s, but no one had written a musical.

Every day I'm bowled over by a new thing. I remember going to Trinity Church when I was doing research. I saw Hamilton's gravestone, and I knew Angelica's gravestone was in there because the biography said so, but there was nothing to mark it. Now if you go down to Trinity Church, there's a marker for Eliza's grave, there's a marker for Angelica, there's a marker for Philip. That's because of the musical! There are weird real-world effects of just a greater awareness of these stories and these very flawed people who shaped our country. I'm kind of blown away by some new detail someone shares with me every day. We know what these people look like—they're on our money; they're on statues. Our goal was to take them off of the statues and off of the money and mess with them a little bit.

**ALEX LACAMOIRE:** Lin was so clear about how the songs in *Hamilton* needed to be. If you hear his original demos, there's such clarity in the direction. "You'll Be Back" was always going to be a Brit pop song. "Right Hand Man" was always going to be a nasty hip-hop groove. I helped to find a way to clarify what the instruments were going to be doing and how a band could play together and make something that served the story [and was] fun to play and musically exciting. It was like a crossword puzzle in a way. It took me about eight months to orchestrate *Hamilton*. I took my time. I made demos for myself. I questioned everything. I wanted it to be tight—all killer, no filler.

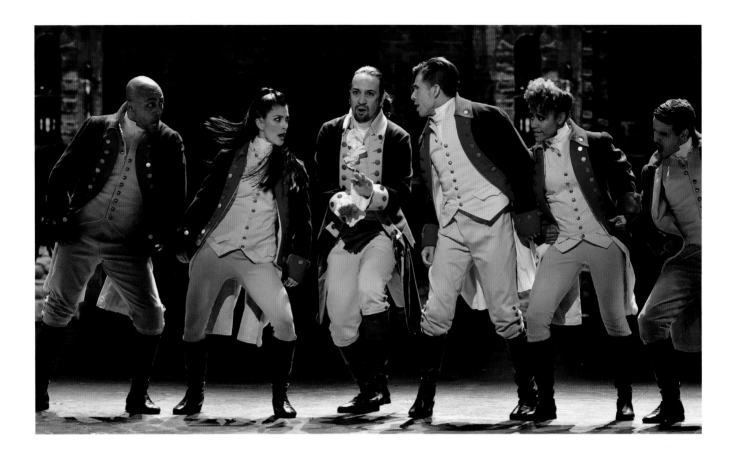

**PAUL TAZEWELL:** Winning a Tony was always a huge dream. I was nominated for a Tony for my first Broadway show, *Bring in 'da Noise, Bring in 'da Funk*. The next nomination was for *The Color Purple*. That was one that I really wanted, but it didn't happen. Years passed, and there were a few more nominations. Then came the process of creating *Hamilton*. There were years that went into that, and I developed relationships with Tommy Kail, Lin-Manuel Miranda, and Andy Blankenbuehler. Seeing the way the show took off was like no other show I'd experienced. *Hamilton* was deeply meaningful to me, and I had also by that point come to clarity around awards for my work. It meant that much more to win the Tony for *Hamilton* because I was now at a place where it wasn't a surface desire. It wasn't a qualifier for the value of my work. I already valued it, and I knew that my collaborators valued what I brought to the work. It was a much more adult relationship to receiving the award.

The Tony has always been near and dear to me and seemed more accessible than other awards. The idea of being nominated for an Oscar before Steven Spielberg asked me to design *West Side Story* seemed unattainable. There will always be a very dear place in my heart around the Tony Award and how it speaks of the importance of our theatre community and industry. It also reinforces my position within that theatre community.

Most of my work has been musicals, so it's always been important for me to help to realize characters that have an emotional reality, so they are accessible to an audience. That's why musicals are moving; there is an expression of emotion that happens through breaking into song and dance that you don't get in any other art form. The work that I do as a costume designer helps to underscore that. I hope to render characters that ring true, whether it's subtly or in obvious ways, by manipulating color and shape and silhouette, and the way my designs move through space. All of that together is hopefully transcending a straightforward story and becomes poetic.

I work to create an intimate space that is a safe space. It's intimate because I'm putting forward what my idea is

Seth Stewart, Carleigh Bettiol, Lin-Manuel Miranda, Jon Rua, Ariana DeBose, and David Guzman of *Hamilton*, costumes by Paul Tazewell

and seeing if it jibes with what the actor's idea is. That's a vulnerable place. The actors are literally shedding clothing and putting on other clothing to take on this character that I'm hopeful will work for them. As my idea is being created in the moment I'm standing and watching their body language and seeing what subtle messages they're sending through the mirror and how they relate to what I'm asking them to wear. That conversation is both silent and also encouraging conversation about what the choices are, how we can make the choices clearer, what works and what doesn't work. That goes alongside of making sure the clothing fits and has the same design lines that I drew in my sketch. There's a lot that needs to be accomplished in a fitting, and we're working on multiple levels.

In *Hamilton* the cast starts out in the parchment tone, an off-white neutral color palette, so we see them as a group all on the same level. They line up as unidentified characters, except for Burr. Hamilton is revealed by putting on a coat in a costume-specific moment. We continue to add pieces on top of this neutral palette that are specific colors, have a certain kind of texture or cut. The three sisters' colors work together. They each have their own individual color. My husband loves aqua, so I chose to use that color to represent Eliza. They're both creative and personal choices. Most of my choices are how I viscerally feel about a character. The color that I chose to put on Angelica the first time we see her is like the sun. There was this energy that surrounded that iridescent golden rose tone. I felt that spoke of who she was as a character. I think if I have an emotional tie to a costume, there will be enough audience members that will have that same connection to it.

When I first started working with Howell Binkley, he was already an acclaimed designer, and I was a youngster coming up. He was always a gentleman, always the warmest in the room. He was always a beacon of warmth that made me feel welcome and okay in the room and allowed me to settle my spirit enough to be present and do the work that was needed of me. He sculpted and made sense of the color palette that I put onstage. He was able to use color in a way that became dynamic with what I was doing. It was always exciting to see how it evolved. I'm blessed to have had the opportunity to work with him.

The Tonys are hugely meaningful from inside our industry. It's important how we honor our peers and show them that they are valued. It's an opportunity to raise everyone up, whether you're nominated or win. It's celebrating all the work we do of a season and giving that heartfelt applause from people who know how hard it is to do what we do.

**SCOTT SANDERS:** We premiered the original production of *The Color Purple* in 2005, and it earned eleven Tony Award nominations. LaChanze won the Tony for originating the role of Celie. The musical launched its first of three North American tours in 2007 and the show continued to entertain audiences for five more years.

A part of Alice Walker's story follows Celie's sister Nettie to Africa. Once we opened the show on Broadway, Oprah and I had a dream to bring *The Color Purple* musical to the continent of Africa. Oprah was planning the opening of her Oprah Winfrey Leadership Academy for Girls in South Africa. We began to make plans to travel to Johannesburg in 2007. In advance of that trip, I called my friend Tom Schumacher at Disney and asked him if he could introduce me to the local producers in South Africa. I met with two leading producers, and they were very interested in presenting the show in SA, but felt the scale of the Broadway production was too large for it to make business sense for a limited run. My takeaway was that we needed to come up with a smaller, more efficient production of the show. Knowing the reputation of London's Menier Chocolate Factory for creatively reimagining popular musicals for a smaller-scale venue, I reached out to David Babani to ask if they wanted to produce London's first production of *The Color Purple*. David was enthusiastic to reenvision the work for his 180-seat theatre, and plans were made to premiere the show in the summer of 2013. Our director, John Doyle, cast Cynthia Erivo in the lead role of Celie.

When I went over to London to see the first performance in this jewel box of a space, it was so incredibly powerful. We all know that British audiences have a reputation for not giving standing ovations, but after the first performance, every single person in the audience stood up, not only applauding, but also stomping their feet on the bleacher seating. The actors had gone backstage and started to remove their costumes, but the thunderous pounding of feet on the bleachers—sounding like a football game—continued on for so long that they had to re-dress and come back out for a second bow. That night, I told Cynthia, "You're astounding. Broadway needs to see you do this." The next day I had a sobering lunch with my co-producers at the Corinthia Hotel. They said I shouldn't revive *The Color Purple* because it had only closed five years earlier. It was too soon. But the idea just kept burning a flame inside of me. I pursued casting Jennifer Hudson for the role of Shug Avery. In 2015, the planets finally lined up for us to adapt the Menier Chocolate Factory production as the first Broadway revival of *The Color Purple* at the Bernard Jacobs Theatre, starring Cynthia Erivo, Jennifer Hudson, and Danielle Brooks. It was a revelation to see the show in New York with this more intimate scale. Audiences and critics raved.

Cut to Tony Sunday of 2016. *The Color Purple* was nominated for five Tony Awards. Cynthia was nominated and had become the toast of the town. Oprah showed up to present our music performance on the Tony broadcast. The Best Revival of a Musical award is presented earlier than Best Musical. Jeffrey Seller and his husband, Josh, were sitting right next to us. He was there as producer of *Hamilton*. Jeffrey and I were both nervous wrecks, and we both won. It was a monumental night, one that I'll never forget. It was tremendous recognition for Cynthia to win the Outstanding Actress in a Musical Tony in her Broadway debut. It became the ultimate launch-pad for her successful film and television career. The Tony Awards for *The Color Purple* made Oprah Winfrey a first-time Tony winner and Quincy Jones an EGOT.

Our Tonys mean a lot to us. The award is a recognition of craft and talent. Winning the Tony for Best Revival of a Musical was an acknowledgment from our community that this production was unique and special. For all of us who spend our days and weeks and months and years working in the theatre, it is often for love and passion more so than for money. It's because we love telling stories onstage with a live audience. This kind of collaboration is rare and unique from an artistic perspective. When you can get the financial box office and the reviews and the Tony, it's a trifecta of icing on the cake.

Dunnel Brooks, Oprah Winfrey, LaRita Brooks, Danielle Brooks, and Scott Sanders

# WINNERS ⊙ 2017

PLAY: *Oslo*, J. T. Rogers

Produced by Lincoln Center Theater, André Bishop, Adam Siegel, Hattie K. Jutagir

MUSICAL: *Dear Evan Hansen*

Produced by Stacey Mindich, Mickey Liddell, Hunter Arnold, Caiola Productions, Double Gemini Productions, Fakston Productions, Roy Furman, Harris Karma Productions, On Your Marks Group, Darren Bagert, Roger & William Berlind, Bob Boyett, Colin Callender, Caitlin Clements, Freddy DeMann, Dante Di Loreto, Bonnie & Kenneth Feld, FickStern Productions, Eric & Marsi Gardiner, Robert Greenblatt, Jere Harris and Darren DeVerna, The John Gore Organization, Mike Kriak, Arielle Tepper Madover, David Mirvish, Eva Price, Zeilinger Productions, Adam Zotovich, Ambassador Theatre Group, Independent Presenters Network, The Shubert Organization, Wendy Orshan, Jeffrey M. Wilson, Arena Stage, Molly Smith, Edgar Dobie, Second Stage Theatre, Carole Rothman, Casey Reitz

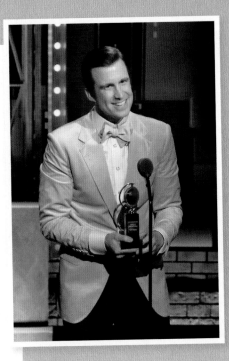

Gavin Creel

BOOK OF A MUSICAL: Steven Levenson, *Dear Evan Hansen*

ORIGINAL SCORE (MUSIC AND/OR LYRICS) WRITTEN FOR THE THEATRE:
Benj Pasek and Justin Paul, *Dear Evan Hansen*

REVIVAL OF A PLAY: *August Wilson's Jitney*

Produced by Manhattan Theatre Club, Lynne Meadow, Barry Grove, Eric Falkenstein, Ron Simons, John Legend/Mike Jackson, Ken Wirth

REVIVAL OF A MUSICAL: *Hello, Dolly!*

Produced by Scott Rudin, Roy Furman, James L. Nederlander, Eli Bush, Universal Stage Productions, Roger Berlind, William Berlind, Heni Koenigsberg, Terry Allen Kramer, Seth A. Goldstein, The John Gore Organization, Daryl Roth, The Araca Group, Len Blavatnik, Eric Falkenstein, Ruth Hendel, Independent Presenters Network, Peter May, Jay Alix & Una Jackman, Jane Bergère, Scott M. Delman, Wendy Federman, Stephanie P. McClelland, Anita Waxman, Al Nocciolino, Spring Sirkin, Barbara Freitag, John Mara Jr. & Benjamin Simpson, Joey Parnes, Sue Wagner, John Johnson

ACTOR IN A LEADING ROLE IN A PLAY: Kevin Kline, *Present Laughter*

ACTRESS IN A LEADING ROLE IN A PLAY: Laurie Metcalf, *A Doll's House, Part 2*

ACTOR IN A LEADING ROLE IN A MUSICAL: Ben Platt, *Dear Evan Hansen*

ACTRESS IN A LEADING ROLE IN A MUSICAL: Bette Midler, *Hello, Dolly!*

ACTOR IN A FEATURED ROLE IN A PLAY: Michael Aronov, *Oslo*

ACTRESS IN A FEATURED ROLE IN A PLAY:
Cynthia Nixon, *Lillian Hellman's The Little Foxes*

J. T. Rogers

Sound designers Gareth Fry and Pete Malkin accepting a Special Tony Award for *The Encounter*

**ACTOR IN A FEATURED ROLE IN A MUSICAL:**
Gavin Creel, *Hello, Dolly!*

**ACTRESS IN A FEATURED ROLE IN A MUSICAL:**
Rachel Bay Jones, *Dear Evan Hansen*

**SCENIC DESIGN OF A PLAY:** Nigel Hook, *The Play That Goes Wrong*

**SCENIC DESIGN OF A MUSICAL:** Mimi Lien, *Natasha, Pierre & the Great Comet of 1812*

**COSTUME DESIGN OF A PLAY:** Jane Greenwood, *Lillian Hellman's The Little Foxes*

**COSTUME DESIGN OF A MUSICAL:** Santo Loquasto, *Hello, Dolly!*

**LIGHTING DESIGN OF A PLAY:** Christopher Akerlind, *Indecent*

**LIGHTING DESIGN OF A MUSICAL:** Bradley King, *Natasha, Pierre & the Great Comet of 1812*

**DIRECTION OF A PLAY:** Rebecca Taichman, *Indecent*

**DIRECTION OF A MUSICAL:** Christopher Ashley, *Come from Away*

**CHOREOGRAPHY:** Andy Blankenbuehler, *Bandstand*

**ORCHESTRATIONS:** Alex Lacamoire, *Dear Evan Hansen*

**SPECIAL TONY AWARD FOR LIFETIME ACHIEVEMENT IN THE THEATRE:** James Earl Jones

**ISABELLE STEVENSON AWARD:** Baayork Lee

**REGIONAL THEATRE AWARD:**
Dallas Theater Center

**SPECIAL TONY AWARD:**
Gareth Fry and Pete Malkin

**TONY HONOR:**
Nina Lannan; Alan Wasser

James Earl Jones and Mark Hamill

**BENJ PASEK AND JUSTIN PAUL:**
The Tony Awards is more than just
an award show. It's a window into

Benj Pasek and Justin
Paul accepting for
Original Score

an incredible world for every theatre kid who wonders if
they'll ever find their place. It's a night where we cheer
on music, dance, stories, and songs and celebrate the folks
who make it all possible. To think that we were once just
kids watching that world from afar and now we get to be
part of the community that inspired us to create musicals
is almost beyond comprehension. The Tonys will always be
that permission-giving event for the kids who spontaneously
break out into song and put on plays in their backyards,
inviting them to be part of it all one day too.

**J. T. ROGERS:** I had been told by wiser, older theatre
artists that if you win, you're going to be relieved,
and they were right. For whatever the reasons, I was
the front-runner, which made me incredibly nervous,
having never been the front-runner in anything having
to do with the arts in my entire career. As Tony night
got closer, I became quite anxious. When they called my
name I was gobsmacked as I walked up to the stage,
desperately trying to remember who to thank in the four
seconds I had to speak.

I never thought that *Oslo* (A) would transfer to
Broadway, or (B) would run the table of every award
with the capstone being this extraordinary honor,

the Tony Award. When I was writing it, I don't think
anyone would have bet that a fourteen-actor, Israeli-
Palestinian conflict play with Yasser Arafat in spiritual
form onstage—and that's three hours long—would go to
Broadway. All to say, as a playwright, it's a fool's errand
to try and pick which of your plays is going to have a
commercial life.

But I will say that a key reason for *Oslo*'s success was
the brilliant choreography of Bartlett Sher's staging and
the visual splendor of his design team. Steve Sondheim
told me over drinks that he thought Bart's production
was the single best staging of a play he'd ever seen.
Agreed.

**BRADLEY KING:** The most important use of lighting in
*Natasha, Pierre & the Great Comet of 1812* was to make
sure the audience knew where to look and what was
going on. There were physical challenges to that show.
We first did the show at Ars Nova, and we were in a
room with a nine-foot ceiling. Typical theatrical lighting
was too big for it. That's where the idea for the light
bulbs and table lamps came in. We figured out how to
do the show more architecturally than theatrically. That
ended up working out well and became the base for the
Broadway production.

**SANTO LOQUASTO:** The intention of this production of
*Hello, Dolly!* was to do as beautiful a revival as we could. I
certainly acknowledged the nineteenth-century look in the
same way that Oliver Smith did in the original. Often, we
used the same engravings of New York but executed them
differently. It was really about doing a lush version of it that
embraced the 1880s.

The first time we were onstage in costume and Bette
Midler entered, everyone was elated. But *I* sensed that
Bette had issues, so I went down to the edge of the stage.
She said, "Ask them if we can do it again, and this time
I want to watch." Bette came down the aisle and stood
near me. We did the number again, and the assistant
choreographer stood in. Bette said she had to talk to me.
She kept clutching at her mic saying, "Am I off? I want to
make sure no one can hear me. Is the goddamn thing off?"
We went into her dressing room, and she said, "They all

Michael Aronov

look *too* good. They look just as good as I do. I worry I don't stand out." Early on we had discussed the notion that Dolly was an independent woman and should be in more of a suit like a businesswoman. Sadly, we had drifted away from that. This more distinctive character choice was now missing. Bette was right! So, we put her in a dress we loved—a bright blue dress in the midst of all this confetti. Now she stood out.

**ANDRÉ BISHOP:** *Oslo* was developed under our very own roof from scratch. It was *Oslo* the workshop, and then *Oslo* the play at the Mitzi Newhouse. The we moved it to the Beaumont, and it became *Oslo* the Broadway play.

**MIMI LIEN:** I never even dared to dream that winning a Tony would be something to strive for, much less anything that would happen to me in my lifetime. To have one means going beyond what I ever dreamed possible.

The hallmark of the design for *Natasha, Pierre & the Great Comet of 1812* is its environmental aspect, which was ultimately about set design and architecture coming together. I had to learn everything about building code for that design, because every bit of space that the actors inhabited was also inhabited by the general public…the entire set had to be up to code.

Because of the particular journey of *Natasha, Pierre & the Great Comet of 1812*, it became a lesson in how to maintain the spine of the design through very different spatial contexts and venues. We were in so many different spaces, from an eighty-seven-seat cabaret space to a twelve-hundred-seat Broadway house. How do you maintain the same spirit of the design in such vastly different spaces? That was a very specific lesson that I could only have learned from this show.

**ALEX LACAMOIRE:** *Hamilton* ended its run at the Public at the top of May, and we started rehearsals for *Dear Evan Hansen* a month later. In that month I orchestrated most of *Dear Evan Hansen*. I don't know how I did it, but there were things about the show that just flowed out of me. I was in the zone because I had lived with that music long enough that I understood where it needed to go. I had had a lot of writing practice because of *Hamilton*. I was just off the heels of being creatively inspired, so I was in a place where I could crank out charts quickly in a short amount of time.

*Natasha, Pierre & the Great Comet of 1812*'s Mimi Lien, Bradley King, and Paloma Young

*Dear Evan Hansen*'s Michael Park, Steven Levenson, Jennifer Laura Thompson, Michael Greif, Ben Platt, Kristolyn Lloyd, Alex Lacamoire, Rachel Bay Jones, Justin Paul, Ben Pasek, Stacey Mindich, Laura Dreyfuss, and Will Roland

It's amazing being a Tony winner, particularly because orchestration is not a category that's been around for a very long time. I'm honored that orchestration is considered a creative art, because it is, and I'm honored to be recognized for it. The community of orchestration is very small, and to be even a fraction of a thought in any of those people's minds and to be part of that circle is hugely rewarding and overwhelming. To be recognized by the whole industry in that way is fantastic and makes me proud. It's not why I do it, but it's a wonderful piece of recognition. It encourages you to keep going and feel there's care in what you cared about.

Actress winners Laurie Metcalf and Bette Midler

# WINNERS ◎ 2018

**PLAY:** *Harry Potter and the Cursed Child, Parts One and Two*, Jack Thorne

Produced by Sonia Friedman Productions, Colin Callender,
Harry Potter Theatrical Productions

### MUSICAL: *The Band's Visit*

Produced by Orin Wolf, StylesFour Productions, Evamere Entertainment, Atlantic
Theater Company, David F. Schwartz, Barbara Broccoli, Frederick Zollo, Grove • REG,
Lassen Blume Baldwin, Thomas Steven Perakos, Marc Platt, The Shubert Organization,
The Baruch/Routh/Frankel/Viertel Group, Robert Cole, deRoy-Carr-Klausner,
Federman-Moellenberg, FilmNation Entertainment, Roy Furman, FVSL Theatricals,
Hendel-Karmazin, HoriPro Inc., IPN, Jam Theatricals, The John Gore Organization,
Koenigsberg-Krauss, David Mirvish, James L. Nederlander, Al Nocciolino,
Once Upon a Time Productions, Susan Rose, Paul Shiverick, Allan Williams

**BOOK OF A MUSICAL:** Itamar Moses, *The Band's Visit*

**ORIGINAL SCORE (MUSIC AND/OR LYRICS) WRITTEN FOR THE THEATRE:**
David Yazbek, *The Band's Visit*

**REVIVAL OF A PLAY:** *Angels in America*

Produced by Tim Levy for NT America, Jordan Roth, Rufus Norris & Lisa Burger for the
National Theatre, Elliott & Harper Productions, Kash Bennett for NT Productions, Aged in
Wood, The Baruch-Viertel-Routh-Frankel Group, Jane Bergère, Adam Blanshay Productions,
Catwenjam Productions, Jean Doumanian, Gilad-Rogowsky, Gold-Ross Productions,
The John Gore Organization, Grove Entertainment, Harris Rubin Productions, Hornos-
Moellenberg, Brian & Dayna Lee, Benjamin Lowy, Stephanie P. McClelland, David Mirvish,
Mark Pigott, Jon B. Platt, E. Price-LD Ent., Daryl Roth, Catherine Schreiber, Barbara Whitman,
Jujamcyn Theaters, The Nederlander Organization, The Shubert Organization

### REVIVAL OF A MUSICAL: *Once on This Island*

Produced by Ken Davenport, Hunter Arnold, Carl Daikeler, Roy Putrino,
Broadway Strategic Return Fund, Sandi Moran, Caiola Productions, H. Richard
Hopper, Diego Kolankowsky, Brian Cromwell Smith, Ron Kastner, Rob Kolson,
Judith Manocherian/Kevin Lyle, Jay Alix/Una Jackman/Jeff Wise, Witzend
Productions/Jeff Grove/Wishnie-Strasberg, Mark Ferris/Michelle Riley/Marie
Stevenson, Silva Theatrical Group/Jesse McKendry/Dr. Mojgan Fajiram, Conor
Bagley/Brendan C. Tetro/Invisible Wall Productions, Silverwalport Productions/
Tyler Mount/Ushkowitzlatimer Productions, The Harbert Family/Reilly Hickey,
Keith Cromwell/Red Mountain Theatre Company, 42nd.club/
The Yonnone Family/Island Productions

**ACTOR IN A LEADING ROLE IN A PLAY:**
Andrew Garfield, *Angels in America*

**ACTRESS IN A LEADING ROLE IN A PLAY:** Glenda Jackson,
*Edward Albee's Three Tall Women*

Glenda Jackson

*Carousel*'s Lindsay
Mendez and Justin Peck

Catherine Zuber, Katrina
Lindsay, and Christine Jones

**ACTOR IN A LEADING ROLE IN A MUSICAL:** Tony Shalhoub, *The Band's Visit*

**ACTRESS IN A LEADING ROLE IN A MUSICAL:** Katrina Lenk, *The Band's Visit*

**ACTOR IN A FEATURED ROLE IN A PLAY:** Nathan Lane, *Angels in America*

**ACTRESS IN A FEATURED ROLE IN A PLAY:** Laurie Metcalf, *Edward Albee's Three Tall Women*

**ACTOR IN A FEATURED ROLE IN A MUSICAL:** Ari'el Stachel, *The Band's Visit*

**ACTRESS IN A FEATURED ROLE IN A MUSICAL:** Lindsay Mendez, *Rodgers & Hammerstein's Carousel*

**SCENIC DESIGN OF A PLAY:** Christine Jones, *Harry Potter and the Cursed Child, Parts One and Two*

**SCENIC DESIGN OF A MUSICAL:** David Zinn, *SpongeBob SquarePants: The Musical*

**COSTUME DESIGN OF A PLAY:** Katrina Lindsay, *Harry Potter and the Cursed Child, Parts One and Two*

**COSTUME DESIGN OF A MUSICAL:** Catherine Zuber, *My Fair Lady*

**LIGHTING DESIGN OF A PLAY:** Neil Austin, *Harry Potter and the Cursed Child, Parts One and Two*

**LIGHTING DESIGN OF A MUSICAL:** Tyler Micoleau, *The Band's Visit*

**SOUND DESIGN OF A PLAY:** Gareth Fry, *Harry Potter and the Cursed Child, Parts One and Two*

**SOUND DESIGN OF A MUSICAL:** Kai Harada, *The Band's Visit*

**DIRECTION OF A PLAY:** John Tiffany, *Harry Potter and the Cursed Child, Parts One and Two*

**DIRECTION OF A MUSICAL:** David Cromer, *The Band's Visit*

**CHOREOGRAPHY:** Justin Peck, *Rodgers & Hammerstein's Carousel*

**ORCHESTRATIONS:** Jamshied Sharifi, *The Band's Visit*

**SPECIAL TONY AWARD FOR LIFETIME ACHIEVEMENT IN THE THEATRE:** Chita Rivera; Andrew Lloyd Webber

**ISABELLE STEVENSON AWARD:** Nick Scandalios

**REGIONAL THEATRE AWARD:** La MaMa E.T.C., New York, New York

**SPECIAL TONY AWARD:** John Leguizamo; Bruce Springsteen

**TONY HONOR:** Sara Krulwich; Bessie Nelson; Ernest Winzer Cleaners

Lifetime Achievement winners Andrew Lloyd Webber and Chita Rivera

**NATHAN LANE:** I was at a point in my life and career where I felt I really needed to shake things up. I was doing *The Addams Family* on Broadway at the time, and in a lovely piece about me for the *New York Times* Charles Isherwood referred to me as "The greatest stage entertainer of the decade." Now I can find the dark cloud in any silver lining, and I found that word *entertainer* disturbing. At that point I had been a professional actor for thirty-five years, but I thought, was that the perception? Is that all I am? An entertainer? Like I was opening up for Wayne Newton in Vegas! Look, people always tend to put you in a box, but I refused to stay in it. I felt I had more to offer as an actor, and I needed to challenge myself and the audience and see if I could shift people's perception, even just a little. So, I went to Chicago and played Hickey in *The Iceman Cometh* for Bob Falls at the Goodman Theatre with my old friend the late great Brian Dennehy as Larry Slade. It was the best thing I could have done for myself as an actor. It was scary, it was thrilling, it was a life-changing experience. O'Neill can do that to you.

Rufus Norris, the head of the National Theatre, had come to New York to meet with actors because he wanted there to be more of an exchange between our acting communities. During our dinner, in passing he mentioned Marianne Elliott was doing *Angels in America*, and that I could possibly play Roy Cohn, and then we went on to discuss other things. I thought for sure some famous British actor would be playing that part, but when I eventually met with Marianne, she said, "I sent him over here to get you. He's just so shy he kept that to himself." She really wanted an American actor to play Roy Cohn.

*Angels in America* is a masterpiece, one of the greatest plays of the twentieth century, right up there with *Streetcar* and *Salesman*. It's an extraordinary piece of writing, and that part is just a huge gift to any actor. [Cohn is] seductive, he's charming and funny, but he's a vile human being. To go onstage and have those scenes to play is inspiring and thrilling every night, and a great challenge just to live up to the writing and not get in its way.

I felt like I'd never really seen the kind of disintegration physically of what AIDS is doing to him in a very specific

Bruce Springsteen

way. The first chapter of the biography *Citizen Cohn* chronicles what happened to him in the hospital, with hospital reports and everything. He had a tremor in his hand, so I started with that. He had thrush, so I wanted his voice to be affected. He was famous for having a strong voice. He was always yelling on the phone—it was an effective weapon of his—so I made his voice much weaker in the hospital scene with Joe Pitt, when he pulls out the IV. Then he has these full-body seizures, and Belize has to hold him down on the bed. It's an awful thing to go through. When you physically create that night after night, it feels like it's happening to you. It's very real and very emotional. As horrible a person as he is, I wanted the audience to see the fragility of the human being underneath all that. He once said, "I can lick anything, but I can't lick this." It sounds like a line from the play.

Ken Davenport accepting with Roy Putrino, Corey Brunish, Hunter Arnold, and Jenna Ushkowitz

*The Band's Visit*'s Kai Harada, Jamshied Sharifi, Tony Shalhoub, Itamar Moses, Ari'el Stachel, David Yazbek, Katrina Lenk, Orin Wolf, John Styles, and Tyler Micoleau

Sergio Trujillo and
Jack Noseworthy

# WINNERS ◎ 2019

PLAY: *The Ferryman*, Jez Butterworth

Produced by Sonia Friedman Productions, Neal Street Productions, Ronald Frankel, Gavin Kalin Productions, Roy Furman/Benjamin Lowy, Scott M. Delman, Stephanie P. McClelland, Tulchin Bartner Productions, Ron Kastner, Starry Night Entertainment, Kallish Weinstein Creative, Scott Landis, Steve Traxler, Richard Winkler, Rona Delves Broughton/Bill Damaschke, 1001 Nights, Burnt Umber Productions, Rupert Gavin, Scott Rudin, Jamie deRoy/Catherine Adler, Sam Levy/Lauren Stevens, Ramin Sabi/Christopher Ketner

MUSICAL: *Hadestown*

Produced by Mara Isaacs; Dale Franzen; Hunter Arnold; Tom Kirdahy; Carl Daikeler; Five Fates; Willette & Manny Klausner; No Guarantees; Sing Out, Louise! Productions; Stone Arch Theatrical; Benjamin Lowy/Adrian Salpeter; Meredith Lynsey Schade; 42nd.club; Craig Balsam; Broadway Strategic Return Fund; Concord Theatricals; Laurie David; Demar Moritz Gang; Getter Entertainment; Deborah Green; Harris Rubin Productions; Sally Cade Holmes; Marguerite Hoffman; Hornos-Moellenberg; Independent Presenters Network; Jam Theatricals; Kalin Levine Dohr Productions; Phil & Claire Kenny; Mike Karns; Kilimanjaro Theatricals; Lady Capital; LD Entertainment; Sandi Moran; Tom Neff; MWM Live; Patti Sanford Roberts & Michael Roberts; Schroeder Shapiro Productions; Seriff Productions; Stage Entertainment; Kenneth & Rosemary Willman; KayLavLex Theatricals; Tyler Mount; Jujamcyn Theaters; The National Theatre; New York Theatre Workshop

BOOK OF A MUSICAL: Robert Horn, *Tootsie*

ORIGINAL SCORE (MUSIC AND/OR LYRICS) WRITTEN FOR THE THEATRE:

Anaïs Mitchell, *Hadestown*

REVIVAL OF A PLAY: *The Boys in the Band*

Produced by David Stone, Scott Rudin, Patrick Catullo, Aaron Glick, Ryan Murphy

REVIVAL OF A MUSICAL: *Rodgers & Hammerstein's Oklahoma!*

Produced by Eva Price, Level Forward, Abigail Disney, Barbara Manocherian & Carl Moellenberg, James L. Nederlander, David Mirvish, Mickey Liddell & Robert Ahrens, BSL Enterprises & MagicSpace Entertainment, Berlind Productions, John Gore Organization, Cornice Productions, Bard Fisher/R. Gold, LAMF/J. Geller, T. Narang/ZKM Media, R/F/B/V Group, Araca/IPN, St. Ann's Warehouse, Tamar Climan, Brad Summerscape

ACTOR IN A LEADING ROLE IN A PLAY: Bryan Cranston, *Network*

ACTRESS IN A LEADING ROLE IN A PLAY: Elaine May, *The Waverly Gallery*

ACTOR IN A LEADING ROLE IN A MUSICAL: Santino Fontana, *Tootsie*

ACTRESS IN A LEADING ROLE IN A MUSICAL:

Stephanie J. Block, *The Cher Show*

ACTOR IN A FEATURED ROLE IN A PLAY: Bertie Carvel, *Ink*

Judith Light and Bob Mackie

**ACTRESS IN A FEATURED ROLE IN A PLAY:** Celia Keenan-Bolger,
*To Kill a Mockingbird*

**ACTOR IN A FEATURED ROLE IN A MUSICAL:**
André De Shields, *Hadestown*

**ACTRESS IN A FEATURED ROLE IN A MUSICAL:** Ali Stroker,
*Rodgers & Hammerstein's Oklahoma!*

**SCENIC DESIGN OF A PLAY:** Rob Howell, *The Ferryman*

**SCENIC DESIGN OF A MUSICAL:** Rachel Hauck, *Hadestown*

**COSTUME DESIGN OF A PLAY:** Rob Howell, *The Ferryman*

**COSTUME DESIGN OF A MUSICAL:** Bob Mackie, *The Cher Show*

**LIGHTING DESIGN OF A PLAY:** Neil Austin, *Ink*

**LIGHTING DESIGN OF A MUSICAL:** Bradley King, *Hadestown*

**SOUND DESIGN OF A PLAY:** Fitz Patton, *Choir Boy*

**SOUND DESIGN OF A MUSICAL:** Nevin Steinberg and Jessica Paz, *Hadestown*

**DIRECTION OF A PLAY:** Sam Mendes, *The Ferryman*

**DIRECTION OF A MUSICAL:** Rachel Chavkin, *Hadestown*

**CHOREOGRAPHY:** Sergio Trujillo, *Ain't Too Proud:
The Life and Times of The Temptations*

**ORCHESTRATIONS:** Michael Chorney and Todd Sickafoose, *Hadestown*

**SPECIAL TONY AWARD FOR LIFETIME ACHIEVEMENT IN THE THEATRE:**
Rosemary Harris; Terrence McNally; Harold Wheeler

**ISABELLE STEVENSON AWARD:** Judith Light

**REGIONAL THEATRE AWARD:** TheatreWorks Silicon Valley,
Palo Alto, California

**SPECIAL TONY AWARD:** Marin Mazzie; Sonny Tilders and
Creature Technology Company; Jason Michael Webb

**TONY HONOR:** Broadway Inspirational Voices; Peter Entin;
FDNY Engine 54, Ladder 4, Battalion 9; Joseph Blakely Forbes

André De Shields and guest

Santino Fontana

**SERGIO TRUJILLO:** I do my work because it's part of who I am; it's something that I need to do. To be able to win the Tony Award, especially in 2019, was so significant and important. It gave me the platform to speak about things I would have never been able to talk about before.

Harold Wheeler and Rosemary Harris

I choreographed about ten shows before I was first nominated for a Tony Award. I had to wonder why I was being overlooked. Was it personal? I never thought it was about race; I just thought maybe the work had not lived up to what people expected. My first nomination was for *On Your Feet*. That nomination was incredibly special because it was a show about something I knew. I was basically putting my family onstage. It meant a lot. I realized it was meant to be that that would be my first nomination.

When I won four years later for *Ain't Too Proud*, in my acceptance speech I was able to publicly speak about something that was very much part of who I am and where I'd come from. That was the immigrant story, and more important the undocumented immigrant story. I couldn't believe that the entire theater stood up. That ovation was worth more than a Tony Award, because it said that the community has always stood behind me. The community has always been there for me. That moment demonstrated that. The work that the American Theatre Wing and the Broadway League are doing continues to prove that to me. Not only did I win the Tony Award, but I was invited to be part of the advisory board, to be part of a group of colleagues that are trying to make a difference in trying to change the landscape of American theatre today. That win has empowered me because it gave me a voice, and given Latinos, Latine, or Latinx a voice. I take this win, this responsibility, this opportunity very seriously. I want to be on the front lines to ensure that our stories are being told in the theatre.

**RACHEL CHAVKIN:** Winning a Tony has been profoundly impactful in terms of the calls I get and how seriously my ideas are taken, particularly as I've expanded into having film and television conversations.

I consider a key part of my job to work with the writer to architect a process. Most writers I know value someone helping provide structure. I serve as a connection point between the producers, who of course are looking for outcomes, and the writers, who are working it out. I try to be practically oriented while also loving jumping in the mystery of something that doesn't know what it's trying to be yet. I never take for granted that anything is going to work the way anything that already exists does. I would hate to ever be limited by my own imagination, or to limit anyone else's imagination.

During preproduction, I try as much as possible to meet with all the designers together because I think there's so much synergy that comes from solving each other's problems. That jamming is part of the joy.

Clockwise from left: *Hadestown*'s Hunter Arnold, Rachel Chavkin, Dale Franzen, Jordan Roth, Mara Isaacs, Anais Mitchell, Tom Kirdahy, Reeve Carney, Eva Noblezada

**BRYAN CRANSTON:** What I wanted to convey in playing Howard Beale was a deeply wounded man, not just an angry man. I wanted the anger (I'm mad as hell) to be a manifestation of his depression and emotional wounds.

I'm exceedingly proud to be a Tony winner. I've been very fortunate to have won several things, and I don't take it for granted. I hold them in very high esteem and honor. I think the reason for that is because I don't expect it. I don't expect, or feel entitled that anything should come my way. I just want to do the work, keep my head down, and hope that we're telling a good story for audiences to enjoy. If someone taps me on the shoulder and says, "Guess what? We want to nominate you for an award," I want to be legitimately surprised and delighted. No one knew when we started what this show was going to become. All I knew about *Network* was that I was attracted to the character and the story was solid, prescient in a way. It was striking a nerve in the seventies, and it was still doing that over forty years later.

Bryan Cranston

*Rodgers and Hammerstein's Oklahoma*'s Justin Mikita, Eva Price, James Nederlander, and John Gore

James Corden and Bertie Carvel

*The Ferryman*'s Jez Butterworth, Sonia Friedman, and Caro Newling

Audra McDonald presents the Leading Actress in a Musical Tony to Stephanie J. Block

**EVA PRICE:** *Oklahoma!* was my least favorite Rodgers and Hammerstein musical until I saw Daniel Fish's production of *Oklahoma!* on the campus of Bard College, part of the Bard SummerScape festival. My mind was blown that someone had reinvented and reimagined *Oklahoma!* for today in such a visceral way without changing a single word or lyric. It was incredibly thought provoking. It dealt with the way communities respond to outsiders, toxic masculinity, what it means to be at the start of nation building, and how we treat our fellow man. I wanted to follow this artist and produce his vision. I researched the original 1943 production, where I learned that everything about *Oklahoma!* was completely modern for its time in the way our version was. Agnes de Mille as its choreographer was a modern idea, a dream ballet was modern. The idea of music pushing forward story in the way musicals do today was a very radical idea back then.

The show grew from the production I saw at Bard. We developed it further and cast it differently and kept expanding on the vision. Every time we took risks and made bold choices, I thought back to the bold choices that were made when the production was created. The groundwork was there when the show first existed for us to create our version.

We tried very hard in our advertising to make it clear this was not your grandmother's *Oklahoma!* Sometimes people didn't understand that when they came to see it and would leave early. They would say, "This is *Oklahoma!* This isn't what I grew up watching." We'd just say, "Fair enough. But you can be open to something different." One of my favorite things was to watch the audience's reaction. I'd sit there amongst the audience and hear thoughtful debate, which was incredible.

When the show won the Tony Award, it was exciting and surprising. It was one of the greatest moments of my career to know that hard risk and hard work can pay off to something so successful and joyous.

**HAROLD WHEELER:** The Lifetime Achievement Award is an honor and a privilege. It is a recognition for six decades of my work as an orchestrator. I never set out to win awards. The job itself is rewarding in so many ways. The first orchestra rehearsal, when I hear the music live in a rehearsal hall, is thrilling, and then the ultimate is three days later when the cast comes in. They are so used to hearing the music with just piano, so when they hear it with all the musicians they are surprised and shocked and excited. I love the process. Sometimes I'll have four different orchestrations in my head ready to go. During the rehearsal period with the orchestra, I refine what I had in my head to what I call the final, final orchestration. Sometimes a number can be simple, and you don't want to cloud it with a bunch of orchestra. As long as I've done this, and as many times as I've done this, it is still exciting. I get choked up thinking about it.

**JESSICA PAZ:** Nevin Steinberg and I had worked together for five years prior to *Hadestown*, so we had a rapport and a language. We knew what each other's styles were. I was nervous going into *Hadestown* because I was used to being his associate. I didn't know what to expect working as his equal for the first time. I read Tina Fey's book *Bossypants*. She talked about doing improv and saying yes to things instead of no. I found that very inspiring. I realized instead of saying no to an idea, I could say yes, which would allow Nevin and I to riff off each other. It led to exploring what the possibilities could be. Nevin always treated me as an equal, even when I was his associate, but even more so as his co-designer. But it was also important for me to feel equal. Not because he treated me equal, but to feel that I am equal. That was important to me especially as a woman collaborating with a man, and someone who I was technically a subordinate to for five years. I definitely have a challenge as a woman in the industry. Sometimes I'll give a note and people don't want to take it. They'll do it, but reluctantly. I've observed those same people interacting with male designers, and they don't do that. The way they react to me and my contemporary male designers is not the same.

These gems of shows like *Hadestown* don't show up often. Everyone became a family. I have never worked on a show in which every design element worked together in such a cohesive whole before. There was something special about the way Rachel brought all the design elements together. We all worked together to make it this gelled thing. That was a by-product of how close we all were and how well we worked together.

My job is to make the audience laugh, to make them cry, and to make them react and feel the energy of the music. The sound enhances the story by giving it more energy and excitement. Sound makes it dynamic and makes it breathe. The ultimate goal of sound design is to make sure that every person in every seat of the audience hears the same thing. Sound design is the only department that points things at the audience. Every other department focuses their energy on the stage. With sound it's about the experience off the stage.

I have a journal entry from twenty years ago where I wrote that I wanted to be the first woman to win a Tony for sound design. That was before there was even a Tony for sound design. I forgot about it and went on my way. Then I was nominated. It means a lot to be the first woman nominated for sound design of a musical. I'm only the second woman ever to be nominated for sound design as a whole, the first woman being Cricket S. Myers for the play *Bengal Tiger at the Baghdad Zoo* a decade ago. It's bananas to me that that's true. I feel proud that my first Broadway musical as lead designer led to my being the first woman to win a Tony for sound design. It was humbling to have in the same category mentors and friends who have been working in this industry for a long time. I felt like I had arrived.

**RACHEL HAUCK:** I find it impossible to describe the experience of winning a Tony. I couldn't believe any of it was happening—the nomination. The fact that I was sitting there in such fancy clothes, in such incredible company. In the moment, I was mostly trying to appear calm while keeping my pounding heart from being audible. Then suddenly I was standing on the stage of Radio City Music Hall in complete shock with my heart pounding for real, looking out at an ocean of faces, with a very heavy, completely incredible piece of recognition in my hand. Just. Stunned.

I am so, so proud of *Hadestown*. I loved Anaïs's music the minute I heard it. It kind of hypnotized me with its beauty and depth. Figuring out how to tell that story took a long time, it was really challenging to find a world that could hold those incredible lyrics and ride the wave of emotion and worlds that she conjures. That show was built by a team of incredible storytellers, starting with Anaïs and Chavkin, all working together for such a long time. Everyone was a rule breaker, all of us trying ideas as the music grew and changed. Some worked, some didn't. The Broadway design has all those layers in it. It is full of passion and poetry and love, failed ideas helping us find the

Michael Chorney, Todd Sickafoose, Rachel Hauck, Jessica Paz, Nevin Steinberg, and Bradley King of *Hadestown*

*The Boys in the Band*'s Matt Bomer, Michael Benjamin Washington, Charlie Carver, Jim Parsons, Ryan Murphy, Mart Crowley, Tuc Watkins, Andrew Rannells, Bryan Hutchison, David Stone, Robin de Jesus, Zachary Quinto, Aaron Glick, and Patrick Catullo

Fitz Patton

Robert Horn

Elaine May

Ali Stroker

Celia Keenan-Bolger (center) with presenters Tina Fey and Jake Gyllenhaal

good ones, and the good ones stronger for it. I am deeply proud of it, this thing we all made together, so to see the production recognized in such a complete way is intensely meaningful and moving.

Awards are hard. When art becomes competitive, it is very, very complicated and deeply problematic. Award season tends to bring out the worst in all of us, I'm sorry to admit. But I will also admit that the idea of being recognized by your peers is intense and moving. It's true, what everyone says, I was so very honored to be nominated with my remarkable peers, whose work I respect deeply. I genuinely was not expecting that the actual award would go my way that night, so much so that as they announced the nominees, I was sitting with my legs crossed. When they called my name, what I remember is the incredible roar in the room—or at least it felt like that to me, but then again, that might just have been my head exploding. I know my jaw dropped. I was totally stunned. I kissed my incredible partner, Lisa, who has a picture of the underside of her seat because she dropped her phone in shock. In one of the most surreal moments of my life, I walked up to the stage of Radio City Music Hall, a truly out-of-body experience. I worried for the cameraman, who was somehow walking backwards while crouching to get his shot. When I got to that podium in front of…what is it, 6,000 people? I looked up, suddenly standing there with a Tony in my hand, and the first person I saw was Rachel Chavkin, and right behind her, Anaïs, both on the aisle. I locked eyes with Chavkin, whose expression I will never forget, it was how I felt. I tried to find my mom in the balcony. No way. And suddenly there I was giving a speech. When I went backstage in shock, one by one by one the cast of *Hadestown* who were waiting in a stairwell to do the opening number snuck backstage to find me and celebrate. They were absolutely not supposed to do that, but they popped their heads around the corner, one than another then a wee flood of Workers and Fates. We cried and cheered (not very quietly, I'm afraid) as we watched on the monitors while Bradley, then Jess and Nevin, then Todd and Michael's names were called. One of our stage managers, Cherie—who is an incredible photographer in her own right—took a picture of us all backstage together, Workers, Fates, stage managers, designers, and all those Tonys in that one moment before we got swept off to do the press and the cast went on to do the opening number for the live broadcast. I cherish that picture.

I feel so lucky my mom was there. I wish my dad could have been there too. My sister was in India on business; one of my strongest, happiest memories of that night was having a probably ill-advised bottle of champagne with her at five a.m. over FaceTime. Lisa and I were finally home, on the roof of our building, watching the sun come up on the George Washington Bridge, so happy, still in our Tony outfits, still so shocked. I cannot imagine what the experience was like for Lisa or for my mother. I'd never have been standing there without a lifetime of support from my family. What must it be like to see that kind of recognition come for the one you've supported so intensely for so many years? The road is hard and long, as the lyric goes. and my partner, Lisa? Well. How do you thank someone for the kind of love and support that gets you through the brutally hard nights, the long days, the self-doubt, the days you're a wreck and hopefully only she knows it. When your work is recognized like this, you share it with everyone in your life. You wouldn't be there without all of them; they are a huge part of it.

Winning a Tony changed my professional life overnight. It opened so many doors that as a woman in this particular field are surprisingly hard to open, still. I can only hope that every step forward on that front helps kick the door open for the many, many folks of immense talent right behind us.

# ACCEPTANCE SPEECHES THROUGH THE YEARS

Greg Morrison and Lisa Lambert

For anyone who may have lived in Toronto between the years 1985 and 1995 and who received a singing telegram set to the tune of "Take Me Out to the Ball Game," you can now say it was written by a Tony Award–winning songwriter.

**LISA LAMBERT (2006)**

**ROBERT PRESTON (1967):** I'm either going to have to break this thing up three ways or let Gower and Mary have custody of it on alternate weekends.

**ELLEN BARKIN (2011):** Performing in *The Normal Heart* is a very profound experience for me. It's the proudest moment in my career. It has transformed me not just as an actor but as a human being, because it taught me something that I never believed in. It taught me that one person can make a difference, that one person can change the world. So thank you to the great, great Larry Kramer. Thank you, thank you, you Jewish boy who always thinks that you can make the world a better place. Thirty years ago this week the world was attacked by a virus, and Larry Kramer went to war. He picked up his most powerful weapon, his pen, and he wrote a play: *The Normal Heart*. Twenty-six years ago, with its first production, he lit a fire, and that fire still burns today down at the Golden Theatre. Thank you to our towering visionary genius of a director, George Wolfe. Thank you for teaching me to play with fire, and thank you for turning this production into a Molotov cocktail that we can ignite every night. Thank you to Joe Mantello, who, like Atlas, carries us across the stage night after night on his slim shoulders just burning through the history of this play. Thank you to the bravest ensemble of actors I've ever had the honor to work with….Larry, this is for you and all the bullets in your belt.

**CHRISTOPHER PLUMMER (1997):** [To] the great Jack Barrymore and Ethel and Lionel, who long ago showed us, all us impressionable youngsters how magical the theatre could be.

**JACK FELDMAN (2012):** When I was around five years old and running around telling everybody I wanted to write Broadway shows, it didn't really occur to me that it would take fifty-six years to actually accomplish that. But it was worth the wait. Look, Ma, a Tony!

**DENNIS KELLY (2013):** When I wrote *Matilda the Musical* I really had no idea how to write a musical. In many ways this award is a ringing endorsement of ignorance and stupidity.

**SONYA TAYEH (2020):** Dance is an art that survives the multiplicity, color, and layer in community. As we steady ourselves again, I hope we can remember what art collectively brings us. It welcomes. As a brown, queer, Arab American woman, I wasn't always welcome. It takes graceful hands to lead people like me to the door. It's been ten years since a woman has won this award. Though I'm honored to be a part of this legacy, this legacy is too small. We need a vastness to break into a new era for all people.

**MARC SHAIMAN (2003):** If anyone in the orchestra cuts me off, there's a virtual orchestra at *Hairspray* on Tuesday.… We have to thank Margo Lion. Margo Lion called me out of the blue. God bless her. I was as depressed as a man can be who gets to make music all the time…Margo Lion, thank you for saving our lives. Our relationship was doing fine without you, but it's never been better. I love this man. We're not allowed to get married in this world; I don't know why. But I would like to declare in front of millions of people I love you and I'd like to live with you the rest of my life.

Marc Shaiman and Scott Wittman

**STEPHEN DALDRY (2020):** We were blessed to have Matthew López's play. What an extraordinary piece he wrote. I would also just take a moment to thank all those young men who were ghosts in our play representing the many tens of thousands of people who died in the city in another pandemic that is shamefully still with us: AIDS.

**DEREK McLANE (2020):** This means more than you could possibly ever know. My father taught me many things. He taught me the value of hard work, the value of patience—which we've all needed a lot of in this last year and a half. He taught me, most importantly, a love of adventure and travel and of foreign cultures. And so when Alex Timbers and Carmen Pavlovic and Bill Damaschke called me about five years ago and described this adventure, this trip—*Moulin Rouge*—this crazy adventure and said, "Would you like to join us?," of course I had to say yes instantly.

> Thank you to Larry Kramer, the great badass of the American theatre, whose play thirty years later reminds us the war is not over. Those of us still standing, Larry, can never repay you.
> **JOHN BENJAMIN HICKEY (2011)**

**JOHN LARROQUETTE (2011):** A very special thanks to Daniel Radcliffe, without whom I know that I would be home in my underwear watching this on television.

**JOEY PARNES (2014):** The little engine that could did. We all do what we do in the theatre because we believe it matters. Theatre nourishes the soul and gets us to feel and think and see things differently. This is what drives us. The goodwill and collaborative spirit that flows through each of us on this show and on all shows everywhere that people make theatre. It's a great gift. Thank you for embracing that gift. Thank you for giving us another one!

**JAMES NAUGHTON (1997):** I heard on NY1 last week that 2 percent of the people who come to New York City to try to make it in the theatre actually succeed. Two out of a hundred. So, to be working is way ahead of the game. And to be standing here and looking at you and to be a part of this community and to call you my colleagues is a great, great honor.

> This award is for every kid who is watching tonight who has a disability, who has a limitation or a challenge who has been waiting to see themselves represented in this arena. You are. **ALI STROKER (2019)**

**MART CROWLEY (2019):** I'd like to dedicate this award to the original cast of nine brave men, who did not listen to their agents when they were told that their careers would be finished if they did this play, and they did it, and here I am, thank you.

**JUSTIN TOWNSEND (2020):** This is for my mother. Thank you for sharing your love of music, painting, and that *Tommy* record, where I discovered that music could tell a story.

Andrew Garfield

**ANDREW GARFIELD (2018):** At a moment in time where maybe the most important thing that we remember right now is the sanctity of the human spirit, it is the profound privilege of my life to play Prior Walter in *Angels in America*, because he represents the purity of humanity. And especially that of the LGBT community. It is a spirit that says no to oppression, it is a spirit that says no to bigotry, no to shame, no to exclusion. It is a spirit that says we were all made perfectly and we all belong. So I dedicate this award to the countless LGBT people who have fought and died to protect that message for the right to live and love as we are created. Tony Kushner, thank you for being the angel of America that

we all wish we could live in, that we all dream of living in one day.

**MARISSA JARET WINOKUR (2003):** My sister made me a painting years ago that said "Fairy tales do come true." If a four-foot-eleven chubby NY girl can be a leading lady in a Broadway show and win a Tony, then anything can happen!

**ROBERT LOPEZ (2004):** When we started writing *Avenue Q* four years ago, Jeff was an intern and I was a temp. Our lives kind of sucked, so we came up with an idea for a show about people like us whose lives all kind of suck. **JEFF MARX (2004):** But we're here to tell you as living proof that things get better. L [LL Cool J] and Carol [Channing] just gave us a Tony Award!

**BRIAN F. O'BYRNE (2004):** There are no such things as competition between actors....What we try to do is be good. The nomination hopefully means that we're good. Any of the actors in this category would be standing here if they had my part. There are great parts. I have the best part on Broadway.

**PETER HYLENSKI (2020):** I grew up working in the theatre since I was a kid, and I never thought there would be a time in my life where theatre wouldn't be there, so the past 560 days has really been a reminder of just how much I cherish this. But also, more so, how much I cherish the people that I get to create with every day.

**JOHN LEGUIZAMO (2018):** Bruce Springsteen is getting the same award as me tonight, and he is the greatest lyrical storyteller in song ever, so this makes this special award even twice as special to me. He was born to run, but I grew up in Queens, so I had to run. And I ran all the way to Broadway, yo. You know how they say awards mean nothing until you win one? Well, it's true. This means a lot to me because it validates my work in the theatre. In order for me to make it in theatre, I had to create my own parts. Otherwise, I was just going to be relegated to playing the gangsters, the janitors, the drug dealers. But we Latin people are so much more than that, and theatre has allowed me to be much more than that, because there are no gatekeepers on Broadway. All you have to write is a great freakin' story, and if you write it, they will come. And if you write it for Latin people and people of color, they will come too. It's even more important with Latin people because we are the least represented minority across all media. That's why theatre has always been my sanctuary. This pervasive exclusion stops there, and it stops here tonight and every night I was on Broadway, because thousands upon thousands of Latin people showed up and paid unreasonable prices just to be able to see themselves reflected back on one night they could feel someone was talking about them to them. My hope is that someday our stories won't be the exception but the rule, that I will live to see a Broadway with our stories written by us, for us, and for all. Tonight I stand on strong shoulders that came before me just as others will surely stand on mine....Single moms are like superheroes. [My mom] gave me the antidote I needed to overcome. With her daily affirmations—"John, you can do anything you set your mind to, mijo," she armed me with a secret shield against the invisible glass ceilings, unspoken quotas, and cheap tokenism. Esto es para todos ustedes mis hermanos y hermanas, nunca retrocedan y nunca acepten menos. And let's never forget the fifteen hundred missing Latin immigrant babies in detention and 4,645 dead American citizens in Puerto Rico. Never forget them.

**JEFFREY SELLER (2016):** *Hamilton: An American Musical* embodies the best values, the best impulses that make our nation a beacon to the world. Inclusiveness, generosity, ingenuity, and the will to work hard to make our dreams come true. Look around. Look around. How lucky we are to be alive right now. Thank you.

## Musical theatre rocks.
### DUNCAN SHEIK (2007)

**CHRISTOPHER ASHLEY (2017):** Most of all, I want to accept this on behalf of the people of Newfoundland and all of the first responders and their families in New York on 9/11; the people who gave their lives and the people who extended their hearts and their homes, who were generous and kind in the worst of moments. To all of you, thank you.

**RON LEIBMAN (1993):** Jessica, the love of my life, thank you. Maybe we can get an apartment with a washer/dryer now.

**CAROL CHANNING (1995):** I can't think of anything more soul fulfilling that I could have done. I mean, it was the only thing to do. An achievement apparently is just doing exactly what you want to do.

**EDWARD ALBEE (2005):** I think the virtue of being given a lifetime achievement award before you have necessarily achieved your lifetime work is probably because if they wait until you have achieved all of your lifetime work you probably will have died. This is better. And I'm grateful. I'm dedicating this to the memory of Jonathan Thomas, my life partner who died only a month ago. He and I were together for thirty-five years, and he made me a happy playwright. And you have made me a happy playwright tonight.

**STEVEN SATER (2007):** Eight and a half years ago, Duncan, Michael, and I set out to give voice to the hopes and the hidden rebellion in the hearts of young people. And it's young people everywhere who first heard our songs and came to see our show and stand outside our stage door to talk about how much it's meant to their lives. So, this is for you, the guilty ones and all our fans of all ages who come again to our show.

When I used to think about if I ever possibly won one of these, would I feel like there was a mistake made—would I feel that way? And I don't.
**MARY LOUISE WILSON (2007)**

the '20 20s

Lauren Patten

# WINNERS ◯ 2020

**PLAY:** *The Inheritance*, Matthew López

Produced by Tom Kirdahy; Sonia Friedman Productions; Hunter Arnold; Elizabeth Dewberry & Ali Ahmet Kocabiyik; 1001 Nights Productions; Robert Greenblatt; Mark Lee; Peter May; Scott Rudin; Richard Winkler; Bruce Cohen; Mara Isaacs; Greg Berlanti & Robbie Rogers; Brad Blume; Burnt Umber Productions; Shane Ewen; Greenleaf Productions; Marguerite Hoffman; Oliver Roth; Joseph Baker/Drew Hodges; Stephanie P. McClelland; Broadway Strategic Return Fund; Caiola Productions; Mary J. Davis; Kayla Greenspan; Fakston Productions; FBK Productions; Sally Cade Holmes; Benjamin Lowy; MWM Live; Lee & Alec Seymour; Lorenzo Thione; Sing Out, Louise! Productions; AB Company/Julie Boardman; Adam Zell & Co/ZKM Media; Jamie deRoy/Catherine Adler; DeSantis-Baugh Productions/ Adam Hyndman; Gary DiMauro/Meredith Lynsey Schade; John Goldwyn/Silva Theatrical Group; Deborah Green/Christina Mattson; Cliff Hopkins/George Scarles; Invisible Wall Productions/Lauren Stein; Sharon Karmazin/Broadway Factor NYC; Brian Spector Madeleine Foster Bersin; UndividedProductions/Hysell Dohr Group; Ushkowitzlatimer Productions/Tyler Mount; The Young Vic

**MUSICAL:** *Moulin Rouge! The Musical*

Produced by Carmen Pavlovic, Gerry Ryan, Global Creatures, Bill Damaschke, Aaron Lustbader, Hunter Arnold, Darren Bagert, Erica Lynn Schwartz/Matt Picheny/Stephanie Rosenberg, Adam Blanshay Productions/Nicolas & Charles Talar, Iris Smith, Aleri Entertainment, CJ ENM, Sophie Qi/ Harmonia Holdings, Baz & Co./Len Blavatnik, AF Creative Media/International Theatre Fund, Endeavor Content, Tom & Pam Faludy, Gilad-Rogowsky/Instone Productions, John Gore Organization, MEHR-BB Entertainment GmbH, Spencer Ross, Nederlander Presentations/IPN, Eric Falkenstein/Suzanne Grant, Jennifer Fischer, Peter May/Sandy Robertson, Triptyk Productions, Carl Daikeler/Sandi Moran, DeSantis-Baugh Productions, Red Mountain Theatre Company/42nd.club, Candy Spelling/Tulchin Bartner, Roy Furman, Jujamcyn Theaters

**BOOK OF A MUSICAL:** Diablo Cody, *Jagged Little Pill*

**ORIGINAL SCORE (MUSIC AND/OR LYRICS) WRITTEN FOR THE THEATRE:**
Christopher Nightingale, *A Christmas Carol*

**REVIVAL OF A PLAY:** *A Soldier's Play*

Produced by Roundabout Theatre Company, Todd Haimes, Julia C. Levy, Sydney Beers, Steve Dow

*American Utopia*'s Tim Keiper, Daniel Freedman, Karl Mansfield, Mauro Refosco, Stephane San Juan, David Byrne, Angie Swan, Bobby Wooten III, Jacqueline Acevedo, Chris Giarmo, Tendayi Kuumba, and Gustavo Di Dalva

**ACTOR IN A LEADING ROLE IN A PLAY:** Andrew Burnap, *The Inheritance*

**ACTRESS IN A LEADING ROLE IN A PLAY:** Mary-Louise Parker, *The Sound Inside*

**ACTOR IN A LEADING ROLE IN A MUSICAL:** Aaron Tveit, *Moulin Rouge! The Musical*

**ACTRESS IN A LEADING ROLE IN A MUSICAL:** Adrienne Warren, *Tina: The Tina Turner Musical*

**ACTOR IN A FEATURED ROLE IN A PLAY:** David Alan Grier, *A Soldier's Play*

**ACTRESS IN A FEATURED ROLE IN A PLAY:** Lois Smith, *The Inheritance*

**ACTOR IN A FEATURED ROLE IN A MUSICAL:** Danny Burstein, *Moulin Rouge! The Musical*

**ACTRESS IN A FEATURED ROLE IN A MUSICAL:** Lauren Patten, *Jagged Little Pill*

**SCENIC DESIGN OF A PLAY:** Rob Howell, *A Christmas Carol*

**SCENIC DESIGN OF A MUSICAL:** Derek McLane, *Moulin Rouge! The Musical*

**COSTUME DESIGN OF A PLAY:** Rob Howell, *A Christmas Carol*

**COSTUME DESIGN OF A MUSICAL:** Catherine Zuber, *Moulin Rouge! The Musical*

**LIGHTING DESIGN OF A PLAY:** Hugh Vanstone, *A Christmas Carol*

**LIGHTING DESIGN OF A MUSICAL:** Justin Townsend, *Moulin Rouge! The Musical*

**SOUND DESIGN OF A PLAY:** Simon Baker, *A Christmas Carol*

**SOUND DESIGN OF A MUSICAL:** Peter Hylenski, *Moulin Rouge! The Musical*

**DIRECTION OF A PLAY:** Stephen Daldry, *The Inheritance*

**DIRECTION OF A MUSICAL:** Alex Timbers, *Moulin Rouge! The Musical*

**CHOREOGRAPHY:** Sonya Tayeh, *Moulin Rouge! The Musical*

**ORCHESTRATIONS:** Justin Levine with Katie Kresek, Charlie Rosen, and Matt Stine, *Moulin Rouge! The Musical*

**SPECIAL TONY AWARD FOR LIFETIME ACHIEVEMENT IN THE THEATRE:** Graciela Daniele

**ISABELLE STEVENSON AWARD:** Julie Halston

**SPECIAL TONY AWARD:** The Broadway Advocacy Coalition; David Byrne's *American Utopia*; *Freestyle Love Supreme*

**TONY HONOR:** Fred Gallo; Irene Gandy; Beverly Jenkins; New Federal Theatre

Julie Halston

**CATHERINE ZUBER:** *Moulin Rouge!* was a true collaboration with the entire team. Alex Timbers is a wonderful director who brought out the best in everyone. He inspired me to delve into all the nuances and possibilities of the costume design, but always in a respectful, collaborative manner. We all felt that his guidance resulted in some of our best work. The fact that we created such a cohesive visual piece is a testament to Alex's amazing direction.

Alex Timbers

Aaron Tveit

**DANNY BURSTEIN:** All I ever wanted to do as a kid was to be able to make a living as an actor and have the respect of my peers. I pinch myself; I know how incredibly lucky I am. There are so many other people who are far more talented than I am that have not been able to make it work.

It's lovely to win, but the real thrill is the whole process, the nomination, and the validation from your peers. The outpouring of love and care that you get from the community means more than any award could ever replace.

Danny Burstein

Derek McLane

**DEREK McLANE:** The fact that my award was one of ten for *Moulin Rouge!* was thrilling. It was exhilarating to see the other designers win, and my buddy Alex Timbers won. Sonya Tayeh won. And Danny Burstein, who I've done a bazillion shows with and have known forever, won his first Tony Award that night. It felt like a crazy party.

**MATTHEW LÓPEZ:** When I was five, I watched my aunt Priscilla win a Tony Award for *A Day in Hollywood/A Night in the Ukraine.* As you can imagine, it was a very big deal in my house. It still takes me by surprise when I look up and see my Tony Award on the shelf. When you grow up obsessed with the theatre like I did, raised in a family in which winning Tonys is not so far-fetched an idea, to win one is just a dream. I remember at the *Inheritance* party later that night, Jesse Tyler Ferguson pulled me into a hug and said, "so many Tonys in the López family." That's when it hit home for me what it meant for me in relation to my aunt. I'm aware of the fact that for most people it doesn't come true. My win means that in some small way I will be remembered, that my play will be remembered, and that enough people decided that my play would be included in a very rarefied list of honored plays. You

Matthew López

Winning for *Moulin Rouge* was very special for me. I had my son there with me. That show was hard fought; it was a lot of work. There were many things that happened during that show. We went out to Boston, and the ceiling of the theatre fell in! At one point it felt like all these strikes were against the show. But we kept on persevering. There was seven months between Boston and when we started rehearsal in New York. And then the pandemic! The nominations came out in the middle of the pandemic, with no date in sight for the show. Then the Tonys finally happened. The weekend of the Tonys we had just reopened *Moulin Rouge.* There was so much happening with the reopening, and working on the number for the Tonys, all the interviews you do—it was a whirlwind. And of course, between the time we closed the show on March 12, 2020, and the reopening, I was taking care of my wife. It was an amazingly difficult time. The entire community was there supporting my wife and me. That just speaks to who the people are in this business. While the awards are fantastic, and an incredible honor, the real honor is to be associated with a group of people that support, love, and take of one another the way that we do. That means more to me than anything else.

Allison and Andrew Burnap

David Alan Grier

do have to look at the past winners—Tennessee Williams, August Wilson, Wendy Wasserstein, Terrence McNally—and remind yourself you will forever be included on that list with them. To be in that company is quite an encouragement!

My favorite memory from Tony night was watching Andrew Burnap win. It was so gratifying because that was the culmination of years of work he and I did together on the role. It was the happiest and most loving and passionate collaboration I've ever had with an actor—occasionally tempestuous but always loving. Whenever an actor wins an award for one my characters, I'm proud and happy for them, but it also feels like a validation of my imagination that went into writing the character. When Lois and Andrew won Tonys for *The Inheritance*, it felt personal, because they were my characters brilliantly interpreted by those actors. Especially given the nature of the role and the unhappy journey Toby takes, it meant more to me for Andrew to win than for me to win. It felt in some way as a validation of Toby's life as a person who started in my imagination who then grew to inhabit Andrew's. I think that night we were both thinking about Toby and missing him and feeling very happy for him.

**DAVID ALAN GRIER:** My first professional job was *The First*, a musical about Jackie Robinson. It ran for about three and a half weeks. When it closed, I thought I was a failure and went back to my life. Then I got a Tony nomination, and that was verification that this had not been a figment of my imagination. Cleavant Derricks won that year, and I was not disappointed. I'm so glad I didn't win then, because I wasn't ready for it.

The year I won was the first season after everything had been shut down for a year and a half due to Covid. The nominations were announced, but no one knew if, how, and when there would be a ceremony. It was great to finally go to the show a year later. They announced my name, and people were trying to hug me as I ran up to the stage. I was dodging them because I didn't want to get Covid! I was also very aware of the time limit. I got very emotional and started to cry as I was making my speech. I had two options at that point. One was to say that I was humbled by the award, and for the other people in my category to keep at it. There were so many people that season who put years into their shows, it finally came to Broadway and had to close in previews because of Covid, and then never reopened because they didn't have the funds. That may have been their only shot in their life. My other option was to make a joke, which I did. Both are a part of me, but I just wanted to lighten that moment up.

To be honored for *A Soldier's Play* is significant for me. I never thought I would have the relationship I ended up having with it. If you'd have told me in 1982, when I was in the Off-Broadway production, that I would end up coming back to it again and again, I would never have believed it. It's been fun to come back to it over and over. I always played a different role, which gave me a whole new perspective on the play. I got to replace Larry Riley in the original production. I worked with Sam Jackson, Denzel Washington, James Pickens Jr., and of course Adolph Caesar, who played the Sarge. It was like being in a club or a fraternity. I knew that a movie was being planned, but I never thought I'd be in it. I thought they'd get actors from Hollywood. But they cast three of us from the show—me, Denzel Washington, and Adolph Caesar. When Kenny Leon offered me the role

Adrienne Warren

of the Sarge in the first Broadway production of *A Soldier's Play*, I had to do it. When I went back to my seat after winning the Tony, I grabbed Kenny and just fell in his arms weeping and thanking him for giving me this role. It was awesome to share the love I felt that night with as many people as I could.

Douglas Turner Ward came to see the show. He and I went way back to when he cast me in the original. As a young actor he and the Negro Ensemble Company were my heroes. He had throat cancer and could barely talk. I had originally planned to go out for my dinner break, but instead I spent that time with Doug. He whispered, but he spoke so loudly and with such resonance. It was just a master class that realigned me and my life mission, what I hoped to accomplish as an actor and an artist.

I talked about that moment with Doug in my speech. When I got back to my seat—I was next to Jane Alexander—she said, "Thank you for acknowledging Doug." It was so sweet and meant so much that she said that. People hear you.

**ADRIENNE WARREN:** I dreamt of winning a Tony my whole life. Every year my parents and I would sit in the living room and watch the Tonys together. They were athletes, and not as much into theatre as I was, but they were always willing to indulge and support me in that aspiration. I'm so grateful for that; not everybody has that family support. I would watch and look up to people like Audra McDonald, LaChanze, and Cicely Tyson. I wanted to be there so badly. I was hyperaware of the work that it took to get there, which inspired me to work harder in my training, even if I was only ten.

Playing Tina Turner was fun and painful and hard and challenging. Tina was a part of the whole process and was in rehearsals with us in London for the West End production. She was my mentor throughout that entire process, which was so special. That does not always happen on these bio musicals. She was so gracious and allowed me to ask her anything. That was the key into the work. I couldn't have done it without her. She put me through my paces because she had to approve the performance. If I didn't have her approval, I wouldn't have gone to Broadway with it. There was no guarantee.

I never realized before speaking with Tina Turner that you can actually see her performing with black eyes in some of her videos. Back then people weren't that aware of her situation. She and I watched a video together, and she said, "Do you see that right there? That's a black eye. He had just thrown a coffee pot at my face before I went onstage." That was horrifying to hear, and my heart broke for her the more I learned. The job itself became more important; I felt more responsibility. She had become someone I cared about, and I now understood she had gone through more pain that we could have ever imagined. The resilience she had in persevering past that is more profound that anyone knows. This was my opportunity to try to portray that for her and honor her in that way. Her insights about what was happening to her internally as opposed to the external entity of Tina Turner were invaluable.

It took a while for me to figure out how to let myself into the character. I ultimately realized I wasn't putting on a Tina Turner Vegas show where I would be impersonating her. It was about the core of a woman, a Black woman from the South whose dad is a preacher. I'm a Black woman from the South and my dad is a preacher. I grew up an athlete; she grew up an athlete. We had so many parallels. Once I started to allow myself in, it allowed me to relax into the role. I started to have fun and started to really listen and be in the scenes. I was cast because they saw something in me, and I learned to allow that to shine through.

It was such a profound moment when Tina Turner said, "You can have her. I'm letting her go to you." I was working so hard, and I didn't know if she was ever going to approve my performance. It was so special when she gave her approval and crowned me in that way. I became part of her legacy.

Having a Tony means the industry sees me, and I'm so grateful for that. It means that another little girl that looks like me can see herself. It means I have a voice that matters, and I have the responsibility to use it for things that I'm passionate about. It means I'm going to keep creating work on Broadway. It's my home. I'm so in love with the community and proud to be a part of it.

Justin Townsend

Peter Hylenski with presenters Jordan Fisher and Jasmine Cephas Jones

## 2021

On March 12, 2020,
Broadway went dark
due to Covid-19.

Thousands of people lost
their jobs overnight,
and many lost their lives.
Most theaters remained
closed until the 2020
Tony Awards were presented
in September 2021, and
no awards were given for
the 2021 season.

# WINNERS ◯ 2022

**PLAY:** *The Lehman Trilogy*, Stefano Massini, Ben Power

Produced by The National Theatre; Neal Street Productions; Barry Diller; David Geffen; Kash Bennett; Lisa Burger; Caro Newling; Ambassador Theare Group; Stephanie P. McClelland; Annapurna Theatre; Delman-Whitney; Craig Balsam/Heni Koenigsberg/John Yonover; Fiery Angel/Seth A. Goldstein; Starry Night Entertainment; Gavin Kalin Productions; Paul & Selina Burdell/Bill Damaschke; 42nd.club/ Phil & Claire Kenny; CatWenJam Productions; Amanda Dubois; Glass Half Full Productions; Dede Harris/Linda B. Rubin; Kallish Weinstein Creative; Kors LePere Theatricals LLC; James L. Nederlander; No Guarantees; Mark Piggott KBE, KStJ; Playing Field; Catherine Schreiber/Adam Zell; Tulchin Bartner Productions; Richard Winker/Alan Schorr/Dawn Smalberg; The Shubert Organization (Robert E. Wankel: Chairman & CEO); Independent Presenters Network; John Gore Organization

**MUSICAL:** *A Strange Loop*

Produced by Barbara Whitman; Pasek, Paul & Stafford; Hunter Arnold; Marcia Goldberg; Alex Levy & James Achilles; Osh Ashruf; A Choir Full Productions; Don Cheadle & Bridgid Coulter Cheadle; Paul Oakley Stovall; Jimmy Wilson; Annapurna Theatre; Robyn Coles; Creative Partners Productions; Robyn Gottesdiener; Kayla Greenspan; Grove Entertainment; Kuhn, Lewis & Scott; Frank Marshall; Maximum Effort Productions Inc.; Joey Monda; Richard Mumby; Phenomenal Media & Meena Harris; Marc Platt & Debra Martin Chase; Laurie Tisch; Yonge Street Theatricals; Dodge Hall Productions/JJ Maley; Cody Renard Richard; John Gore Organization; James L. Nederlander; The Shubert Organization (Robert E. Wankel, Chairman and CEO; Elliot Greene, COO; Charles Flateman, Executive VP); RuPaul Charles; Alan Cumming; Ilana Glazer; Jennifer Hudson; Mindy Kaling and Billy Porter; Presenting the Production by Page 73 (Liz Jones and Asher Richelli: Executive Directors; Michael Walkup: Producing Director; Rachel Karpf: Associate Director); Woolly Mammoth Theatre Company and Playwrights Horizons (Adam Greenfield: Artistic Director; Leslie Marcus: Managing Director)

**BOOK OF A MUSICAL:** Michael R. Jackson, *A Strange Loop*

**ORIGINAL SCORE (MUSIC AND/OR LYRICS) WRITTEN FOR THE THEATRE:** Toby Marlow & Lucy Moss, *Six: The Musical*

**REVIVAL OF A PLAY:** *Take Me Out*

Produced by Second Stage Theater (Carole Rothman, President & Artistic Director; Khady Kamara, Executive Director)

Natasha Katz

**REVIVAL OF A MUSICAL:** *Company*

Produced by Elliott & Harper Productions; The Shubert Organization (Robert E. Wankel: Chairman & CEO); Catherine Schreiber; Nederlander Presentations, Inc.; Crossroads Live; Annapurna Theatre; Hunter Arnold; No Guarantees; Jon B. Platt; Michael Watt; John Gore Organization; Tim Levy; Grove-REG; Hornos-Moellenberg; Levine-Federman-Adler; Beard-Merrie-Robbins; LD Entertainment/Madison Wells Live; Benjamin Lowy/Roben Alive; Daryl Roth/Tom Tuft; Samira Productions/Caiola Productions; Aged in Wood/Lee-Sachs; Berinstein-Lane/42nd.club; Boyett-Miller/ Hodges-Kukielski; Finn-DeVito/Independent Presenters Network; Armstrong-Ross/Gilad-Rogowsky; Boardman-Koenigsberg/Zell-Seriff; Concord Theatricals–Scott Sanders ProductionsAbrams-May; deRoy-Brunish/Jenen-Rubin; Fakston Production/Sabi-Lerner-Ketner; Maggio-Abrams Hopkins-Tackel; Levy & Chauviere and Jujamcyn Theaters (Jordan Roth: President; Rocco Landesman: President Emeritus; Paul Libin: Executive Vice President Emeritus; Jack Viertel: Senior Vice President)

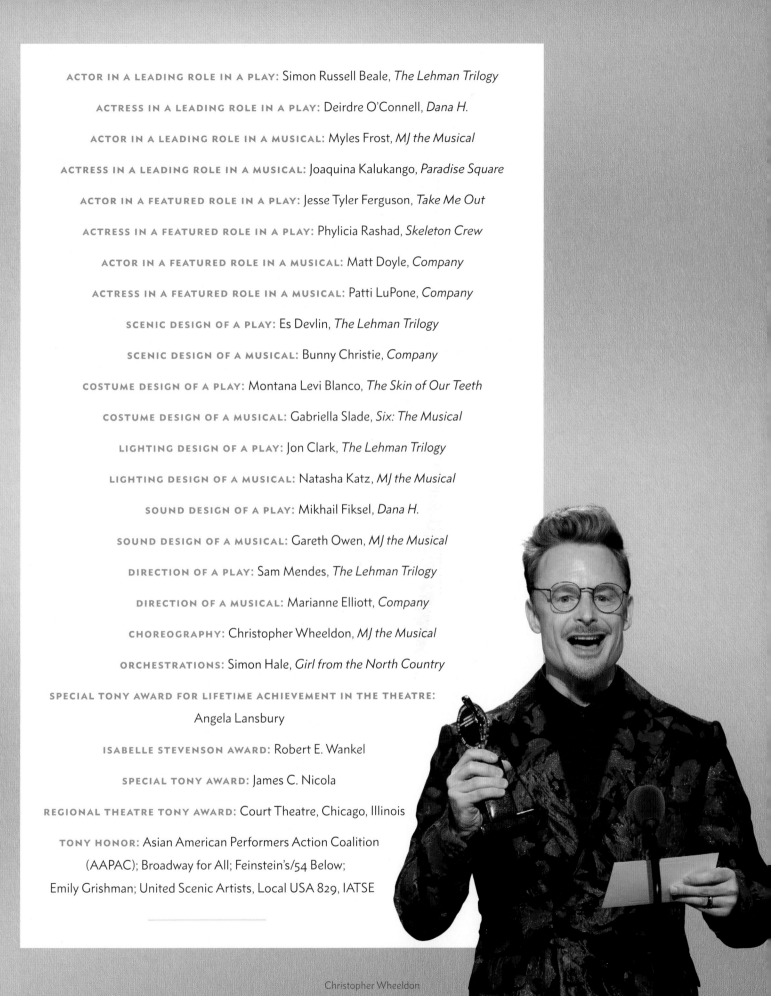

**ACTOR IN A LEADING ROLE IN A PLAY:** Simon Russell Beale, *The Lehman Trilogy*

**ACTRESS IN A LEADING ROLE IN A PLAY:** Deirdre O'Connell, *Dana H.*

**ACTOR IN A LEADING ROLE IN A MUSICAL:** Myles Frost, *MJ the Musical*

**ACTRESS IN A LEADING ROLE IN A MUSICAL:** Joaquina Kalukango, *Paradise Square*

**ACTOR IN A FEATURED ROLE IN A PLAY:** Jesse Tyler Ferguson, *Take Me Out*

**ACTRESS IN A FEATURED ROLE IN A PLAY:** Phylicia Rashad, *Skeleton Crew*

**ACTOR IN A FEATURED ROLE IN A MUSICAL:** Matt Doyle, *Company*

**ACTRESS IN A FEATURED ROLE IN A MUSICAL:** Patti LuPone, *Company*

**SCENIC DESIGN OF A PLAY:** Es Devlin, *The Lehman Trilogy*

**SCENIC DESIGN OF A MUSICAL:** Bunny Christie, *Company*

**COSTUME DESIGN OF A PLAY:** Montana Levi Blanco, *The Skin of Our Teeth*

**COSTUME DESIGN OF A MUSICAL:** Gabriella Slade, *Six: The Musical*

**LIGHTING DESIGN OF A PLAY:** Jon Clark, *The Lehman Trilogy*

**LIGHTING DESIGN OF A MUSICAL:** Natasha Katz, *MJ the Musical*

**SOUND DESIGN OF A PLAY:** Mikhail Fiksel, *Dana H.*

**SOUND DESIGN OF A MUSICAL:** Gareth Owen, *MJ the Musical*

**DIRECTION OF A PLAY:** Sam Mendes, *The Lehman Trilogy*

**DIRECTION OF A MUSICAL:** Marianne Elliott, *Company*

**CHOREOGRAPHY:** Christopher Wheeldon, *MJ the Musical*

**ORCHESTRATIONS:** Simon Hale, *Girl from the North Country*

**SPECIAL TONY AWARD FOR LIFETIME ACHIEVEMENT IN THE THEATRE:**
Angela Lansbury

**ISABELLE STEVENSON AWARD:** Robert E. Wankel

**SPECIAL TONY AWARD:** James C. Nicola

**REGIONAL THEATRE TONY AWARD:** Court Theatre, Chicago, Illinois

**TONY HONOR:** Asian American Performers Action Coalition
(AAPAC); Broadway for All; Feinstein's/54 Below;
Emily Grishman; United Scenic Artists, Local USA 829, IATSE

---

Christopher Wheeldon

**MICHAEL R. JACKSON:** I started working on *A Strange Loop* when I was about twenty-three years old. It was initially a very thinly veiled personal monologue that I wrote for myself. I kept working on it. I went to grad school, I started writing music, and the songs started to work their way into the monologue. The monologue took on another form. I performed a one-man version of the show, that began to take on another form as I continued to work on it. There were many stops and starts over many years until we got to Off-Broadway, and then a pre-Broadway tryout, and finally Broadway. That whole period of time was about eighteen years.

Michael R. Jackson

The first big award I won was the Jonathan Larson grant in 2017. That same week I won the Lincoln Center Emerging Artists award. At the same time the Williamstown Theatre Festival offered me an opportunity to stay there for the summer as the playwright in residence. It was that offer and those awards that led me to quit my job.

I worked as an usher for *The Lion King* and *Mary Poppins*. Watching an audience watch a show night after night gave me an intimate knowledge of how audiences respond to live theatre. They want pleasures delivered to them from the stage, and I had to figure out how to deliver that to them in my own work. What I do in *A Strange Loop* is very different from *The Lion King* and *Mary Poppins*, but the system is the same. There's a relationship between what's happening onstage and the audience. I got to watch that every show that I ushered, and I think I learned by osmosis what was needed for *A Strange Loop*.

The audience is a collaborator. I very much leaned into that in *A Strange Loop*. You have to have respect for the audience. They're the reason you're doing the show.

**BUNNY CHRISTIE:** Bobbie's emotional state was the inspiration for the set for *Company*. The loneliness, the anxiety, figuring out what she wants her life to look like. I think that's recognizable for a lot of people. In New York I've always loved how you can see right into other people's apartments. It's fascinating; it's that *Rear Window* thing, where you see into someone's life. Bobbie is an observer of her friends' relationships. Another inspiration was *Alice in Wonderland*, Bobbie falling down the rabbit hole into a world of memory and imagination, where she is less and less in control of what's happening, until finally she takes control and makes her own decisions, regardless of her friends' opinions.

**PATTI LuPONE:** *Company* was another incredible experience, starting with Marianne Elliott. She's only the second female director I've worked with since 1978, which is not good. Marianne created an equal room. Usually in Broadway musicals there's a hierarchy, but she gave everyone a voice. It was a safe room that allowed us to fail. Marianne showed us great care, respect, and consideration. She cast the show brilliantly; everyone was at the top of their game. My win for *Company* was a hard-earned win. We started previews in New York on March 2, and then on March 12 everything was shut down due to the pandemic. It was a shock. We were allowed to go to the theater to get personal belongings. I went in three times to neutralize my dressing room in case I didn't come back. When I left, I said goodbye to my life in musical theatre. My son helped me put my trunk in the car, and we drove back to Connecticut, and I broke down. I didn't know if I was ever going back. When we finally did return, we were all shell shocked. We were afraid we'd get shut down again. We were tested for Covid every night, and every day somebody was sick. At one point there were more understudies onstage than there were principals. I joked it was like the Jets and the Sharks, because we the principals and the understudies rehearsed separately.

I was a member of the ensemble of *Company*, and I loved being a member of that ensemble. I knew everybody was going to score in this show because everybody was brilliant.

**JESSE TYLER FERGUSON:** I saw the original production of *Take Me Out* three times. A lot of the reason I saw it that many times was because of the performance of Denis O'Hare. I thought his performance was so extraordinary and original. I certainly connected to the character. I'm not a baseball fan, but I was so enamored with that performance and the way he fell in love with the game, it made me want to fall in love with the game as well.

Jesse Tyler Ferguson

When the phone call came with the offer for *Take Me Out,* I never expected it would be for the role of Mason Marzac, because I had heard that Sean Hayes was going to play that role. It turned out that there was a conflict, and now the role was mine if I wanted it. I was just blown away by the fact that this was in my lap. I went to the AIDS Memorial Park in New York City and sat on a bench and reread the play on my iPad. I fell in love with the play again, but what really scared me was that Denis O'Hare's line readings came flooding back to me. I had a bigger job than I expected. Denis O'Hare had given an iconic performance as Mason Marzac, and I had to figure out my own version of the character. It was very intimidating. Before rehearsals even started, I told the director, Scott Ellis, that I felt like I was living under the shadow of Denis O'Hare. He felt the same way about Joe Mantello's direction of the original production! He told me we were in the same boat and would figure it out together. I really put my trust in him to guide us through our new version of this play.

I was the seventy-fifth person to win that award. It means so much to me. This community means so much to me. I never expected to get nominated for any awards and being recognized by a community of people that I just respect so much, and a community of people that I feel saved me. I found my people and became who I was when I became a theatre actor. I was given the tools to find faith in my ability. I was given encouragement and opportunity. They lifted me up and gave me confidence. To be honored by that group of people and stand in front of them at Radio City Music Hall was overwhelming. I was in a state of shock because I'd had the dream of having that moment for so long.

**MONTANA LEVI BLANCO:** The design process starts with conversations with the design team and the director, but the most important person I speak with is the performer. Even if I'm doing a period piece, I really like to include the performer in where the design is at that moment, and what it could be. My ultimate goal is that the performer feels supported and confident, and that they can do the show without even thinking about their clothes. I love including little Easter eggs that the audience may or may not notice. But the actor is aware of it, and it can enhance their performance.

Montana Levi Blanco and presenter Judith Light

Sound Design winners Mikhail Fiksel and Gareth Owen

Sam Mendes

*The Lehman Trilogy*'s Kash Bennett, Sue Wagner, John Johnson, Stefano Massini, Ben Power, John Yonover, Adrian Lester, John Gore, Rufus Norris, and Simon Russell Beale

Joaquina Kalukango

**JOAQUINA KALUKANGO:** It was so surreal when my name was announced as the winner. It was divine. My best friend is Danielle Brooks, and I knew she was going to be there, but I had no idea that Cynthia Erivo was going to present the category with her. To have people who are like my sisters there while my mom and actual sister were there in the audience was incredibly special. It was a night full of love. The Tony is the highest award in this field, and I am honored to have one. It lets me know the stories we're telling are worth telling. It's worth sacrificing and doing eight times a week. There's a huge legacy of people whose footsteps I'm following in, and to be a part of that is extremely meaningful.

**MATT DOYLE:** Stephen Sondheim was there almost every day when we were putting *Company* together in 2020. He was injured at the time, so he had a cane. He would give us notes. Sometimes you'd get an email from him at night reminding you of something or sharing a new idea. I had so much respect for him because he cared so deeply about what was happening with this work, and how much he wanted his work to evolve and not become museum pieces. Every single change that happened in that show went through Stephen. He was such a kind and warm audience member. He would make sure that his laughter was heard, and make sure that you felt received and valued. He knew it must be terrifying to go up in front of him!

He gave me notes about my song "Getting Married Today." He constantly reminded me of the speed and following through the breath. Mixing and marrying that with Marianne's specificity, which is what I think was so groundbreaking about this version of "Getting Married Today," was really special. Sondheim and Marianne worked so well together. He would not have trusted anyone else to make changes to *Company* in that way. With her direction every single thought had to have a new vision; you had to see the idea. Early in the process I was making a lot of grand gestures. Sondheim said that the gestures were too much, and Marianne said, "You need to trust the process. That will all get cut down. He's just trying to find the specificity." They had to figure out each other's process throughout. It was fascinating to work with both of them because they were both right. We did find that middle ground. The party

I'm very honored to be a Tony winner. I was nominated with Jane Greenwood, my mentor, and Sarafina Bush, who assisted me. They are like family, and having my name alongside theirs was one of the most special parts of the night.

*The Skin of Our Teeth* is a play with grit and depth. Because there's so much that goes on in the play, it was important to me to be specific about time. There has to be a clarity with the time shifts and the decades for the story to unfold. A Black family was at the center of our production. They were the nucleus, the compass that guided the audience's experience through those time shifts. For each act we based the design on primary research, looking at images of real Black families of the periods. The hope was that the characters would inhabit an honesty and be vessels of the African American experience through time.

What's interesting about costumes is that even before people speak, they can just present onstage, and we're given information about character, time, mood, state of mind. It's another form of storytelling.

trick of the song is the speed with which it's performed. Marianne was so wise to know and stress that the

Myles Frost as Michael Jackson in a scene from *MJ: The Musical*

words are hilarious and deserve specificity and clarity and each moment given to them. "Getting Married Today" is the most brilliantly written panic attack I've ever heard. Every small irrational thought leads to a bigger irrational thought until you reach that climax and have that final break before you come down. I was diagnosed with a panic disorder when I was a kid, and I was so excited to bring a bit of my identity into this role and celebrate and find the comedy in it. It's so relatable because anxiety is so prevalent in our society. The reaction to the song was huge; it was like a cathartic release for audiences. I wouldn't be surprised if Steve dealt

with panic as well, because of how perfectly it was written.

Matt Doyle

*Company* is the most profound and special accomplishment in my life. I feel like I will always look back on this time as the closest professional family I've ever had and the most life-changing and grounding experience in my life.

I dreamt of winning a Tony since I was thirteen years old and went through so many different rationalizations of how and if it would happen. It felt like it happened in the best way imaginable. Never have I worked so hard for something in my life and believed in something and loved something so much. So, when I was standing on that stage, I had no imposter syndrome whatever. I felt like I had really earned that moment.

Simon Hale

Corey Brunish, Chris Harper, Marianne Elliott, Nick Sidi, Jordan Roth, and Catherine Schreiber

Angela Lansbury and New York City Gay Men's Chorus

Bonnie Milligan and
Miriam Silverman

# WINNERS ◎ 2023

**PLAY:** *Leopoldstadt*, Tom Stoppard

Produced by Sonia Friedman Productions; Roy Furman; Lorne Michaels; Stephanie P. McClelland Gavin Kalin; Delman Sloan; Eileen Davidson; Brad Edgerton; Patrick Gracey; Hunter Arnold; Burnt Umber Productions; Cue to Cue Productions; The Factor Gavin Partnership; Harris Rubin Productions; Robert Nederlander Jr.; No Guarantees; Sandy Robertson; Iris Smith; Jamie deRoy/Catherine Adler; Dodge Hall Productions/Waverly Productions; Ricardo Hornos/Robert Tichio; Heni Koenigsberg/Wendy Federman; Thomas S. Perakos/Stephanie Kramer; Brian Spector/Judith Seinfeld; Richard Winkler & Alan Shorr

**MUSICAL:** *Kimberly Akimbo*

Produced by David Stone; Atlantic Theater Company; James L. Nederlander; LaChanze; John Gore; Patrick Catullo; Aaron Glick

**BOOK OF A MUSICAL:** David Lindsay-Abaire, *Kimberly Akimbo*

**ORIGINAL SCORE (MUSIC AND/OR LYRICS) WRITTEN FOR THE THEATRE:**
David Lindsay-Abaire and Jeanine Tesori, *Kimberly Akimbo*

**REVIVAL OF A PLAY:** *Suzan-Lori Parks' Topdog/Underdog*

Produced by David Stone; LaChanze, Rashad V. Chambers; Marc Platt; Debra Martin Chase, The Shubert Organization (Robert E. Wankel: Chairman and CEO; Elliot Greene: Chief Operating Officer; Charles Flateman: Executive Vice President)

**REVIVAL OF A MUSICAL:** *Parade*

Produced by Seaview; Ambassador Theatre Group Productions; Alex Levy; Kevin Ryan; Eric and Marsi Gardiner; Interscope & Immersive Records; Erica Lynn Schwartz; Creative Partners Productions; Marcia Goldberg; John Gore Organization; Cynthia Stroum; Tom Tuft; Benjamin Simpson; Nathan Vernon; Brian & Nick Ginsberg; Ruth & Stephen Hendel; Roth-Manella Productions; Chutzpa Productions; 42nd.Club; Ahava 72 Productions; The Andryc Brothers; The Array; At Rise Creative; Caiola Jenen Productions; Coles Achilles; deRoy Brunish Productions; Fakston Productions; Federman Batchelder; Level Forward; Pencil Factory Productions; Renard Lynch; Robin Merrie; Rubin Stuckelman; Runyonland Sussman; Kristin Caskey; Mike Isaacson; Bee Carrozzini, New York City Center (Michael S. Rosenberg, President & CEO)

**ACTOR IN A LEADING ROLE IN A PLAY:**
Sean Hayes, *Good Night, Oscar*

**ACTRESS IN A LEADING ROLE IN A PLAY:**
Jodie Comer, *Prima Facie*

**ACTOR IN A LEADING ROLE IN A MUSICAL:**
Harrison Ghee, *Some Like It Hot*

Jodie Comer

Micaela Diamond, Suzan-Lori
Parks, and Ben Platt

**ACTRESS IN A LEADING ROLE IN A MUSICAL:** Victoria Clark, *Kimberly Akimbo*

**ACTOR IN A FEATURED ROLE IN A PLAY:** Brandon Uranowitz, *Leopoldstadt*

**ACTRESS IN A FEATURED ROLE IN A PLAY:** Miriam Silverman, *The Sign in Sidney Brustein's Window*

**ACTOR IN A FEATURED ROLE IN A MUSICAL:** Alex Newell, *Shucked*

**ACTRESS IN A FEATURED ROLE IN A MUSICAL:** Bonnie Milligan, *Kimberly Akimbo*

**SCENIC DESIGN OF A PLAY:** Tim Hatley & Andrzej Goulding, *Life of Pi*

**SCENIC DESIGN OF A MUSICAL:** Beowulf Boritt, *New York, New York*

**COSTUME DESIGN OF A PLAY:** Brigitte Reiffenstuel, *Leopoldstadt*

**COSTUME DESIGN OF A MUSICAL:** Gregg Barnes, *Some Like It Hot*

**LIGHTING DESIGN OF A PLAY:** Tim Lutkin, *Life of Pi*

**LIGHTING DESIGN OF A MUSICAL:** Natasha Katz, *Sweeney Todd: The Demon Barber of Fleet Street*

**SOUND DESIGN OF A PLAY:** Carolyn Downing, *Life of Pi*

**SOUND DESIGN OF A MUSICAL:** Nevin Steinberg, *Sweeney Todd: The Demon Barber of Fleet Street*

**DIRECTION OF A PLAY:** Patrick Marber, *Leopoldstadt*

**DIRECTION OF A MUSICAL:** Michael Arden, *Parade*

**CHOREOGRAPHY:** Casey Nicholaw, *Some Like It Hot*

**ORCHESTRATIONS:** Charlie Rosen & Bryan Carter, *Some Like It Hot*

**SPECIAL TONY AWARD FOR LIFETIME ACHIEVEMENT IN THE THEATRE:** Joel Grey, John Kander

**ISABELLE STEVENSON AWARD:** Jerry Mitchell

**REGIONAL THEATRE TONY AWARD:** Pasadena Playhouse

**TONY HONOR:** Victoria Bailey, Lisa Dawn Cave, Robert Fried

Brandon Uranowitz and Patrick Marber

Kristin Caskey, Alfred Uhry, Jason Robert Brown, and Greg Nobile

Tim Lutkin

2023 ○ 291

**MICHAEL ARDEN:** I've always loved *Parade*. I grew up listening to the cast album, which was my keyhole that I peeked through into the world of musicals. After January 6, it became clear that this was a vital piece of theatre that needed to be shared. It was important for me to examine how easily people can be swept up into something they might not stand behind if they were thinking clearly. I cast Ben Platt and Micaela Diamond in the lead roles. It was exciting to see two people who were the appropriate ages to play Leo and Lucille (who were around 29 and 23), and who were also both Jewish, as the roles had never been cast that way in a major production. It seemed like this was an opportunity to do something really close to the bone.

The night of our first preview there were neo-Nazi protestors outside the theater. It was ugly. I was mostly concerned about our cast. I pushed through the protestors to make my way into the theater. The cast was in a circle onstage getting ready. We had a few moments together and realized if the Nazis were protesting us, we were doing something right. People are still fighting this war.

Shortly before the Tonys I went to the opera with my dear friend Our Lady J, who is trans. I was asking her about her summer plans, and she told me she was supposed to go to Minnesota to visit family, but now she didn't know if she could go. She could be sued or arrested for using the bathroom. So many people and kids are out there and terrified. They may not even be able to speak their truth into existence yet, let alone behave as themselves within a society. I knew there was a connection to *Parade* in this idea of supremacy. It became clear that I would be a fool not to use my fifty-five seconds to speak to that. I grew up being called a faggot all the time. I felt it was important to reclaim that term. My husband gave me the line. He's the real writer. He said, "You were called faggot, now you're a faggot with a Tony Award."

**SEAN HAYES:** It is the most gratifying and meaningful recognition to the dedication of creating a piece of art. And it's super cool.

Michael Arden

Matthew Broderick and Sean Hayes

J. Harrison Ghee

**J. HARRISON GHEE:** The entire season I felt so much love from every direction. I was humbled to be in the running for a Tony, and to receive all that love. I was so happy to share the moment of winning with my mom. It meant everything to me to give her flowers, and to show her that she's made a difference in the world through me. I am the human I am because of her.

I was excited to take the journey of *Some Like It Hot*. It closely mirrors my real-life experience. I'm stepping into this freedom and expansion of who I am as a human, and hoping other people will be encouraged to do the same, whatever that means for them. There's a little Daphne in everybody. It's that part of you that's longing to be free and have joy. The dress I wore to the Tonys was vibrant blue (designed by Jérôme LaMaar), and allowed me to express that freedom and joy in the form of fashion.

Matthew Lopez and Amber Ruffin wrote the script for *Some Like It Hot* and allowed me to be a collaborator. On the show's first meet-and-greet day, everybody introduced themselves, saying our pronouns and who we were going to play. I said, "J. Harrison Ghee, all things with respect. I play Jerry/Daphne." That is how I communicate in my life.

Then those words appeared in the script. There wasn't a conversation about it, but they were listening and paying attention. They understood this was how I live and helped my experience be seen, and in turn helped others to feel seen. That was the same with everyone on the show. No one was too precious about their work, and everyone was open to ideas that would make the experience more authentic.

I don't take it lightly that I get to live in a time when people are more accepting of who I am, and especially that I have a voice in helping others. There have always been non-binary people, but so many were not as fortunate. The day after I won the Tony I casually flew to the White House. I took a moment to stand with the building and touch the brick. I stood there with my Tony and felt my ancestors and the people who built it. I thought that I am beyond their wildest dreams of what was possible.

The fact that Alex Newell and I—two non-binary actors—were even nominated felt like the needle had moved. There was representation, understanding, and the breaking of boundaries and labels and limits. This was a moment to prove and show that if a human is doing good work, honor the work and make space for that in every way.

Beowulf Boritt

**BEOWULF BORITT:** New York City today is not that different from what it was in 1946. There are a lot more tall buildings now, but the tightness of spaces, the vistas you get when you look through a street of fire escapes and suddenly see a skyscraper off in the distance remain the same.

The design of New York, New York changed massively from my original idea to what appeared onstage on opening night. There was an early idea that was much more of a ballet set and more abstract and lyrical. We decided we needed more grit and reality and more of the iron and the roughness of New York City. The whole idea turned out to be too expensive, so at zero hour I had to simplify. I had four weeks to come up with a new idea and get it drafted and to the shop so we could stay on schedule. I was panicky and sitting on the floor of my studio racking my brain for how to do it. I remembered Hal Prince would always say that in a musical you need to leave a lot of empty space, a lot of black space, which leaves room for the audience's imagination and makes them participate in the storytelling. That gave me clarity,

Alex Newell and the cast of *Shucked*

John Kander, Ariana DeBose, and Joel Grey

and I knew what changes were needed. The number of people who have come up to me and said that it's a very Hal Prince set is shocking to me. There's a lot I learned from that man that I'm still putting into practice.

The moment they call your name at the Tonys, you're running down the aisle with a camera in your face. Sam Jackson high-fived me as I walked past him. I got up onstage and gave the speech. Lin (-Manuel Miranda) was standing in the wings and pulled me into a huge bear hug as soon as I came offstage. I was thinking, "Whose life is this? It's not what I ever expected going into this business. I thought I would be lucky to make a living at all. To get to live in the sky this way is something I don't take for granted at all.

# ACCEPTANCE SPEECHES THROUGH THE YEARS

I'm deeply grateful for this recognition of the fact that a new and an original and unheralded work can find its way on Broadway and prosper.

**EDWARD PADULA (1961)**

**KEN DAVENPORT (2018):** This is a business where you hear *no* an awful lot, so this award is dedicated to all of the people that said yes to this production. And lastly, to all of the people who dream about doing what I do and what everyone else in this room does, do not stop asking your question. It is amazing what can happen. You can get to your yes.

**ROB ASHFORD (2002):** Any of you gypsies out there who want to be choreographers, I say go for it. And I hope that you are as supported and blessed and lucky as I am.

Rob Ashford

**ELAINE MAY (2019):** At the end of the play I died. Now my death was described onstage by Lucas Hedges so brilliantly. And he described the death, my death, he described it so heartbreakingly, he was so touching, that watching from the wings, I thought: "I'm going to win this guy's Tony."

**JOHN DOYLE (2006):** I'd like to dedicate this to all the directors and actors and designers and artists out there who knock on doors that don't get answers, and who look for a break that they think is never going to come. And I hope they will remember this moment as living proof of the fact that it's never too late.

**HAL PRINCE (2006):** Thank you for this honor, and thank you for letting me work most of my adult life on Broadway. I've had my successes which have flopped at the box office, my humiliating misfires, and some shows that have run, for which I am extremely grateful. I've also had decades of working with the most brilliant creative artists in the American theatre. I'm a lucky guy.

**JOHN GALLAGHER JR. (2007):** Heaven must feel like this.

**CHARLES NELSON REILLY (1962):** Twelve years ago, I carried a very heavy mail bag in this hotel, and the tips were terrible. The mail bag I carry every night at the 46th Street Theatre is very light. And I hope for all you kids starting out that you find an easy way to get to that light mail bag.

**GENE SAKS (1983):** Neil, if you're watching in California, I have a confession to make. I was going to share this with you tonight, but I just learned that they're changing the name of the Alvin Theatre to the Neil Simon.

**DANIEL SULLIVAN (2001):** There must be some mistake. I had nothing to do with *The Producers*.

**FRANK LANGELLA (2002):** I started in this profession forty years ago, and if I've learned anything it's that the good and bad moments in an actor's career pass. The trick is to stay at the table, play the cards you're dealt, and hope for a winning hand. I got such a winning hand with *Fortune's Fool.*...I have had millions and millions of extraordinary moments standing on a stage acting for you. I'm very grateful to each and every Tony voter who gave me this for this work. This wonderful moment, which I know is about to pass.

**SCOTT WITTMAN (2003):** My mother took me to Radio City every Saturday morning when I was a kid, and she used to say to me, "One day you'll be up there." I always thought she meant a Rockette. I never knew it was going to be this.

**TOM KIRDAHY (2020):** This award is in loving memory for all the beautiful souls lost to AIDS and Covid, and it's dedicated to the love of my life, my husband, Terrence McNally.

**CHRISTINE BARANSKI (1989):** I thank Manny, my producer, who is my friend and the father of my two Tonys.

**JEROME ROBBINS (1989):** I'm so happy that what has arrived here was a part of my history and the theatre's history, which was fading away and being lost. And it meant so much to me that I was able to stop that for a while, bring it all back again, hope to get it recorded and notated and archived. And also got the extra dessert of having a nice big hit, too.

**JUDD HIRSCH (1992):** This makes me feel uniquely qualified to be in a play that is so extraordinary—the play I'm in, *Conversations with My Father*. Herb Gardner, you have written the play of your life. You have written the part of my life. Herb Gardner, you have written what I consider—and you'll have to excuse me for this—the greatest play on Broadway today.

**NATALIA MAKAROVA (1983):** For my husband who didn't help much but wasn't in my way.

**DOUG HUGHES (2005):** I'd like to thank my mother and father, great actors, great parents. I know it must seem like a wild act of Oedipal revenge for the son of two actors to become a director, but I assure you that's not the case. What happened with *Doubt* is very, very simple. John Patrick Shanley wrote a play for our time, and I was given the opportunity to work on it every day in the company of geniuses. So, if you'll indulge me, I'd like to live a fantasy here and simply say I love working in the world of the theatre. Safe and dangerous, small and infinite, I am overjoyed to have a place in it.

*Doubt*'s Doug Hughes and Adriane Lenox

I'm a New Yorker, and my parents took me to Broadway matinees every Saturday, so this means a great deal to me. **WENDY WASSERSTEIN (1989)**

# ACKNOWLEDGMENTS

**EILA MELL:** Emilio Sosa, I can never thank you enough for bringing me this dream project. You are such a dear friend, and working with you was an enormous privilege.

Heather Hitchens, it was a joy to work with you and get to know you.

Ian Weiss, thank you so much for all your hard work. Your contribution was vital to this book, and I loved every moment working with you.

Joe Davidson, you were a wonderful partner on this book. Your enthusiasm for this project made every step of the process easier and even more fun. Thank you for helping me bring this vision to life.

Kayla Williamson, you are a wonder. Your efforts made this book so much easier for me to navigate.

Thank you to everyone at Black Dog & Leventhal, especially Becky Koh, Betsy Hulseboch, Kara Thornton, Seta Bedrossian Zink, Katie Benezra, and Lillian Sun.

Alex Camlin, it was great to collaborate again!

Sue Oyama, you had a big job! Thank you so much for your hard work. It made my job so much easier.

Jack Cesarano, thank you for being the best researcher I could have had on this book.

Darcy Winter, thank you for your contribution to this book. Your enthusiasm and hard work are greatly appreciated, and I am so happy you were a part of my team.

Gary Tifeld, you are an incredible theatre historian. Thank you so much for being on call for so many photo IDs, and for all the tools you generously gave me to research this book.

Mike Cesarano, thank you for all your support and help.

Katherine Latshaw, having you in my corner means the world to me. Thank you so much.

Christie Wagner, thank you for your help. It was an absolute joy to get to know your Dad, and such a privilege to include him in my work.

Bruce Gotlieb and Matt Stashin, thank you so much for your unending enthusiasm and support.

Derek McLane, thank you for all your help.

Audra McDonald, thank you for being such an important part of this book. It was a joy to collaborate with you.

And finally, a huge thank you to Scott Hofer, Stephen Trask, Doug Denoff, Merle Frimark, Kathy Voytko, Daisy Prince, and all the contributors and their representatives.

**AMERICAN THEATRE WING:** The American Theatre Wing would like to thank the entire team who worked tirelessly on this book: Eila, Joe, Katherine, Susan, Heather, Emilio, Ian, and Kayla. Thank you for all your hard work.

Thank you to the entire American Theatre Wing staff for your support: Laura, Melissa, Tracy, Luis, Bryony, Josh, Jacob, Yoanna, Emily, Rachel, and Miranda.

Lastly, we'd like to thank the women who founded and continued to support the American Theatre Wing when we needed them most, especially Antoinette Perry, who took a bet on many artists and gambled on creating a world for the future of theatre.

# SELECT INDEX

# PHOTO CREDITS

American Theatre Wing: viii, 2, 3 (top right and bottom left), 10, 15 (top), 16, 24 (top left and bottom left), 34, 93, 101 (both), 102 (top left), 124 (middle), 129, 131 (both), 135 (both), 139 (both), 140 (bottom); Anthony Casale/NY Daily News Archive/Getty Image: 54 (bottom); Associated Press: 13 (bottom), 17 (top and bottom), 19 (bottom), 32, 41, 48, 59, 69, 71, 73 (bottom), 85; Associated Press/ Aubrey Reuben: 199 (bottom right); Associated Press/ Brian Zak/Sipa: 186 (bottom), 187 (top), 190 (bottom left); Associated Press/Charles Sykes: 210 (bottom right); Associated Press/Dave Pickoff: 44 (bottom); Associated Press/David Goldman: 195 (top), 197 (bottom right); Associated Press/Ed Bailey: 100 (top); Associated Press/ Jeff Christensen: 181, 182 (bottom), 183 (both), 184, 185 (top right), 187, (bottom), 190 (top), 190 (middle right), 190 (bottom right), 192; Associated Press/John Lent: 63; Associated Press/Kathy Willens: 109, 165 (bottom left), 168 (top), 168 (bottom left), 169; Associated Press/Marty Lederhandler: 14, 31 (top), 123 (bottom); Associated Press/ Mary Altaffer: 269; Associated Press/Richard Drew: 18, 72, 73 (top), 76, 82 (middle and bottom), 84, 86, 87, 89, 90, 94, 108 (bottom), 113 (top), 119, 122, 126 (left), 149 (top), 151, 163 (bottom right), 165 (top), 166 (top), 185 (top left), 185 (bottom); Associated Press/Ron Frehm: 95 (bottom), 96, 130 (top); Associated Press/Seth Wenig: 195 (bottom), 197 (top), 197 (bottom left); Associated Press/Stuart Ramson: 186 (top), 188; Associated Press/Suzanne Plunkett: 148 (right), 149 (bottom), 153 (right), 155, 156, 157 (bottom); Associated Press/Suzanne Vlamis: 66 (bottom); Associated Press/Tina Fineberg: 161 (top right); Associated Press/Tom

Fitzsimmons: 11, 15 (bottom); Bettmann/Getty Images: 20, 23, 25, 68, 102 (middle right), 145; Billy Rose Theatre Division, The New York Public Library for the Performing Arts: 3 (bottom right); Bruce Glikas/FilmMagic/Getty Images: 184 (right), 196, 226 (bottom), 229 (bottom left), 286 (top left); Cewzan Grayson/PA Images/Getty Images: 152 (bottom); Charles Sykes/Invision/AP: 78, 215, 216, 217, 219 (top right), 219 (bottom right), 223, 225, 240 (bottom), 261 (bottom), 262 (bottom), 266 (top left and top right), 282, 283, 284, 285 (both), 286 (top right), 287, 288 (both), 289 (all); Cindy Ord/Getty Images for Tony Awards Productions: 276 (top right), 277 (left); Courtesy of John Lee Beatty: 83; Courtesy of Robin Wagner: 74 (bottom); CSU Archives/Everett Collection: 4; Dan Farrell/NY Daily News Archive/Getty Images: 24 (right); Dennis Van Tine/ Sipa USA/AP: 253 (top); Dimitrios Kambouris/WireImage/ Getty Images: 161 (bottom right), 162 (left); Disney General Entertainment Content/Getty Images: 56 (top), 57, 60; Evan Agostini/Getty Images: 138, 140 (top), 163 (top); Evan Agostini/Invision/AP: 51, 214, 220 (left), 221, 228 (right), 257 (bottom), 274 (both), 275, 277 (right), 279; Everett Collection: 6, 19 (top), 45 (top); Express Newspapers/ Associated Press: 249 (bottom); Frank Micelotta/Getty Images: 161 (left), 162 (right), 164, 165 (bottom right), 166 (bottom); James Devaney/WireImage/Getty Images: 163 (bottom left), 296; Jamie McCarthy/Getty Images for Tony Awards Productions: 278 (left); Jenny Anderson/Getty Images for Tony Awards Productions: 254 (middle left), 254 (bottom left), 278 (right); Jim Mooney/NY Daily News/ Getty Images: 38, 39; JIMI CELESTE/Patrick McMullan/

Getty Images: 190 (top right); Kevin Kane/WireImage for Tony Awards Productions/Getty Images: 210 (bottom left), 212; Kevin Mazur Archive 1/WireImage for Tony Awards Productions/Getty Images: 177, 250 (bottom); Larry Busacca/WireImage for Tony Awards Productions/Getty Images: 222; LARRY C. MORRIS//The New York Times/Redux: 49; Leo Friedman/Photofest: 33 (top); Mary Kouw/CBS/Getty Images: 286 (bottom); Michael Zorn/Invision/AP: 249 (top), 250 (top), 252 (left), 253 (bottom), 254 (top left), 255, 256, 257 (top), 270; Mike Albans/NY Daily News Archive/Getty Images: 136 (bottom), 137; Mike Coppola/WireImage/Getty Images: 208 (bottom), 210 (top right), 213 (top right and bottom right); New York Times Co./Getty Images: 12 (top); Paul Hawthorne/Getty Images: 268; Photo by Bob Deutsch: 65, 70, 75; Photo by Friedman-Abeles © The New York Public Library for the Performing Arts: 61; Photo by Rob Rich/Everett Collection: 168 (bottom right); Photo by S. Sarac/Everett Collection: 167; Photofest: 7, 13 (top), 21, 31 (bottom), 32 (top), 33 (bottom), 37, 42, 44 (top), 47, 64, 66 (top), 74 (top); Photofest (Reproduced with the permission of the Aronson-Budhos Collection): 12 (bottom); Photograph courtesy of Cameron Mackintosh Ltd.: 36; Used by Permission. All rights reserved, Playbill Inc: 5, 35; Reuters/Alamy Stock Photo: 134 (top); Richard Corkery/NY Daily News Archive/Getty Images: 77, 136 (top), 153 (left), 296 (bottom); Ron Galella/Ron Galella Collection/Getty Images: 46 (top and bottom), 54 (top), 55, 56 (bottom), 58, 92, 95 (top), 97, 98, 102 (bottom right), 107, 109 (left), 115 (top), 120 (top), 124 (top left and bottom right), 125, 126 (right), 127, 128, 134 (middle right), 141, 142, 199 (top right); SARA KRULWICH/ The New York Times/Redux: 82 (top), 144; Scott Gries/ ImageDirect/Getty Images: 148 (left), 152 (top), 158, 160; Shevett Studios: vi, 26, 27, 100 (middle and bottom), 102 (top left and right), 103 (all), 104, 105, 106, 108 (top), 112, 113 (bottom left and bottom right), 114 (all), 115 (bottom), 116, 117 (all), 118, 120 (bottom left and right), 121 (all), 123 (top), 143, 170, 171, 172, 173 (both), 174, 175, 176 (all), 178 (bottom), 180 (top left), 194, 198, 199 (left), 202 (both), 203 (both), 204 (all), 206 (both), 207 (all), 208 (top), 210 (top left), 213 (top left and bottom left), 218 (all), 219 (middle), 220 (right), 226 (top), 227 (bottom), 228 (left), 229 (top), 229 (bottom right), 231, 232, 233, 234, 235, 236, 237, 238 (both), 239 (both), 240 (top left and right), 241 (all), 242 (all), 243, 244, 245, 248, 252 (right), 258 (both), 259 (both), 260 (both), 261 (top), 262 (top left and right), 264, 265 (all), 266 (bottom), 290, 291, 292, 293, 294, 295, 297; Sonia Moskowitz/IMAGES/Getty Images: 50; Stan Honda/PA Images/Getty Images: 157 (top), 159; Stephen Lovekin/WireImage for Tony Awards Productions/Getty Images: 178 (top), 180 (bottom left), 180 (right); Theo Wargo/Getty Images for Tony Awards Productions: 227 (top), 246, 251, 276 (bottom right), 280 (both); TIMOTHY A. CLARY/AFP via Getty Images: 130 (bottom), 133, 153 (bottom right); Udo Salters/Sipa USA/AP Images: 276 (left); Walter McBride/Corbis/Getty Images: 134 (middle left)

Black Dog & Leventhal Publishers
Hachette Book Group
1290 Avenue of the Americas
New York, NY 10104

www.hachettebookgroup.com
www.blackdogandleventhal.com

First Edition: April 2024

Published by Black Dog & Leventhal Publishers, an imprint of Hachette Book Group, Inc.
The Black Dog & Leventhal Publishers name and logo are trademarks of Hachette Book Group, Inc.

The publisher is not responsible for websites (or their content) that are not owned by the publisher.

The Hachette Speakers Bureau provides a wide range of authors for speaking events. To find out more, go to hachettespeakersbureau.com or email HachetteSpeakers@hbgusa.com.

Black Dog & Leventhal books may be purchased in bulk for business, educational, or promotional use. For more information, please contact your local bookseller or the Hachette Book Group Special Markets Department at Special.Markets@hbgusa.com.

Print book interior design by Alex Camlin

Library of Congress Cataloging-in-Publication Data
    Names: Mell, Eila, 1968- author.
    Title: The Tony Awards: a celebration of excellence in theatre / Eila Mell.
    Description: New York, NY: Black Dog & Leventhal, 2024. | Includes index. | Summary: "Officially sanctioned by the American Theatre Wing, The Tony Awards: A Celebration of Excellence in Theatre will commemorate 75 magical years of Broadway's biggest night, featuring photographs and interviews with a cavalcade of stars and a foreword by Audra McDonald" —Provided by publisher.
    Identifiers: LCCN 2023001209 (print) | LCCN 2023001210 (ebook) | ISBN 9780762484416 (hardcover) | ISBN 9780762484423 (ebook)
    Subjects: LCSH: Tony Awards—History. | Theater—Awards—New York (State)—New York.
    Classification: LCC PN2270.A93 M45 2024 (print) | LCC PN2270.A93 (ebook) | DDC 792.079/7471—dc23/eng/20230519
    LC record available at https://lccn.loc.gov/2023001209
    LC ebook record available at https://lccn.loc.gov/2023001210

ISBNs: 978-0-7624-8441-6 (hardcover), 978-0-7624-8442-3 (ebook)

Printed in China

IM

10  9  8  7  6  5  4  3  2  1

THE TONY AWARDS